THE PULITZER PRIZE PLAYS

The First Fifty Years ❖ 1917–1967

A Dramatic Reflection of American Life

PAUL A. FIRESTONE

An Imprint of Hal Leonard Corporation
New York

Published in 2008 by Limelight Editions
An Imprint of Hal Leonard Corporation
7777 West Bluemound Road
Milwaukee, WI 53213

Trade Book Division Editorial Offices
19 West 21st Street, New York, NY 10010

Printed in the United States of America

Book design by Mark Lerner

Library of Congress Cataloging-in-Publication Data

Firestone, Paul A.
The Pulitzer Prize plays: the first fifty years, 1917–1967: a dramatic reflection of American life / by Paul A. Firestone.
    p. cm.
    Includes bibliographical references (p.).
1. American drama–20th century–History and criticism. 2. Pulitzer prizes.
I. Title.
    PS351.F47 2008
    812'.509–dc22
2008039963

ISBN 978-0-87910-355-2

www.limelighteditions.com

THE PULITZER PRIZE PLAYS

With deepest love—
For my wife, Pearl, and Lydia and Ted

Contents

Part Two: Social Protest

Part Three: Political Heroes

Part Four: Morality and Survival in a Materialistic Society

Part Five: The Spiritual Condition of Humankind

Joseph Pulitzer (1847–1911) *Photo courtesy of Culver Pictures, Inc./Superstock*

Introduction

The Pulitzer Prize for Drama

It is likely that Joseph Pulitzer's initial concept for the Pulitzer Prize as set forth in his will in 1904 was inspired by the publicity the world was giving the Nobel Prize, established in 1901 by Nobel, the inventor of dynamite. Competitive and ambitious, Pulitzer conceived the brilliant idea of endowing Columbia University with a journalism school and awarding annual prizes in journalism, based upon comprehensive and accurate reporting. In the new twentieth century, he hoped excellence in news reporting would become equated with the name Pulitzer. In August 1902, after giving two million dollars for the establishment of a school of journalism at Columbia University, Pulitzer stated his intention to provide annual prizes not only to journalists, but to writers "for various accomplishments, achievements and forms of excellence."

A Hungarian-born Jewish immigrant, Joseph Pulitzer began his career as a reporter for the German daily *Westliche Post* in St. Louis in 1868. Enterprising and energetic, he became a lawyer and was elected to the Missouri state legislature. He became part-owner of the newspaper and learned firsthand that a newspaper could be the people's watchdog, a medium that could alert the public to all societal matters, and especially to the political corruption of local and state politicians.

Over the next two decades, Pulitzer bought newspaper companies in St. Louis and New York, becoming owner-editor of the *St. Louis Post-Dispatch* and the *New York World*. As the owner and business manager of two important newspapers in two metropolitan areas, he was eager to reach a readership circulation of more than a hundred thousand and reduced the price of his dailies to one cent. When he achieved his readership goal, he sold the idea of large-scale advertising to retail stores, greatly increasing his papers' revenues.

Critics of Pulitzer described him as self-interested and self-promoting, intent on increasing newspaper circulation through sensationalist reporting and gossip. His bitter business competition with William Randolph Hearst, owner-editor of the *New York Journal*, first inspired the term "yellow journalism" in reference to both publishers' wildly irresponsible and sensational reporting. Each day spuriously sensational headlines on page one of the *Journal* and the *World* were meant to promote sales and garner greater income from advertisers. They also had graver consequences, as their jingoistic stories about the Cuban insurrection and the sinking of the U.S. Battleship *Maine* urged the country into the Spanish American War.

In the late 1890s after a long, competitive newspaper-war with Hearst, Pulitzer, because of poor health, retired from active control of his newspapers.

It is ironic that Pulitzer, who won his hard-earned success as an editor of sensational urban dailies, conceived the notion of integrity in journalism as his legacy to the America he came to love. But Pulitzer felt he was a champion of the people, with a mission to provide vital information to his readers—who were mainly new immigrants, the poor, the politically unrepresented, and especially women, whom he encouraged to become literate in many editorials. Pulitzer wanted to be remembered as a benefactor to America just like Andrew Carnegie, who had benevolently established more than twenty-five thousand libraries.

He did not conceive of his gift of millions of dollars to establish the Columbia University School of Journalism as a self-indulgent monument like the castle San Simeon, which newspaper tycoon Hearst built for himself in California. However, he must surely have been aware that, after a decade or two, the association of his name with Columbia would help remove whatever criticism might have tarnished his reputation as a sensationalist newspaper owner-editor. The Pulitzer name would come to be conjoined with excellence in journalism and signify honest, accurate, and objective news reporting.

Tracking the footprints of the Nobel Prizes, Pulitzer offered a broad range of annual prizes for excellence in "public service, public morals, American literature and the advancement of education." When he died on October 28, 1911, he bequeathed a fund of several million dollars for prizes to honor the best newspaper editorial, the best example of a reporter's work, the best American novel, the best book of the year dealing with United States history, the best American biography, and the best American stage play.

From its inception in 1917, the Pulitzer Prize for a best play invited controversy.

There is no objective, universally approved standard by which to measure excellence in drama beyond the rigid structure of the "Unities" conceived by Aristotle in his *Poetics*. The original wording of the Pulitzer Prize proposed that truly qualified "jurors" should see and evaluate the plays entered as candidates, and that the winning play should satisfy Joseph Pulitzer's best-play criteria. In his will he established what he believed was a unique and appropriate basis for judging the competition: "For the original American play, performed in New York, which shall best represent the educational value and power of the stage in raising the standard of good morals, good taste, and good manners—$1,000.00."

The determination of the prize-winning play does not take place today as Pulitzer once envisioned it, with the final choice made by drama-specialist jurors. The jurors, usually a trio of critics, often including a playwright or novelist, come to a judgment, but they must yield the ultimate decision to an advisory board whose secretary appoints the jurors, and whose thirteen members include the president of Columbia University and a select group of newspaper editor-owners or journalists.

Originally, advisory board members lived in cities throughout the United States, far from Broadway, and were not required to view any of the candidate plays. The board was to consider the merit of candidate plays and name one based on an analysis of the jurors' evaluative report.

Though the proceedings of the advisory board have never been made known to the public, the controversies that have arisen in the committee have often been reported in newspapers and in magazine articles. And there have been outspoken critics of the board who have given clues to the biases, shortcomings, and politics of that body. Ever sensitive to criticism, the Pulitzer committee has always responded rapidly to correct any areas of oversight or seeming unfairness that might suggest neglect or bias in the selection of the prize play.

The advisory board constitutes a remarkable group, including notable publishers, editors, drama critics, and professors. And today, using videos and printed texts of the candidate plays, the advisory board is fully acquainted with the play that is proposed as prizeworthy by the jurors.

The Pulitzer Prize Office, established in 1912 in the Columbia School of Journalism, was finally ready to function five years later in 1917 when the first four prizes were awarded: (1) to Herbert Bayard Swope, a reporter for the *New York World* for a series of articles, entitled, "Inside the German Empire"; (2) to the editors of the *New York Tribune* for an article remembering the anniversary of the sinking of the trans-Atlantic passenger ship *Lusitania*, (3) to J.J. Jusserand, Ambassador of France to the United States, for his history, *With Americans of Past and Present Days*; and (4) to Laura E. Richards and Maude Howe Elliott for their biography, *Julia Ward Howe*. In 1917 there were no awards for the novel, the drama, or poetry.

In 1918 the jurors agreed on the first Pulitzer Prize play, *Why Marry?* by Jesse Lynch Williams. In this comedy of manners, a young woman states her case against the marital vow "to honor and obey." The jurors' choice was unanimous. In subsequent years, however, the process of selection became more complicated. Theater season after theater season, the task of choosing a best play that reflected "good morals, good taste, and good manners" perplexed the jurors.

When *Anna Christie* by Eugene O'Neill received the prize in 1922, a change in the directive seemed imperative: the heroine Anna is a former prostitute. But it took six years of dialogue and contention before the advisory board of the School of Journalism at Columbia changed the provision of Pulitzer's will to omit the offending moralistic phrase and amend the will's criteria: "For the original American play, performed in New York, which shall best represent the educational value and power of the stage, one thousand dollars."

Six years later, in 1934, the advisory board faced another controversy when the highly praised but British-themed *Mary of Scotland* was refused the honor, and again revised the provision, adding that the play should preferably be one dealing with American life.

In the first fifty years of Pulitzer awards, 1917 to 1967, there were forty-two prize-winning plays. (There were eight years when no award was made.) The jurors honored plays that ranged widely in dramatic treatment: realistic, tragic, satirical, farcical, historical, fantastic, and musical. But all, no matter how diverse or unique in style, were selected as best representing to the public "the educational value and power of the stage."

Historically, the years from 1917 to 1967 were momentous, reshaping and redefining American society. During these five decades, the United States endured vast political, social, and economic changes, brought about by world wars and a series of world depressions. And through these years, American plays have reflected those changes. The playwrights writing in their time held up their individual mirrors to American life, revealing at times a cause for celebration, at others a call to arms.

Each of the forty-two Pulitzer Prize plays included here has been grouped for analysis according to its major theme—the theme that, in the words of drama critic Henri Fluchere, "poses a conflict which the development of the dramatic situation has to solve."[1]

This theme is intricately woven into the drama's psychological, sociological, and philosophical design. Like a coordinating nerve center sending commands from the brain to every part of the body, the play's major theme commands, directs, and controls the entire action of the play. It reflects the emotional and intellectual processes of the playwright from the conception of the dramatic conflict to its resolution.

The comparative study of major themes is like fitting together jigsaw pieces of a puzzle to create the image of a society's social values. The completed picture gives us an understanding of that society's vision, its reality. The drama's action and dialogue, characters and conflict, and resolution to the conflict all serve to illustrate the playwright's vision of a culture.

There are five broad categories into which the major themes fall. Each one reflects a social institution within the construct of a culture and may serve as a basis for a dramatic exploration of that culture's mores and beliefs. While the Pulitzer Prize plays represent aspects of American culture, the categories below form the societal infrastructure of all modern cultures.

The categories are these:
1. Family Life
2. Social Protest
3. Political Heroes
4. Morality and Survival in a Materialistic Society
5. The Spiritual Condition of Humankind

Since many readers will not recognize some of the titles and/or will have only vague memories of some of the plays, the following chapters will include story lines and character analyses in addition to sociocultural assessments. The chapters are of unequal lengths by the very nature of each play's substance and scope. Each play is evaluated for its unique power as it presents a portrait of American life.

THE PULITZER PRIZE PLAYS

PART ONE

Family Life

CHAPTER ONE

Youth in Parental Conflict

Among the Pulitzer Prize plays there are more than a dozen portraits of adolescent youths seeking independence from parental authority. But unique among all of these are the serious-minded youths of *Look Homeward, Angel*, *Long Day's Journey into Night*, and *The Subject Was Roses*. In these plays the adolescent sons are bound intrinsically into a family constellation, respectful of parental authority by necessity, but anxious for the independence from the family that promises a new life.

The essential conflict in each of these plays is sparked by the differences between an idealistic son and a materialistic, authoritarian parent, the sensitive youth attempting in vain to influence a dominating parent to reestablish the family on a solid basis of commitment and love.

Both parents in *Long Day's Journey into Night* and *The Subject Was Roses*, and the mother in *Look Homeward, Angel*, are antagonists whose actions have negatively affected the lives of their families. Confronted by their sons, these parents rationalize their shortcomings and continue to fail to meet their family's needs.

In each play, the mother's role is subtly characterized by how well she feeds her family. In Eliza Gant's boarding house Dixieland, in *Look Homeward, Angel*, the children are served the paying boarders' stale leftovers. In the Tyrone house of *Long Day's Journey into Night*, no one is hungry and little food is eaten, to the consternation of Catherine, the cook. In the Cleary house of *The Subject Was Roses*, the mother's anxieties are reflected in the ill-prepared food:

the waffles stick, the coffee is weak. Indifferent, careless, or hostile, these mothers seem to fail to nourish their families both physically and emotionally.

While there is an absence of food in these plays, there is a great quantity of liquor consumed, bordering on alcohol addiction, especially by the fathers. Booze is the approved drug used as an escape from the pain of introspection and the daily pressures of economic reality. Inebriated, each father can temporarily abandon his responsibility to his family, and even express the hostility he normally hides from his wife and children.

In each of these Pulitzer Prize plays, the youthful protagonist has the same hope for his life: to become a writer. And each one, in his earned success and maturity in virtual time, has looked backward to examine his early years, remembering his family and the serious conflicts he had with one or both of his tyrannical parents. Out of that conflict comes the writer's compassionate insight into human nature. Thus the plays represent a writer's coming to terms with his past, probing the negative and positive power of his family as it has shaped his character and destiny. Like Freud's talking cure, each playwright conjures up in memory the conversations and actions in which he was involved and objectifies himself, examining the issues and the persons that impacted his life. And in the end, each playwright forgives all those who acted with selfishness, ignorance, and tyranny.

In these dramas American youth is not motivated to usurp the power of the parent as in the cultural models of Elizabethan Shakespeare's Prince Hal and the Attic Greek myth of Daedalus and Icarus. Rather, the American youth's objective is to attain psychological, social, and intellectual maturity through education, to develop self-reliance and independence in a new role or enterprise, and to make a meaningful, artistic contribution to society.

The authoritarian character of the American parent changes as each play unfolds, the parent yielding to the need to let go when he or she is confronted by the strong-willed offspring. None of these antagonist-parents serves as models for the youths to emulate. Rather, each serves as a model to avoid becoming.

The chrysalis struggles to be free of the web in which it has been encased.

Overcoming entrapment, breaking free, gives the emerging butterfly its impetus to spread its wings and fly high. And when the drama is done, the rancor is gone, lost in time, and the artist is fine-tuned to the realities and the possibilities of life, its pleasures and its pains.

Look Homeward, Angel (1957–1958)
by Ketti Frings

A Play in Three Acts. Produced by Kermit Bloomgarden and Theater 200, Inc. Opened on Broadway at the Ethel Barrymore Theater, November 28, 1957.

The Original Cast

Ben Gant	Arthur Hill
Mrs. Marie "Fatty" Pert	Florence Sundstrom
Helen Gant Barton	Rosemary Murphy
Hugh Barton	Leonard Stone
Eliza Gant	Jo Van Fleet
Will Pentland	Tom Flatley Reynolds
Eugene Gant	Anthony Perkins
Jake Clatt	Joseph Bernard
Mrs. Clatt	Mary Farrell
Flory Mangle	Elizabeth Lawrence
Mrs. Snowden	Julia Johnston
Mr. Farrell	Dwight Marfield
Laura James	Frances Hyland
W. O. Gant	Hugh Griffith
Dr. Maguire	Victor Killian
Tarkington	Jack Sheehan
Madame Elizabeth	Bibi Osterwald
Luke Gant	Arthur Storch

Ketti Frings' play *Look Homeward, Angel* is a dramatized adaptation of Thomas Wolfe's autobiographical novel, illuminating significant persons and experiences in the life of young Eugene Gant in the late summer of 1916. The settings are Eliza Gant's boardinghouse, Dixieland, and old man W. O. Gant's stonemason's workshop in Altamont, a "hick" town in the back country of North Carolina.

The title of the play comes directly from a line in John Milton's elegiac poem *Lycidas*, written in 1637. It honors the memory of Milton's Cambridge schoolmate who drowned in the Irish Sea, and according to Milton the youth's pure spirit has given him angelic wings to fly to his home in heaven. Milton took the title for his elegy from the Roman Virgil's pastoral poem about a shepherd, Lycidas, who dies young and goes to heaven.

Look Homeward, Angel is, in fact, an elegiac tribute to Wolfe's brother Ben, a pure spirit who also died young. In the play Brother Ben encourages the youthful Eugene to be a writer, and on his death provides Eugene with the money to go off to college to begin to realize his dream. And like the Milton poem, the play ends on a note of optimism: of renewal and of the rededication of the artist to his work.

The Angel addressed in the title of the play has two significances, or "objective correlatives" as defined by T. S. Eliot.

First, it refers to the Carrara marble statue of an angel that stands in W. O. Gant's stonemason yard. This work of art inspired Gant when he was a young man to want to become a stone sculptor, not simply a carver of gravestones. After an apprenticeship as a carver, he acquired the stone yard and the beloved Angel.

Over the years, obsessed with its beauty, old man Gant has tried on at least twenty occasions to duplicate the figure—in vain; he is, indeed, a frustrated Pygmalion wanting to prove his artistic talent by recreating the Galatea-angel, the eternally beautiful maiden of stone, the thing he loves most in this world. No earthly woman he has known—the women at Madam Elizabeth's whorehouse, which he frequented when he was younger; his hag of a first wife, Cynthia; or his second wife, Eliza, whom he has come to hate after thirty-one years of marriage—can possibly compare with his ideal, a dream-model of timeless femininity, undemanding and uncomplaining.

Eugene Gant, too, has a personal angel: his brother Ben, who is correlated with Milton's deceased Lycidas. This identification is made in the very first scene of the play when Ben is sitting on the front porch of the boarding house with his inamorata, Mrs. Marie "Fatty" Pert. It is 1916, the war in Europe is raging, and Ben, who writes for a small-town newspaper, recounts his dream of becoming a pilot in the air corps to fly high in the sky with the angels.

Yet Ben's military enlistment is denied because his frail body has contracted the fatal disease tuberculosis. Though he is thwarted in his earthly dream, Ben is Eugene's undying Angel—the embodiment of everything positive and supportive—and in that form looks protectively on him from heaven.

Tragically, Eugene must face the loss not only of his beloved brother, but of the woman he wants to marry, the beautiful boarder Laura James. Laura leaves Dixieland forever after Eliza reprimands her for consorting, at twenty-three years of age, with her seventeen-year-old son. Confessing her love for Eugene but concerned about the differences in their ages, Laura goes off to marry an older man whom she does not love. She never explains her reasons to Eugene, and he is shattered.

Bitterly unhappy with the prospect of a life without love, Eugene longs to escape the family business and go to college. Yet, though Eliza favors Eugene, she refuses to pay the modest tuition at the state university. Instead, she wants Eugene to follow in her footsteps and learn the family boardinghouse operation.

With its electric sign and advertising handbills, Dixieland is very much a business rather than a home. Eliza caters to her boarders with home cooking and freshly laundered napkins at table; meanwhile, she has raised her family in dank rear bedrooms and fed them the boarders' leftovers. Everything about Eliza proclaims a victory of materialism over maternalism.

Eugene hates his mother's marketing orientation, deeming it a form of begging. But Eliza is determined to have her way, and to win every altercation with delaying tactics, tears, fabrications, threats, commands, and complaints.

An atypical American mother in the literature of the first quarter of the twentieth century, Eliza Gant is as iron-fisted as a man. She has attained economic independence through her business initiative and owns a considerable amount of real estate in Altamont. Operating within the framework of a male-dominated business society, she has tried to teach her children that they must work hard to earn money, that gain comes with driving a hard bargain, and that shrewdness and self-seeking are the guidelines she has followed to her success.

Cunning and ruthless in her dealings with her own family as she is with strangers, Eliza has neither respect nor love for her aesthetic husband. She demands that he sell the stonemason property where he earns his meager living—a transaction that would generate a sizable profit for her but would deprive Gant of a place where he can work and live in the solitary peace he needs. The sale of the yard is thwarted by Ben and Eugene.

To escape Eliza's power, her oldest son, Luke, has joined the Navy. Her only daughter, Helen, is enslaved in the Dixieland kitchen as cook and bottlewasher, but hopes that soon she and her husband will have saved enough money to move away and buy a house of their own. Only Eugene escapes from Eliza's tyranny to set out on the life he dreams of, thanks to the insurance money he inherits on Ben's death.

Realizing that Eugene with his inherited monies will surely leave and never come to see her again, Eliza is shamed into selling one of her properties to pay for her youngest son's college tuition at Chapel Hill. But she cannot suppress her misgivings, and suddenly, in an emotional reversal, she tries to convince him to postpone his plans. She even promises to build a proper family house for the Gants on one of her lots. Standing his ground, Eugene bravely says, "Good-bye."

In the epilogue, the drama captures Thomas Wolfe's voice, expressing Eugene's feelings of loneliness and alienation as, far from Altamont, he too looks homeward, back to earlier years, to examine where he came from and where he now finds himself. From offstage, Ben's ethereal voice urges him to live with courage, to look forward and to accept the reality: like Ben himself, the child-Eugene is gone forever, never to be found again.

Eugene is free to live his life. The major theme of escape from the tyranny of the parent has been resolved.

Long Day's Journey into Night (1956–1957)
by Eugene O'Neill

A Play in Four Acts. Produced by Leigh Connell, Theodore Mann, and Jose Quintero. Opened on Broadway at the Helen Hayes Theater, November 6, 1956.

The Original Cast

James Tyrone	Fredric March
Mary Cavan Tyrone	Florence Eldridge
Jamie Tyrone	Jason Robards, Jr.
Edmund Tyrone	Bradford Dillman
Cathleen	Katharine Ross

Long Day's Journey into Night is an autobiographical drama that reveals the destructive environment of playwright O'Neill's dysfunctional family and the powerful conflict between Edmund Tyrone, the playwright's undisguised alter ego, and his tyrannical father, James Tyrone, the major force in the shaping of the playwright's life.

Before he died, in 1953, O'Neill wrote in his will that the play's production was to be withheld from the stage for twenty-five years after his death to avoid hurt to any person. But three years later, in 1956, his widow, Mrs. Carlotta O'Neill, who had been willed control of all the playwright's works, decided that the play should be produced and that no living person would be defamed or injured.

When he finished writing the play in 1940,[1] O'Neill dedicated it to his beloved Carlotta on their twelfth wedding anniversary, confessing that through the years he had been tormented by the ghosts of his immediate family—his father, James; his mother, Mary; and his older brother, Jamie—and that this work was a final liberation from that torment and a forgiveness for their injury. Eugene O'Neill, America's greatest playwright, is deeply in touch with the inner confusion and depression of each of his characters in this memory play.

A natural actor—like James O'Neill, his matinee idol father—O'Neill was noted for writing detailed stage directions and descriptive settings. In his setting for *Long Day's Journey into Night*, he cites

the well-read library of philosophical, sociological, and literary authors lined up on the bookshelves of the Tyrone summer home. Most
noteworthy by virtue of his absence is Sigmund Freud. Why is Freud
missing from the list? No answer is forthcoming. O'Neill is a Freudian
playwright, profoundly influenced by *Beyond the Pleasure Principle*,
as he indicates in his Work Diary entry in January 1925 when he was
writing *Strange Interlude*. Freud's *Group Psychology and the Analysis
of the Ego* was also in his library.[2] The play's powerful psychological
insights evidence full understanding of Freud's theories.

Long Day's Journey into Night is set in the living room of the
Tyrones' seaside house in Connecticut, during one single day and
night in August 1912. Breakfast is over, and James Tyrone, the famous actor, star of *The Count of Monte Cristo*, has his arm around
his wife Mary's waist as they enter the living room. They have left
their two sons Jamie, thirty-four, and Edmund, twenty-four, talking in the dining room. James, sixty-five, admires his wife's recent
weight gain, which he takes as a sign of health after her stay in a
program to cure morphine addiction. Yet Mary's trembling hands
and uneasy self-consciousness reveal a deep psychological distur-
bance. She attributes her nervousness to her concern for Edmund,
her younger son, who has the hacking cough of the consumptive—a
cough she tries to comfort herself by attributing to a summer cold.

Laughing uproariously as they come from the dining room,
Jamie and Edmund tell the story of the ongoing contest between
their neighbors, the lower-class shanty Irishman Shaughnessy and
the oil-rich millionaire Harker. Shaughnessy's pigs found a break in
the fence between the properties and went wallowing in Harker's
mucky pond. As a result, the pigs have died of pneumonia and chol-
era. And Shaughnessy, after a fistfight and name-calling, is bringing
a court action against Harker.

This narrative that attempts to assign culpability to either
Shaughnessy or Harker is the ironic metaphor of the drama: Who is
responsible for the sickness and hopelessness in the Tyrone-O'Neill
house? The play asks the philosophical question: Who is responsible for life's tragedies? for the Tyrones? for the pigs?

As the Tyrones' lives are revealed, it becomes difficult, almost impossible, to assign the blame for the tragic events to any one person

or to any single, thoughtless action or mistaken judgment. Just as in life, each person must find his own strength to negotiate his journey between Scylla and Charybdis. And just as in Greek tragedy, Fate and the Furies relentlessly turn joy to sadness and hope to despair.

From the moment the curtain rises, the wailing foghorns outside the house are like the voices of ghostly demons retelling the tragic events of the Tyrone family's past. To begin with, one family member is missing: another Tyrone, baby Eugene, died in infancy after catching measles from young Jamie while their parents were away on tour. (Here Eugene O'Neill, his parents' third son, surrenders his name to the dead second child and, in a psychologically self-destructive maneuver, merges his persona into the character of Edmund.)

Mary Tyrone's addiction began on that tour after giving birth to her third son, Edmund. James called in the cheap hotel doctor, who gave Mary morphine to ease her pain. Though Edmund was an innocent child, he is implicated with his father in Mary's addiction, and has assumed much of the associated guilt: his psychological anguish has lowered the defenses of his immune system, making him susceptible to the tubercle bacillus. James, on the other hand, however many times this history is told, will not accept the fact that his miserliness, a residual from his extreme poverty as a boy, is the main cause of his family's anguish.

An accomplished, self-made, and self-disciplined actor, the handsome James Tyrone was amazingly successful from the start in getting bookings and attracting audiences. But the promising young Shakespearean stopped learning new roles when he realized he was making a small fortune with the popular success of his singular hero in *The Count of Monte Cristo*. Shaped by a penniless, fatherless childhood, James perpetually feared the poorhouse and chose financial success over artistic fulfillment. But in his eagerness to secure his fortune, he invested the monies he earned in real estate, which always turned out to be run-down pieces of property bought at bargain prices from con men.

As the play begins, it is clear that James resents being saddled with total financial responsibility for his family. When Mary censures him for trusting the hateful but inexpensive Dr. Hardy, who has treated her in the past, to oversee Edmund's care now, he willfully denies that Edmund is ill, despite the obvious truth.

Edmund, with the tubercular's persistent cough and lack of appetite, knows he must abstain from drinking hard liquor. Yet throughout the long day's journey, father and sons consume bottle after bottle of whiskey. Near the end of the play older brother Jamie admits that he has always had a deep feeling of hostility toward his younger brother and has tried insidiously to lead him onto the same destructive, alcoholic path he has chosen for himself. James, who trained Jamie for the stage, is angry and ashamed of his ne'er-do-well older son and his drug-dependent wife.

Mary scoffs at Doctor Hardy's suggestion of strengthening her willpower as she abandons herself to her addiction and the comfort offered by the ghost world of her past. Wandering the house like a ghost herself, she recalls her adolescent dream of becoming a nun, put aside when she first fell in love with James Tyrone—a recollection that evokes pitiful regret for misbegotten children. As she disregards the wifely and motherly responsibilities of the present, her son Jamie bitterly describes her as a drug fiend, painting her as a devilishly hostile and cunning presence behind the motherly mask.

It is in this smothering environment that the youth Edmund reveals his deepest feelings that his life is meaningless. In a raw-edged confession he tells his father that he tried to commit suicide.

Scorning Edmund's cowardice and his lack of appreciation for all the good things he has, James tells of the poverty and insecurity of his early life, deserted by his father when he was ten. Hungry, deprived of schooling, often without a roof over his head, James found in himself the courage to become an actor, and his determination and natural gifts brought him success.

In the same mood of self-examination, Edmund confesses, in the most heartfelt, poetical terms, his feelings of inadequacy to face life. Like Hamlet he expresses his wish that his "too, too solid flesh" would dissolve itself in the foam and depths of the ocean as he recounts his awareness of himself as a failure, unloved and unloving—on board the rigger bound for Buenos Aires.

The monologue questions the meaning and value of human existence. Edmund is plagued by feelings that he can never belong to the world of humankind, with death offering the only avenue out of the dilemma. Though it lacks Shakespeare's succinctness, O'Neill's monologue fathoms human consciousness of being and non-being in emotional images that no contemporary dramatist has ever expressed so powerfully.

In *Long Day's Journey into Night*, alienation, loneliness and the specter of death stalk the Tyrone house day and night; this morbid, depressing *anschauung* is the light and shadow of the human condition. The final view of Mary, almost lunatic in the throes of her addiction, closes the play in one of the most poignant mad scenes of all drama, recalling Lady Macbeth's sonambulist madness.

Long Day's Journey into Night begins with laughter over the death of Shaughnessy's pigs, but the Tyrone-O'Neills' own predicament cannot be laughed at. Unlike the stupid porcine creatures, the Tyrones know they are ingesting poison, but they are helplessly hooked, moving inexorably toward anomie and death.

The Greek philosopher Heraclitus envisioned the duality of all matter in nature: night and day, good and evil, life and death, all opposing forces—existing as inseparable halves of the one, like yin and yang, or the masks of Comedy and Tragedy. In O'Neill's *Long Day's Journey into Night*, the duality of laughter and tears reflects the journey of the desperate Tyrones.

The Subject Was Roses (1964–1965)
by Frank D. Gilroy

A Play in Two Acts. Produced by Edgar Lansbury. Opened on Broadway at the Royale Theater, May 25, 1964.

The Original Cast

John Cleary	Jack Albertson
Nettie Cleary	Irene Dailey
Timmy Cleary	Martin Sheen

The Subject Was Roses begins on a Saturday morning and ends three days later on a Monday. The scene is the Clearys' modest Bronx apartment. John and Nettie Cleary are thrilled their son Timmy has returned home without a scratch from service in the infantry in the European theater of World War II. Familial warfare is the theme of this play.

Timmy is still asleep when the play begins and Nettie serves John his breakfast before he leaves for a business meeting. Nettie's breakfast sequence with Timmy evidences a powerful, Oedipal magnetism between mother and son that manifests itself in a guilty awkwardness in body language: Nettie holds her son's hand so long he begins to feel uncomfortable and breaks away. She begins to cry over the ruin of Timmy's favorite waffles and the emotional turmoil she feels over his rejection. When he remarks that the light on the waffle iron has gone out, she pauses, perhaps considering that extinguished light as a metaphor for the one-time, subconscious flame of passion between mother and son.

But Timmy assures her he will keep the strangely Oedipal promise he made before he went to war: he will dance with her on the morning of his return. Starting with a slow dance, they begin a polka whose pounding rhythms accelerate until mother and son fall to the floor, breathing laboredly. At that moment, John re-enters, perplexed at discovering the pair on the floor.

Then the battle between the parents to possess Timmy begins: John tells Timmy he is going to skip the meeting and take him to the ball game, and orders him to kiss his mother good-bye. This is a strangely ironic request, since John himself has not so much as *touched* his wife in seventeen years—ever since Timmy was six!— when Nettie gave birth to a premature infant who died in a hospital incubator. Timmy knows about the hostility that precipitated from that death and senses that the same hostility has been continuous through the years, even to this day. This conflict is the focus of the play.

That afternoon, when John and Timmy return home from the ball game, Timmy carries a bouquet of red roses, having heard his mother tell many times how *her* father used to give her roses every birthday. The major dramatic crisis of the play commences when Timmy asks his father to lie, to say that *he*, not Timmy, bought the roses for her, hoping that the gift of flowers will resolve the years of contention between them.

When the talk turns to war and Timmy's war experiences, John reveals his deeply disturbed character in his animated admiration for the ruthless cunning of his Uncle Mike, who, grazed by a bullet in the Spanish American War, exchanged the *yellow tag* on his wrist for the *blue tag* on a soldier lying next to him. He explains the tags: the yellow-tagged are to be considered casualties of war and ignored, left to die; and the blue-tagged are to be treated immediately. Callously, John disregards the fate of the once blue-tagged soldier, only admiring Uncle Mike's cleverness and his will to survive. John adds that one of the big regrets in his life was his rejection when he went to enlist in World War I, because he claimed that he was the sole support of his family.

Timmy's comment that John would have been a great soldier, that he was a born fighter, inspires John to tell how he beat up two friends who teased him as a slacking draft dodger. Timmy recalls a war experience to which he gives serious weight. The bravest thing he did as a soldier, he says, was to sleep with his boots off during his first night in combat. If he'd stayed battle-ready with his boots on, he says, he wouldn't have been able to sleep, and it was the men who couldn't sleep who eventually cracked up. The quirky superficiality of Timmy's soldiering comes through again later when John mentions casually to Nettie that Timmy was present at the liberation of one of the Nazi concentration camps. Timmy offers no comment in the play about what this horrendous experience meant to him. Did he really have this experience? If so, did it have any impact or significance?

Now, as a civilian, Timmy talks about his plans for college under the GI Bill. When John says he will pay any amount to help Timmy through the finest college, over and above the GI Bill allowance, Timmy asks his father's net worth, wondering whether his father can afford to make such a promise. As a coffee salesman working for the same company all his life, John has always been singularly tight-fisted in giving Nettie money for household expenses or for refurbishing the apartment. Unable to bring himself to reveal the meager dollar amount of his savings, he suggests they change the subject. Timmy then presses John to talk about what he deems a noncontroversial subject: how he and Nettie first met and fell in love.

As the reluctant John warms to the story over a beer, Nettie returns to the apartment. John presents her with the roses, moving her to tears. With sudden bravado, John invites his family to celebrate Timmy's return with dinner at the expensive Hotel New Yorker and an evening at the Diamond Horseshoe and Sawdust Trail night clubs. For Timmy, the evening seems to promise reconciliation within the marriage.

The playwright's stage directions, however, reveal the emotional distance between husband and wife: Nettie touches John's shoulder, and at that moment both respond by jumping apart as if shocked by an electric prod.

It is past midnight, Saturday, when the Clearys return to a dark house after a night of drinking, and after a liquor-inspired, silly vaudeville act, Timmy goes to bed.

Suddenly, John attempts to kiss and embrace Nettie, who rebuffs him, saying that the marital problems that have grown from years of neglect cannot be solved in one night. When he persists, she accuses him of expecting her to behave like a prostitute, and he seizes her angrily. Breaking free of his embrace, Nettie picks up the vase of roses and hurls it against the floor. She is deeply offended, having believed that the gift of roses signified a change of heart in her husband. John confesses that the roses weren't his idea at all, but Timmy's. The phallically symbolic roses delineate the sexual dilemma of the neurotic and confused male Cleary family members.

The following morning, Sunday, John is openly hostile at the breakfast table, criticizing Nettie's coffee and baiting Timmy with anti-Semitic bluster. When Timmy fails to respond to this blatant prejudice, John orders him to get into his uniform and accompany him to Sunday mass. Timmy's response that religion doesn't answer his needs, and that he hasn't considered himself a Catholic for quite a while, fuels John's anger, inciting him to rant that he is the master of the house and that as long as Timmy stays under his roof he'll have to do what he's told to do.

When Timmy finally agrees to go, John answers peevishly that he wouldn't drag anyone to church, that only those seeking Jesus' love of their own volition should go. He exits, slamming the door.

Feeling guilty for having allowed the conflict with his father to rage, Timmy decides to go to church on his own to find his father and apologize for his insolent behavior. He blames himself and his mother for ganging up on John over the past twenty years and says they should begin to consider his father's point of view.

Nettie wants to take Timmy instead to visit her disabled brother, Willis, but Timmy refuses to go, adding with an acerbic cruelty reminiscent of his father's belligerence that it's a waste of time to visit Willie, a man who will always have the mentality of a four-year-old. Just as with his father, he immediately regrets his harshness and tries to apologize. Without answering, Nettie takes her pocketbook, heavy with a collection of coins saved from household expenses, and leaves the house.

At ten o'clock that evening, Nettie still has not come home. The dialogue runs on two separate and individual tracks: while John tells of his efforts to locate Nettie, Timmy recalls events surrounding the death-at-birth of his brother John at a hospital seventeen years ago, a most unusual, even unbelievable memory accomplishment!

Timmy recalls that the Jewish Dr. Goldman, and not his father, came and took Nettie to the hospital in the medical emergency that unfortunately ended in the infant's death. John's lack of caring at this traumatic time turned Nettie's love for him to cool indifference. Subsequently, he punished her coolness by coming home very late every night, spending his time in bars.

Wistfully, Timmy recalls constantly phoning bars as a youngster, trying to locate his father, whom he always suspected of consorting with prostitutes. But at the same time he dreaded his father's homecoming, when he would have to listen to the fighting between his parents that kept him awake and made him sick.

Callously, John makes light of Timmy's recollection of hard times, countering sarcastically that only he knows what hard times really are, as he often went hungry and had to leave school when he was ten to find work to support the family when his father became disabled.

Suddenly, after an absence of twelve hours, Nettie re-enters the apartment, offering, when challenged, that she spent the day at the movies. Her husband is still infuriated by her unprecedented absence, but Nettie announces that in the past twelve hours she has enjoyed the only freedom she's ever known.

At two o'clock on Monday morning Timmy and Nettie, both unable to sleep, meet unexpectedly in the living room. Nettie intuits that Timmy is planning to leave the apartment. His departure is clearly necessary if he wants to escape from the tyranny of his authoritarian father and the perversity of an Oedipal relationship with his over-possessive mother.

With plaintive nostalgia, Nettie looks back in time to the days before John entered her life, recounting how a shy boy who liked her threw an apple core at her, giving her a black eye on the first day of a new job. This circumstance moved her to a second job, where she was fated to meet John. She remembers feeling his gaze and being drawn to his sexual energy—sensing however even then that they were not suited as a couple.

Nettie asks Timmy to turn off the light. The playwright implies that Nettie has accepted the fact that Timmy must leave and she must let go, so that the flame of Timmy's Oedipal complex will be extinguished.

As he obeys her request, Timmy speaks a universal forgiveness for each of his parents and for himself. He declares that no blame for any hardship or pain can be leveled at anyone of the Cleary trio.

At breakfast time, John, momentarily humbled by the past weekend's realizations, tries to convince Timmy to stay. But when his son gives in and tells him for the first time that he loves him, it's more than John can take. Frightened by his own emotion, he announces that Timmy had better leave after all. Launching into another diatribe about Nettie's coffee, he seems determined to restore the familiar dynamic of the household. But all three characters' eyes have been opened to the destructive power of the parents' conflict, and to Timmy's need to break free.

CHAPTER TWO

The Unmarried Woman

In the fourteenth century the term *spinnesterre* was the Middle English word for a woman who earned money working alone in her house, sitting at a foot-pedal-driven spinning wheel, turning wool into yarn. Through the centuries, this home industry was one of the very few economic opportunities available to women, besides for-hire domestic household cleaning, infant care, or the disrespected oldest profession in the world.

Yet such employment did not mean independence for a woman as we might understand it today. Because mean minds were always quick to paint women who lived alone as witches or whores, an un-married woman, young or old, often took refuge under a relative's roof (usually a parent or sibling). She shared in the domestic chores: cooking, laundry, mending, and caring for children. And when evening came and all the chores were done, she would take her place at the spinning wheel.

By the mid-nineteenth century, the Industrial Revolution had replaced the spinster's home industry with large, factory-driven enterprise, and the term spinster had long since taken on a new meaning. Once describing a woman's occupation, it had now become synonymous with being unmarried, an old maid, which was—in American society—a generally accepted term of contempt, derision and/or pity.

It is the life of an old maid that the unmarried, twenty-seven-year-old Jean Graham most fears in the first Pulitzer Prize play, *Why Marry?* (1917–1918). In Act III, Jean complains that society is unfair to women since it trains them only for marriage, to be subservient to men, and to understand that any other useful or absorbing endeavor makes them less desirable in the marketplace of marriage.

Indeed, upper- and upper-middle-class women of that time could not simply go to work in a factory if they wished to earn their independence. If economic pressures forced her, a well-brought-up young woman could engage (though society still raised an eyebrow) in a service career such as teaching or nursing, and, if creative, in writing, painting, or singing. But a young woman's entering service was a sure mark of the inadequacy of the father or brother as economic supporter. And since male-dominated nineteenth- and early twentieth-century society regarded the ideal unmarried woman as "the sheltered lady swathed in innocence and propriety,"[1] such women were generally forced to stay at home—either with a mother or a married sister or brother—to live out their lives as patiently as they could until the right man came along.

Most often the right man did not come on his own, and arrangements by parents frequently proved inadequate. As a consequence, the young woman was consigned to a celibate and lonely fate. If a woman dared to face the disapproval of her family and society, she might strike out for an independent life, but her means for economic survival were limited and restricted.

Portraits of never-married women who would not yield to the loneliness of the spinster's life, and of others who did succumb to its bitterness, are presented in three Pulitzer Prize plays: *The Old Maid*, by Zoe Akins; *Alison's House*, by Susan Glaspell; and *Miss Lulu Bett*, by Zona Gale. These plays all focus on the single, unmarried woman's struggle against the oppressive social rules that denied her, as a woman, the right to live the kind of life she wanted.

Most sympathetically drawn by the three female playwrights— Ms. Zona Gale is the only playwright who did not marry—the old maid heroines in these plays are not embittered, prune-faced stereotypes. Each is a woman fully capable of loving and being loved. In fact, she is more sensitively in tune with love than any of the other female characters of the play. In a sentimentally melodramatic way, the spinster is drawn as a romantic spirit who is self-sacrificing in her pursuit of love.

Each play's dramatic conflict is centered on the heroine's dilemma of having loved unrequitedly and sometimes not too wisely. The family has placed severe restrictions on her, demanding her continued celibacy and respectability as a spinster. Emotionally torn, she longs for personal fulfillment in sexual love and adventure in society, but fears the consequences of condemnation by the family she loves.

The three plays are made of the romantic, histrionic stuff that especially inspired the daily soap-opera radio serials of the 1920s and '30s. Alison, Charlotte, and Lulu are all lonely, lovable women, living within the framework of a bustling family. Enterprising and creative, cheerful, long-suffering, and lively, each woman is the efficient manager of the house and the true caregiver of the family's offspring. Each is taken for granted by all family members—young and old—but thrives within herself, believing that her presence and contribution to the family are indispensable.

These heroines also inhabit a world that reveres love in marriage as the essential ingredient of the fulfilled, female life. In these three plays, each of the heroines is marriage-directed (there is no hint of lesbianism, which may sometimes be the unspoken reason for a woman's choice of the single life, often to the consternation of her unsuspecting family), and each validates Alfred Lord Tennyson's proverbial "better to have loved and lost, than never to have loved at all."

Yet this triptych of feminine portrait plays, reflecting the sexual morality and immorality of the first two decades of the twentieth century, also traces the historical evolution of what feminists hailed as the new freedom for women in America, in terms of occupation and marriage. With the ratification of the Nineteenth Amendment to the Constitution in 1920, women were enfranchised citizens with the right to vote, and with this right, for which they had rallied for more than a century, came a significant social and political power.

Many women courageously went to college to prepare for professional careers without stigma, while others entered the marketplace to compete with men for employment. Marriage and housekeeping were no longer the only culturally allowable endeavors in the life of a woman. With the means for economic independence, a woman was no longer forced to choose a mate as an alternative to spinsterhood. Whether she married at all, and whom she would marry if she did, was her choice, and hers alone.

It is important to note that the younger female characters in these three plays move far away from the Victorian model of woman as a passive and shy flower to be plucked. They dare to challenge the prescribed standards of society, particularly in the matters of love and marriage. In *The Old Maid*, the young Tina has a heavy romance that ends in a socially correct marriage; in *Alison's House*, the young Elsa has an adulterous affair with a married man, indifferent to the hurt they are causing his family; and in *Miss Lulu Bett*, high-school-age Diane coquettishly enjoys back-porch heavy petting with boyfriends.

These young women are simply in harmony with their times. Having come of age in a more oppressive day, their seemingly meeker old maid relatives are the true rebels against conformity, struggling to stand up for their rights, refusing to submit to moral codes imposed by their male-dominated society. For love or for sex, they are willing to break the rules and suffer the consequences.

However, in the last analysis, the plays—even though written by women—prove that this is a man's world. The standard of sexual freedom, though contested, is not proved equal. No man suffers any disgrace or punishment for his sexual activity. He is free to love 'em and leave 'em, with no recriminations, no rebuke, no remorse, no societal condemnation, and no child-support obligation. All psychic suffering and social stigma fall upon the unmarried female, who has defied the moral code. It is she who, according to the social dictates designed by men, has to pay the price.

Alison's House (1930–1931)
by Susan Glaspell

A Play in Three Acts. Produced by the Civic Repertory Company. Staged by Eva La Gallienne on Fourteenth Street. Transferred to the Ritz Theater on Broadway.

The Original Cast

Ann Leslie	Florida Friebus
Jennie	Leona Roberts
Richard Knowles	Robert Ross
Ted Stanhope	Herbert Shapiro
Louise	Josephine Hutchinson
John Stanhope	Walter Beck
Eben	Donald Cameron
Elsa	Eva La Gallienne
Miss Agatha	Alma Kruger
Hodges	Howard da Silva
Mrs. Hodges	Mary Ward

Alison Stanhope, having fallen in love with a married man, retreats into a self-imposed spinsterhood, in the tradition of the Victorian literary ladies Christina Rossetti and Emily Dickinson. As a recluse from society, Alison cries out her longing for love in sensual poetry that society finds shocking and offensive.

The action of the play takes place during the last few hours of the nineteenth century, December 31, 1899: a dramatic termination of the Victorian-dominated century and a metaphor for the end of the angelic Victorian lady.

When the play begins, we learn that Alison's house has been sold. Though Alison has been dead for twelve years, it is only now that the dismantling of her house initiates a re-examination of her love life. A reporter from the local newspaper, anxious to write a feature article, has come to visit the house, and is intent on learning and writing about the poet Alison's secret heart.

The playwright paints contrasting figures of sacred and profane loves in the persons of Alison and her niece, Elsa. The virtuous lady, Alison, tormented by unrequited love for another woman's husband, voluntarily withdrew from society. The young, profane, and insensitive Elsa, who lusts after a married man, runs away with him, destroying the foundations of another woman's marriage and family.

In the play, Miss Stanhope is called "an architect of the soul," her house a metaphoric blueprint for moral living to guide the generations of women of the approaching twentieth century. Two of Ralph Waldo Emerson's moralist poems, "Forbearance" and "The House," are quoted, expressing the socio-sexual philosophy of the Victorian era: "Avoid any adulterous liaison. Stay in joyous harmony with the Sun and the Stars. Be abstinent."

Yet the work of twentieth-century doctors and social scientists (Freud, Kinsey, and Masters and Johnson) suggests that Alison's blueprint for a life of sexual repression may have resulted in a condition of female hysteria and neurosis like that of Anna O., Freud's first major study of female sexual anxiety resulting in a form of paralysis.

The single female poet in American culture is traditionally depicted as a heroine of remarkable purity. Looking backward from the beginning of the twenty-first century to the last days of the nineteenth century, one might hold Alison's role-playing of Miss Purity suspect. Can such an untouchable model—almost a caricature—be real? One recalls W. S. Gilbert's Oscar Wilde lookalike, the pretentious, Victorian Bunthorne in *Patience* as he makes his way down Piccadilly with a lily in his hand, adoring his own pose as a very pure young man.

However, there is no hint of satire in the straight and serious exposition of *Alison's House* and the painful, plaintive poetry that brought its heroine fame, all decorously, posthumously published, like Emily Dickinson's. Alison's poetic outpourings ache with longing for the sexual love that she so piously has denied herself.

In Act III, Alison's brother, John Stanhope, admiringly toasts her sacrifice of her whole sensual life for purity's sake. Yet he, as a man, need not obey the same strict standard. The English or American man of his day could, without social penalty, maintain a mistress or two—if he had the money—or, to satisfy his lust, he could handily pay a casual visit to one of the well-frequented local brothels. But he was conditioned to assume a lack of sexual feeling in respectable women, most of all in that most respectable of women, the queen herself—despite her having been romantically linked with her prime minister, falling deeply in love with her cousin Prince Albert, and bearing nine children during their marriage!

Slowly, pompously, the action of *Alison's House* progresses toward the moral reformation of the profligate niece Elsa with sentimentally flavored Victorian dialogue that conjures up yesteryear's soap operas. As the century closes, Stanhope and his daughter Elsa weigh the morality of that past era against what they see as a loosening of morality in the changing times, in this beginning of a new century. The play ends with a contrived, happy reconciliation between father and daughter, rising to a maudlin note of joyful tears as Stanhope gives Elsa a portfolio of Alison's poems, memorializing her aunt's morally correct, sexually repressed life.

The tribute to Alison's sexual abstinence in this 1930–1931 Pulitzer Prize play poses the cryptic question to the young American woman playgoer of that year: Who will be the model woman of the new century, Alison or Elsa? Which are you? Which would you prefer to be?

The resounding answer to the question "To be Alison or not to be Alison?" comes from Hollywood, loud and clear. Throughout America, Clara Bow is the most popular *it* girl, and American moviegoers—mainly swooning women—come crowding into the cinema palaces to see Ramon Navarro and Rudolph Valentino make love to glamorous vamps. In 1931, Rudy Vallee is crooning about the love life of the short-skirted cheerleader Betty Co-ed—with lips of red for Harvard—every collegiate's sex kitten, fifty years before Debbie is hot enough to do Dallas.

The Old Maid (1934–1935)
by Zoe Akins

A Play in Three Acts. Based on a novella by Edith Wharton. Produced on Broadway, January 7, 1935, by Harry Moses. Staged by Guthrie McClintic.

The Original Cast

Delia Lovell	
(Later Mrs. James Ralston)	Judith Anderson
Charlotte Lovell	Helen Menken
Mrs. Jennie Meade	Mary Ricard
Bridget	Hope Landin
Clementina	Yvonne Mann
Dr. Lanskell	George Nash
Mrs. Mingott	Margaret Dale
Joseph Ralston	Robert Wallsten
James Ralston	Frederick Voight
Servant	Gail Reade
Dee	Florence Williams
John Halsey	John Crowell
Tina	Margaret Anderson

"'Tis better to have loved and lost than never to have loved at all." The subject matter of *The Old Maid* places heavy emphasis on the "lost" of Alfred Lord Tennyson's well-known Romantic poem *In Memoriam*. Based on a 1924 novella by Edith Wharton, the sentimental story of Charlotte Lovell's self-sacrifice was further adapted by Casey Robinson into a popular Warner Brothers film, *The Old Maid*, starring Bette Davis and Miriam Hopkins, in 1939.

The Old Maid examines the psychological and societal punishment that the polite society of late nineteenth-century America inflicted upon an unmarried woman who surrendered her virginity to a callous male who abandoned her, even as she bore his child.

Recklessly in love, Charlotte Lovell has sexual relations with Clem Spender, her cousin Delia's ex-fiance, and goes away by herself to give birth to the child, Tina. On her return, Charlotte attempts to support the child and keep her close by, showing courageous enterprise in opening a nursery school. But the prospect of an impoverished life for her daughter without the privileges of class convinces her to accept an arrangement with Cousin Delia.

Ruthless in her concealed jealousy, Delia proposes a plan to take charge of the child as if she were her own and promises never to reveal Charlotte's secret shame. She invites Charlotte to move into her house, where she can be near her child as she grows. But the price of this privilege is a change in status: the young mother must become Aunt Charlotte, the old maid.

Without resentment or envy, Charlotte helps manage Delia's household. Though they are outwardly respectful to each other, Delia, whose husband has died, is inwardly resentful of Charlotte—especially of her having had the affair with her one-time suitor Clem Spender, whom she secretly still loves.

Had his sins been made known, Spender would have found himself branded a villainous cad by the society of his time. But in this play, this Don Juan, who has captured forever the hearts of both Charlotte and Delia, goes completely unpunished. It is the women who love him who suffer for his mistakes and support his child through life.

Is the failure to censure Spender's immorality in some way an oversight of the female playwright Akins? Is the focus of the playwright sentimentally blurred, placing the dramatic emphasis entirely upon the competitive hostility of the two women? *The Old Maid* is essentially a story of women's lives and their feelings about motherhood and children over more than two decades. However, in prescribing no punishment for Spender, does the playwright imply that society feels no punishment is due him? That his siring the child Tina is such a blessing that he can be let off the moral hook?

The action of *The Old Maid* begins on Delia's wedding day, and ends on Tina's wedding day twenty years later. The years in between are heartbreaking for Charlotte, who has sacrificed the joys of motherhood for her daughter's sake. The playwright constantly pumps up pathos, pity, and admiration for the long-suffering and uncomplaining Charlotte, especially in the climactic scene when Tina, unaware that she is giving the most intense hurt to her birth-mother, angrily demands that the dour and withered old maid Aunt Charlotte stop finding fault and meddling with her life.

Beyond the stoicism of Charlotte's silent forbearance, the play offers no realistic solution to the social problems of the unwed mother. The character never considers having an abortion or leaving her child at an orphanage. The mere, close presence of her child gives Charlotte happiness, and she willingly sacrifices her life in a lonely spinsterhood.

It is Charlotte's romantic belief that, in a woman's lifetime, it is a heavenly cherished Destiny to have loved one, and *only* one special man with unconditional love. Charlotte tells Delia that her love for Clem brought her to full womanhood in the realization of motherhood and that Delia could never imagine the joy she felt in Clem's arms. The constancy of her love for Clem is embodied in the love-child. For Charlotte, even if she was not to be wed, having a child with the man she loved was the be-all of her life as a woman.

Her love child, Tina, will never know the true circumstances of her birth, but through her adoption by Delia she becomes eligible for marriage to a respected, successful member of the upper classes. And her mother, Charlotte, has redeemed her sexual sin through self-sacrifice, enduring alone the utmost in self-denial and pain as an old maid.

Miss Lulu Bett (1920–1921)
by Zona Gale

A Play in Three Acts. Opened on Broadway on December 7, 1920.

The Original Cast

Monona Deacon	Lois Shore
Dwight Herbert Deacon	William E. Holden
Ina Deacon	Catherine Calhoun Doucet
Lulu Bett	Carroll McComas
Bobby Larkin	Jack Bohn
Mrs. Bett	Louise Closser Hale

Diana Deacon   Beth Varden
Neil Cornish   Willard Robertson
Ninian Deacon   Brigham Royce

Miss Lulu Bett is a heart-winning play based on Zona Gale's earlier, open-ended novel of the same name. For the stage, Ms. Gale fashioned the story into a comedy that portrays a caring but unassertive woman, forty and plain, who would like to find the right man to love and marry. But how Lulu is to find Mr. Right in her repressive, Midwestern society presents a dramatic social and moral problem.

Lulu Bett dreams of romantic love and having her own home. She considers her spinsterhood a slavey, unfulfilled life. Unabashedly, she wants to know the joys of sex. A courageous heroine, Lulu takes the problematic matter of matrimony into her own hands and fortuitously realizes a happy ending.

Lulu has given a lifetime of domestic service to the household of Dwight Deacon, her droll brother-in-law, a dentist and something of a leading figure in their small, staid community. His wife, Ina Deacon, Lulu's sister, is a vain, helpless scatterbrain of a woman who has two daughters: Diana, sixteen, is a high school student interested in teasing the boys, and Monona, the impish mischief-maker, is a smart, funny, eight-year-old brat. Mrs. Bett, Ina and Lulu's hilariously batty old mother, is good-humoredly forgiven by everybody for her forgetfulness and her ludicrous misunderstandings.

After many years of cooking, washing dishes, and scrubbing floors to earn her bed and board in her sister's house, Lulu secretly hopes that one day a romantic lover will come and take her away from all the drudgery. Her dream-prince happens to be Ninian, Dwight's older brother. For nearly two decades Lulu has been lovingly dusting Ninian's picture, which stands on the piano.

One day, Ninian comes to visit his brother—and, just as she has dreamed, for the first time in her life Lulu is admired for herself, not for her cooking. Ninian is the first man who sees her completely—inwardly and outwardly—a natural beauty.

For entertainment this particular evening, the Deacons play a parlor game in which it happens—serendipitously—Ninian and

Lulu must declare their love for each other. Dwight, who is a justice of the peace, says that their declarations, even though spoken in a game, are tantamount to vows in a wedding service, and, given all the witnesses present, a legal ceremony. Unaccountably, neither Lulu nor Ninian rejects this strange turn of events; both take it seriously, and Lulu agrees to go away with Ninian as a bride on a honeymoon.

A few days into their trip together, Ninian tells Lulu that many years ago he married a singer but later separated from her and lost contact with her. He believes he has read that his wife died in an accident while traveling in South America, but he is not sure—and that's the reason he can't agree that he is really married to Lulu.

Conscience-stricken and heartbroken, Lulu has no choice but to return to her brother-in-law's home and kitchen. But she does not return to her drab, unattractive, cotton housedress and apron. She has transformed herself into a fashion plate, in the high style of the Roaring Twenties, having seen in her travels how the outside, voguish world lives and dresses.

Dwight has neither understanding nor compassion for the abandoned and crestfallen Lulu. He is only concerned with saving his family's reputation by telling everyone that his brother Ninian didn't want Lulu, didn't love her, and therefore shipped her back. This lie, Dwight asserts to Lulu, is necessary for public dissemination, because if brother Ninian is considered guilty of bigamy—even if it were merely an inadvertent act or a game—he could land in jail.

In self-defense, alone with Dwight, Lulu declares the constancy and mutuality of the love she shares with Ninian, but she is willing to be silent about their marriage to protect the man she loves from being accused of a criminal offense. She had a wonderful honeymoon with Ninian and saw the way people enjoyed life in the big cities of America. She declares she has the right, just as much as anybody else, to enjoy a full life.

The playwright may be accounted guilty of creating stock, two-dimensional, characters. She portrays the Deacon brothers, Dwight and Ninian, as completely opposite in character and morality. Dwight is authoritarian and self-centered, careful of the Deacon reputation and his status among his peers. Ninian is a devil-may-care, aging Don Juan who likes to travel in a sophisticated world. Lulu is goodness personified, her forbearance, generosity, and competence contrasted with the selfish ineffectuality of the entire Deacon household, including her own humorously inane mother. Lulu is so unrealistically forgiving that, even when confronted by the possibility of her lover Ninian's duplicity, she returns to Dwight's household with no anger or hostility, remembering only the happiness of her honeymoon.

The play's resolution to Lulu's dilemma is a contrivance, a *deus ex machina* that brings about a happy ending. Ninian arrives to say that he has had official confirmation that his other wife died in South America, and he has come to deliver Lulu from her kitchen bondage, to make her his one and only.

Lulu is symbolic of the liberated American woman who defies society's disdain for the assertive female. She flouts its old, restrictive conventions, to seek out—on her own—a man to marry. She has transformed herself from a dreary, kitchen Cinderella into a sophisticated woman of the world wearing the latest in modish dress, with the hemline above her silk-stockinged knee. The middle-aged Lulu Bett is the champion of the courageous, independent woman of the twenties, declaring her sexual freedom and seeking love unabashedly on her own terms.

CHAPTER THREE

The Conflict of the Sexes

Throughout the history of Western culture there has been a deep underlying conflict between the sexes, controlled always by the institutions of society designed by men. According to the social anthropologist Ashley Montagu in his essay "Marriage—A Cultural Perspective," it is the disillusions and frustrations of married life that tend to destroy the ideals of married love.[1] Two Pulitzer Prize plays, *Craig's Wife* and *The Shrike*, illustrate Montagu's thesis: they dramatize the tortured relationships between a neurotic wife and her almost faultless husband.

Craig's Wife is set in a luxurious, urban drawing room, *The Shrike* in a mental hospital. Both plays focus on the destructive character of a vengeful, emasculating female, a repudiation of the conventional portrait of woman as the gentler sex.

The anti-heroine in *Craig's Wife* is the avaricious and emotionally disturbed Harriet Craig. George Kelly paints her as a savagely self-centered creature without a hint of human kindness.

For that matter, precious little kindness characterizes playwright Kramm's identification of the grotesque Ann Downs with the shrike—a bird that "impales its prey on thorns or suspends it from branches of trees to tear it apart more easily." In both plays, the female antagonist seeks total domination of the male protagonist to command all that he possesses. She seems to intuitively recognize the boy-infantilism of her husband, who, conditioned to regard the female as the weaker sex, in need of masculine support and gentle treatment, finds himself fighting for his life on new and horrifying ground.

The skirmish that explodes into open warfare between the un-suspecting man and his scheming wife is dramatically alike in both plays. In each case the female character declares battle, threatening her husband's reputation, career, masculinity, and life itself. She prevents his advancement in his career and, to support her calculated aggression, enlists a societal institution: the police in *Craig's Wife* and the medical profession in *The Shrike*. Strategically, each woman proceeds to separate her husband from all former friends, and checkmates him in his every move to assert his independence.

Craig's Wife (1925–1926)
by George Kelly

A Play in Three Acts. Produced by Rosalie Stewart. Directed by George Kelly. Opened on Broadway at the Morosco Theater, October 12, 1925.

The Original Cast

Miss Austen	Anne Sutherland
Mrs. Harold	Josephine Williams
Mazie	Mary Gildea
Harriet Craig	Chrystal Herne
Ethel Landreth	Eleanor Mish
Walter Craig	Charles Trowbridge
Mrs. Frazier	Josephine Hull
Billy Birkmire	Arling Alcine
Joseph Catelle	Arthur Shaw
Harry	J. A. Curtis
Eugene Fredericks	Nelan Jaap

Craig's Wife is a dramatic Freudian study analyzing a neurotic woman's inordinate need for absolute control of everything and everybody in order to guarantee her security. Harriet Craig's obsessive attention to orderliness is attributed to her troubled childhood and her hatred for her father. She recalls that her father cheated on her mother, who discovered his duplicity and died of a broken heart. The other woman immediately married him and took control of all her father's assets. Harriet tells Craig how she suffered her step-mother's cruelty and how her father failed to protect her and her sister Estelle in her own house.

All the female characters in the play serve as foils highlighting Harriet's twisted personality. Ethel, Harriet's niece, is a charming young woman, in love with Eugene Fredericks and, according to Harriet, imbued with foolish, romantic notions. To educate Ethel in the realities of marriage, Harriet tells her to make a contract with Fredericks to protect her property rights and her security. She declares that her own marriage to Mr. Craig is an unromantic, *quid pro quo* contract in which each partner gets what he wants: he, a wife and she, security.

Miss Austen, Walter Craig's kind-spirited maiden aunt, describes Harriet as a totally selfish woman, who wants to exclude the whole world because she cannot impose her order upon it. The very walls of the Craig home, she observes, are a symbol of that selfish exclusion—so different from the kindliness and warmth the house exuded when Walter's mother was alive. The change in the house's ambience has proved too much for Miss Austen, who after two years of staying with the married couple feels compelled to leave.

Drawn in sharp contrast with Harriet is Mrs. Frazier, the charming widow who lives next door. The playwright uses the symbol of roses to illuminate their characters: Mrs. Frazier has lived fully, as a loving wife, mother, and grandmother. Her house is full of pink roses that suggest the warmth of the Eternal Feminine. The roses in Harriet's house are snow white, the symbol of the frigidity of Harriet's barren life.

As icy as is Harriet Craig, so passionate is Rita Passmore, the unfaithful wife to Fergus Passmore, Craig's friend. In the morning newspaper Harriet learns about the double murder of Rita and her husband, Fergus. By chance, that very night Walter Craig had been invited to play poker with the Passmores. At midnight, three hours before Rita came home, Craig left the Passmores' house.

When Harriet reads that the police report that a car was seen leaving the Passmore house around midnight, she immediately senses a way to implicate Craig in what might be an adulterous triangle. The papers report that Fergus Passmore, a jealous husband, may have killed his errant, adulterous wife, Rita, and then himself.

The hostility between Walter Craig and Harriet explodes into bitter warfare after she scolds him for not shunning the Passmores as she has always insisted he do. He complains that she has driven away all of his friends.

When Craig learns later that the police came to his house to interrogate him, Harriet lies about not having placed the phone call that brought the police and voices her concern that she might suffer some possible notoriety because of her husband's having been present in the Passmores' house.

In a brutally dramatic exchange, Harriet reveals her dislike of Walter Craig's very presence in the house she treasures, unable to tolerate his fingerprints on furniture or the cigarette ash that he may have dropped accidentally. In this climactic scene, Harriet leaves the living room in a fury. Walter, bitterly angry, smashes her treasured vase that graces the mantle of the fireplace, in effect, destroying the *penates*, the household gods of their fruitless marriage.

Walter Craig's smashing of the vase symbolically parallels Passmore's crime. In effigy, the woman who torments his life has been removed, destroyed. Both Craig and Passmore are self-and-other-destructive, grown-up boys who naively expect all women to behave in the way they believe their idealized mothers did.

When Harriet calls Craig a fool, he realizes that he was, indeed, foolish ever to have had romantic feelings for her. Realizing she lied about the phone call she made that brought the police to implicate him in the Passmore crime, he understands that she is his dangerous enemy.

Then Harriet discloses the psychological problems of her early life in a confession of deep-rooted hatred of men in power. This shocking revelation confounds Craig, and he leaves the house.

Now Harriet has what she has always wanted—sovereignty over her possessions, without any interfering persons who might scratch the furniture or cause wear and tear on the carpets. She has won aloneness, with no need for anyone's affection. Harriet, entombed in her living room, believes she has triumphed. But we in the audience would prefer to have pity on her.

The Shrike (1951–1952)
by Joseph Kramm

A Play in Two Acts. Produced by Jose Ferrer, with Milton Baron. Staged by Jose Ferrer. Opened on Broadway at the Cort Theater, January 15, 1952.

The Original Cast

Miss Cardell	Phyllis Hill
Fleming	Tom Reynolds
Miss Hansen	Jeanette Dowling
Dr. Kramer	Stephen Elliott
Perkins	James Hawthorne Bey
Grossberg	William Bush
Dr. Barrow	Isabel Bonner
Patient	Vincent Donahue
Ann Downs	Judith Evelyn
Jim Downs	Jose Ferrer
Dr. Schlesinger	Somer Alberg
Sam Tager	Will Lee
George O'Brien	Martin Newman
Joe Major	Joe Comadore
Don Gregory	Philip Huston
John Ankoritis	Will Kuluva
Frank Carlisle	Leigh Whipper
William Schloss	Billy M. Greene
Dr. Bellman	Kendall Clark
Miss Wingate	Mary Bell
Harry Downs	Edward Platt
Tom Blair	Arthur Jarrett

The Shrike dramatizes the conflict between Ann Downs and her estranged husband, Jim, as she malignantly takes control of his life after his attempted suicide.

Set in the psychiatric ward of a large urban hospital, the play follows Ann's machinations to enlist the support of the staff as gradually she undermines Jim's will and his sense of reality. At the end of the play he will be allowed release from the psychiatric ward only in her custody. The alternative is a transfer to the state insane asylum, from which he believes there can be no hope of discharge.

The play's three acts and fourteen scenes present a harrowing account that raises doubts as to the operational integrity not only of this psychiatric unit, but of actual asylums across America.

As the protagonist in the play, Downs is a psychiatric case study, fighting to prove that he is sane and losing the battle because of his wife's crafty maneuverings. The medical profession gives him no choice but to submit to Ann's wishes. In the marital struggle, Ann is symbolically that murderous, flesh-eating bird, the shrike.

What is missing is the background of this marriage. It is interesting to conjecture how Downs, a theater director, might have been deceived by Ann, obviously a superlative actress, into entering a loveless marriage that he eventually fled to pursue an extramarital romance. Now Ann is moved by a double vengeance, having been disgraced by Jim's moving out of the apartment and humiliated by his sexual involvement with another woman. She is determined to destroy that liaison and to prevent her rival, Charlotte, from visiting or communicating with Jim in any way. Charlotte never appears in the play, but through Jim's eyes, the contrasting characters of the women—the angel and the harpy—are evidenced.

In his first interview with the psychiatrists, Jim is rational as he describes the causes of the depression that prompted his suicide attempt: his incompatibility with his unloving wife, Ann; his failure to find work as a director in the theater; and his inability to earn enough as a schoolteacher to meet his financial obligations. Ann, from whom he has been separated for over three months, was pressing him for money and he had less than a dollar to last him until the end of the month when his teacher's salary check was due. His GI life- insurance policy would have provided Ann with $10,000.

With superb cunning and malevolent guile, Ann wins over the doctors and nurses, portraying herself as the long-suffering, loving wife of an unstable, even violent husband. She directs the psychiatrists to disbelieve what Jim asserts as he attempts to prove his sanity in order to be discharged. The doctors, for their part, are shown as easy dupes to Ann in their unquestioning acceptance of her presentation of the facts of the case. They do not consider the possibility of any interpretation other than Ann's, nor do they look to other sources for confirmation of the facts. When Jim realizes that everything is working against the possibility of his ever being released, he begins to play a game of deceit with Ann, who to his chagrin is his hospital-approved, sole guardian.[2]

It is the cruel dramatic action in Nurse Wingate's ward that provides Jim with the essential understanding that on the psychiatric ward, one can be punished unfairly. During a seemingly harmless dialogue exchange at bedtime, a patient, Schloss, provokes another patient, O'Brien, by announcing that O'Brien's mother is a whore. Angrily, O'Brien threatens to break his neck, and Schloss calls in Nurse Wingate to report the threat. Summarily, without a thorough investigation, Nurse Wingate uses her power to punish, summoning attendants to move O'Brien to the terrors and tortures of the violent ward, the dreaded Ward 7.

Nurse Wingate's unfair punishment of O'Brien can be likened to Ann Downs's grotesque punishment of Jim, establishing the major theme of *The Shrike*: life is a dangerous game played with shifting rules, and the most evil contestant determines the outcome. Jim Downs discovers this truth as he observes that Schloss' evil, championed by Nurse Wingate, is triumphant over the innocuous, forthright O'Brien.

After giving Jim a telegram from Charlotte, Nurse Wingate cautions him to give up his lover, because now only Ann has the power to effect his release. Now, he comes to realize he must also deceive the psychiatrists and convince them that he loves Ann.

The drama ends with Downs's awareness that he has lost the battle, that he is trapped in Ann's power. But it is hoped that he has learned the rules of Ann's game, and that when he is outside the hospital ward he will confront her craftily, with a more potent guile than hers, on a level battlefield. When she has lost the support of his captors, this director of theater's real-life confrontations and denouements may be able to orchestrate a scenario wherein he can clip the shrike's wings. Yet Harry's speech that closes Act III, Scene 1, suggests that Jim's new criminal record will make escape difficult or impossible; that he will be dependent on Ann's good graces for the foreseeable future. Given this, do we, and does Jim, still have much reason for hope?

The ill-fated triangle of Jim Downs with two women, his destructive wife Ann and his lover Charlotte, ends on stage with the emasculation of the helpless male, high drama in the battle of the sexes.

CHAPTER FOUR

The Drive for Generation

As humans, our full knowledge of the significance of the sexual act in procreation, and our willingness to mate in any season, separates us from all other creatures. The begetting of children to secure an inheritance or to ensure the continuity of a family bloodline is the major theme of five Pulitzer Prize plays: *They Knew What They Wanted*, by Sidney Howard; *Strange Interlude* and *Anna Christie*, by Eugene O'Neill; *All the Way Home*, by Tad Mosel; and *Cat on a Hot Tin Roof*, by Tennessee Williams.

The dramatic action centers on the mystery of a child to be begotten, who will be responsible for new and unique features in the generation of humankind. The circumstances surrounding the conception of the hero-to-be are exceptional in each play.

In *They Knew What They Wanted* and in *Strange Interlude*, the pregnancy is a result of insemination not by the husband, but by a substitute male. In *All the Way Home* and *Cat on a Hot Tin Roof* the conflict concerns some of the most difficult responsibilities surrounding procreation—in the one, the widow carries her deceased husband's child, and in the other a sexually deprived wife aches to be impregnated by an emotionally confused and possibly homosexual husband. And in *Anna Christie*, the heroine struggles to overcome her hatred of men and sex, learned from a bitter life experience, that keeps her from embracing love and motherhood.

The matter of insemination by a selected male substituting for an impotent, absent, or sterile husband is an ancient theme, reflected in both Hebrew and Greek literature.[1] In Genesis, the barren marriage of Sarah and the aged patriarch Abraham is miraculously made fruitful after the advent of the three angels, informing the couple of God's promise of a son.

The Greek myths frequently recount the affairs of Zeus cohabiting with mortal women to produce various offspring, his visitation expressed in poetic metaphor: a shower of gold, a cloudy-white mist, a white swan, a muscular bull. Zeus' appearance in human form is the basis of the dramatic conflict in the Zeus-Amphytrion-Alcmene triangle that ends in the birth of Hercules. Both *They Knew What They Wanted* and *Strange Interlude* have their origins in a marital triangle modeled after the Alcmene myth. Both are similar in the notion that a fated woman is to be inseminated by an extramarital donor to produce a child with transcendent qualities.

In *Anna Christie*, the appearance of Matt Burke, the stoker, fished out of the ocean, is a dramatic miracle, and for Anna and Matt, it is a fateful love destined by nature. The supernatural factor seems to be O'Neill's sense that the god of the ocean has engineered the meeting of Matt, an ocean-man, with Anna, an ocean-woman, to insure that she will give birth to ocean-loving progeny

There are no spiritual or transcendent birth-happenings in *All the Way Home* or in *Cat on a Hot Tin Roof*. Both plays are realistic explorations of America's basic cultural and moral values as they dramatize the desire for the continuity of one's family name, inheritance, and tradition.

In his philosophical overview of the human being, Nietzsche accounts each newborn individual an "unobjectionable opportunity for a new possession."[2] But in these plays the child is always reckoned more than a property or a responsibility. The conceived child is Nature's gift to humanity, promising the improvement of the species, even as it guarantees continuity to the human family. And each of these plays, whose major theme is the birth of a child, looks hopefully to the new generation as the basic insurance for the preservation of the American heritage.

They Knew What They Wanted (1924–1925)
by Sidney Howard

A Play in Three Acts. Produced by the Theater Guild. Staged by Philip Moeller. Opened on Broadway at the Garrick Theater, November 24, 1924.

The Original Cast

Joe	Glenn Anders
Father McKee	Charles Kennedy
Ah Gee	Allen Atwell
Tony	Richard Bennett
The R.F.D.	Robert Cook
Amy	Pauline Lord
Angelo	Hardwick Nevin
Giorgio	Jacob Zollinger
The Doctor	Charles Tazewell
First Italian Mother	Frances Hyde
Her Daughter	Antoinette Bizzoco
Second Italian Mother	Peggy Conway
Her Son	Thomas Scherman

The character of the foolish and cuckolded husband, popular in Greek and Roman phallic comedies, has survived through the Italian *commedia dell' arte*. He is represented in this Pulitzer Prize comedy by the illiterate, loveable, cursing, great-hearted Tony Patucci, who speaks broken English and has brought to Napa, California, from his native Italy his knowledge of successful wine-making. The exuberant spirit of a happy, reveling, once-sexual Bacchus—in the person of Tony—emanates throughout the play.

Past sixty, Tony has decided to take a young wife in order to have a child, preferably a son. He admits that he has waited a long time to get married, to be rich enough to give his wife-to-be everything, and despite Father McKee's concern, he doesn't care whether the woman he's selected, a pretty waitress who recently served him in a San Francisco restaurant, is a Catholic or not.

To make himself desirable and win Amy, Tony has enlisted the help of the handsome migrant fruit picker Joe to write the letter that proposes marriage. He has also included a photograph—of the youthful Joe, who has been working as Tony's vineyard foreman for the past five months and who, Tony says, is like a son.

The deception works. Joe writes a series of letters to Amy and signs them "Tony." Impressed with the offer of security from a young, rich, and strikingly handsome husband-to-be, Amy enthusiastically heads for the Napa Valley to become Tony's mail-order bride.

On the day set for the wedding, with Amy scheduled to arrive by train, the comic complications begin. Tony has celebrated with too much wine, but he is determined to meet Amy himself and to have Joe leave the premises immediately and forever so that Tony's duplicity with the photo can be explained as a mix-up. Joe and Father McKee caution Tony that he is too drunk to drive, and Joe offers to go to the station to meet the bride. Disregarding Joe, Tony drives off and has a serious accident, breaking both legs.

Meanwhile, the man in charge of the R.F.D. (Rural Free Delivery) at the railroad station has driven Amy to Tony's house, where gradually she learns the truth about Joe and Tony. Angry and disappointed, she is determined to go back to San Francisco, but is forced to change her mind because she doesn't have the money for the fare. She has also given up her job at the restaurant, and jobs are hard to find. When she hears that Tony was taken by ambulance to the local hospital where his legs were to be put into casts, she decides pragmatically that the lesser of two evils is to stay on.

On the night of the wedding Tony lies in bed in pain. But, just as in Roman phallic comedy, the two young people have sex and Amy becomes pregnant. In the six months that follow, Amy nurses Tony devotedly. But as her pregnancy begins to show, she announces that she must leave. When Tony demands an explanation, she confesses that she is carrying Joe's baby.

On hearing this, Tony grabs his gun from the wall and tries to shoot Joe, who manages to get the gun away from him. He pleads with Amy to stay and not go off with Joe, who as an organizer for the Wobblies will not be well equipped to support a wife and baby. He explains in broken English he truly wants the child and will provide all the advantages that money can supply.

In keeping with the theme of Nature's fertility, the comedy begins in the early spring of the year, when the grapes in Tony's vineyard are small and green. And in the last act, months later, the grapes are large and purple. Like the grapes, the characters' dreams grow to a ripe sweetness; everyone in *They Knew What They Wanted* ultimately gets what they want. Joe has had the joy of a sexual liaison with Amy without any subsequent parental responsibility. Amy gets the economic security she longs for, for herself and her child. And Tony realizes his dream of an heir.

As a Pulitzer Prize play, *They Knew What They Wanted* creates a new image of the Italian as a lover of America. The stereotype of the Italian as a tough gangster, anarchist, or communist is happily repainted as a happy-go-lucky, harmless entrepreneur and benefactor. Tony has hung the portraits of Giuseppe Garibaldi and George Washington, the two Fathers of their respective countries, in his living room; they represent his dual allegiance and he rejoices in the prospect that his offspring will inherit both the humanism of Italy and the democratic principles of America.

Creating an all-American family out of an adulterous escapade, Tony is all heart, the model of the lucky greenhorn adapting to American ways. A comic masterpiece of cultural integration, *They Knew What They Wanted* announces its own positive message. Its major theme of generational begetting is realized in that special Italian-American child-to-be-born, like a new variety of grape in the vineyard, promising to bring a joyous, zestful diversity to America.

Strange Interlude (1927–1928)
by Eugene O'Neill

A Play in Nine Acts. Produced by the Theater Guild. Staged by Philip Moeller. Opened on Broadway at the John Golden Theater, January 30, 1928.

The Original Cast

Charles Marsden	Tom Powers
Professor Leeds	Philip Leigh

Nina Leeds	Lynn Fontanne
Sam Evans	Earle Larimore
Edmund Darrell	Glenn Anders
Mrs. Amos Evans	Helen Westley
Gordon Evans, as a boy	Charles Walters
Madeline Arnold	Ethel Westley
Gordon Evans, as a man	John J. Burns

The notion of eugenics and the upward-spiraling development of the human species echoes in *Strange Interlude*. In nine acts, and four and a half hours of playing time, *Strange Interlude* is a Freudian exploration of the psyches of each of the sexually driven characters in complex dramatic conflicts as they grow older and more savage. Through O'Neill's unique reinvention of the dramatic aside, suggesting an adaptation of the Greek chorus or a Shakespeare soliloquy, the audience hears the subconscious thoughts of each character articulated for the audience's ears alone.

The major theme of *Strange Interlude* is the begetting of a special child in a miraculous reincarnation, destined by fate to be endowed with a morality and creative vision far above the common herd. This child, Gordon Evans, grows into the embodiment of the *Uebermensch*, or Superman, who appears in Nietzsche's philosophical treatise *Thus Spake Zarathustra*. In keeping with the idea of breeding selection in Darwinian evolution, Gordon Evans represents the embodiment of a new generation of human beings who will come to shape the planet's destiny.

The dramatic structure of the play is triangular, making *Strange Interlude* one of the most inventive and mysterious of O'Neill's plays. According to the Greek philosopher Pythagoras, three is the perfect number; in the series one, two, three, the number three represents the perfect incorporation of the beginning and the middle in the end. The Greeks conceived the world in a trinity of deities: Zeus (heaven), Poseidon (sea), and Hades (Underworld). Christian theology incorporates into the mystery of the Holy Trinity the individual forms of God the Father, the Son, and the Holy Ghost.

Strange Interlude is a play of an unprecedented (three-squared) nine acts, and O'Neill seems obsessed with formulating and then restructuring the triangle of characters in conflict, adding a sense of symbolic and mythic otherworldliness to his narrative.

The first of the threes is the dramatic triangle that tells of the life-death-rebirth of Gordon Evans. O'Neill gives new life to the secret rituals of the Greek Eleusinian Mysteries of Dionysus, the God of Wine and Vegetation. As in these Mysteries Dionysus is resurrected from the dead, Gordon Evans is reborn in the person of Gordon Evans Shaw.

The second dramatic triangle is constructed around the Greek idea of the power of the curse. The evildoer and his victim are the first two elements, while the avenging Furies or Harpies, who have been summoned by the intoning of the curse, make up the third. They are vulture-like, ruthless spirits demanding revenge—blood for blood—and they bring the inevitable suffering and death to the members of the cursed House.

The third triangular construct is the sexual trio of Sam, Nina, and Dr. Darrell as they are involved in sexual immoralities allowable only to the gods as they function in Greek myths. Though the woman in the myth is married, lustful Zeus takes possession, impregnating her in order to produce exceptional offspring: Hercules, Apollo, Diana, Dionysus, etc. The miracle births in the Greek myths, like the Egyptian Isis-Osiris myth, parallel the Christian Annunciation.

In *Strange Interlude* Nina Leeds, shunning her husband, Sam, deliberately selects a genetically sound male, her doctor, Dr. Darrell, to sire the offspring she wants. The play is an epic drama because it announces and portrays the coming of an epic hero: the reborn Gordon Evans Shaw, whose soul has evolved through Nina Leeds' womb.

Nina is a complex incorporation of the best and the worst of three great women in Greek mythology: Penelope, who is faithful in her love, though besieged by suitors; Medea, who discovers her husband's adulterous entanglement and destroys his lover as well as their sons; and Jocasta, who falls in love with her own son, Oedipus. Nina plays Penelope to her beloved Gordon Shaw, Medea to her husband, Sam, and Jocasta to her son, Gordon Evans II.

According to the Greeks, tragedy has its roots in a sin committed against the natural order. The House of Atreus is cursed by Thyestes when he discovers that his brother Atreus has committed adultery with his wife. In revenge, Thyestes serves Atreus a stew made up of Atreus' own sons' flesh. The sin is the taboo against cannibalism. For successive generations the family is cursed with cruelties of hatred and murder. The source of the conflict of *Strange Interlude* originates in the curse that Nina Leeds puts upon her father when he confesses he prevented her liaison with her lover, the late Gordon Shaw, because he himself was perversely drawn to her.

Subsequently she marries Sam Evans, but aborts his unborn child when she discovers that his house is cursed with an inherited madness. Then, rejecting conventional sexual morality, Nina has an affair with Dr. Darrell—a perfect specimen of a man—and conceives his child.

But Nina remains obsessed with the martyrdom of flying ace Gordon Shaw, shot down in combat during World War I. Gilbert Murray writes in his *Five Stages of Greek Religion*:

> . . . there is nothing that stirs men's imagination like the contemplation of martyrdom, and it is no wonder that the more emotional cults of antiquity vibrate with the worship of this dying Savior . . . who in so many forms dies with his world or for his world, and rises again as the world rises, triumphant through suffering over Death and the broken *Tabu*.[3]

The death of Gordon Shaw represents to Nina the beautiful sacrificed Savior of the twentieth century, and she is driven to find in herself the instrument of his rebirth, the miraculous son. Hence she sees in her son the image not of his biological father, Dr. Darrell, but of her former lover. And at the end of the play, Gordon Shaw and his promise of a brave new world are clearly resurrected in the person of young Gordon Evans.

Not only the play's structure but also its poetical symbolism involves the triad. Gordon Evans is a child of three fathers—Dr. Darrell, his biological father; Sam Evans, his supporting father; and Gordon

Shaw, his spiritual father. Three vehicles appear in the action of the play: two boats and an airplane, which configure the emotional and psychic relationship of Gordon to each of his fathers.

At the end of Act V, the biological father, Dr. Darrell, is unwilling to assume paternal responsibility for his unborn son. He escapes by sailing for Europe. In Act VI, on Gordon's eleventh birthday, Darrell has returned to America. He gives the youth a magnificent model boat. Seeing his mother and Dr. Darrell kissing, the boy smashes the boat. To Gordon, the embrace is evidence of his mother's betrayal of his beloved father, Sam Evans. In Freudian terms, Gordon's destruction of the boat is the symbolic murder of his biological father, Darrell—like Oedipus' killing Laius: retributive justice for the father's having abandoned the son to die.

In Act VIII, Gordon is a full-grown man, proving himself the winner of a boat race as his fiancee, Madeline, cheers him with his parents from their yacht. Ecstatic at the victory, Sam is given pause by Nina's possessive anxiety and stops to soothe her. Cheerfully admitting that his supposed son resembles him not at all, he agrees with Nina that Gordon seems instead to have inherited her former love Shaw's body and spirit. Then, suddenly, he collapses to the deck, having suffered a stroke that will end his life.

In Act IX, the twenty-two-year-old hero has finally emerged as Superman, the winner of all competitions, flying high in his airplane above all that is mundane. Sensing the airplane is the spirit of his father—Gordon Shaw's soul—he takes off into a serenely peaceful sky with his beloved Madeline as the play ends in the distant year 1939.[4]

By now all the loves of Nina's life have moved away, leaving her alone. Dr. Darrell recognizes Nina's jealousy of her daughter-in-law, Madeline, and sternly advises her to give up meddling in others' lives and trying to own them.

Having assumed many female roles—daughter, wife, mistress, mother, mother-in-law, widow—Nina Leeds believed the meaning of her life lay in her role as the birth-mother of the Superman. Nina identifies her womb as the bridge linking the past with the present and into the future via Gordon Evans. She defines her existence as a moment in time, a strange interlude, prefaced by a remembered past, envisioning a future that bears witness to the fact of having lived.

Strange Interlude dramatizes generation as the mystery of the transmigration of souls, and predicts the advent of a whole new race of supermen who will take possession of the earth.

All the Way Home (1960–1961)
by Tad Mosel

A Play in Three Acts. Produced by Fred Coe, in association with Arthur Cantor. Staged by Arthur Penn. Opened on Broadway at the Belasco Theater, November 30, 1960.

The Original Cast

Rufus	John Megna
Boys	Larry Provost, Jeff Conaway, Gary Moran, and Robert Ader
Jay Follet	Arthur Hill
Mary Follet	Colleen Dewhurst
Ralph Follet	Clifton James
Sally Follet	Lenka Peterson
John Henry Follet	Edwin Wolfe
Jessie Follet	Georgia Simmons
Jim Wilson	Christopher Month
Aunt Sadie Follet	Dorrit Kelton
Great-Great-Granmaw	Lylah Tiffany
Catherine Lynch	Lillian Gish
Aunt Hannah Lynch	Aline MacMahon
Joel Lynch	Thomas Chalmers
Andrew Lynch	Tom Wheatley
Father Jackson	Art Smith

Based on the Pulitzer Prize–winning, posthumous novel *A Death in the Family*, by James Agee, *All the Way Home* by Tad Mosel recreates for the stage the life of the Lynch and Follet generations, traumatized by the untimely death of the significant father.

The major theme and action of *All the Way Home* focus on the everyday home-life of the Follets of Knoxville, Tennessee, during four days in May 1925. The conflict that despoils the harmony of the Follet family is Jay Follet's alcoholism, an addiction that has been constantly undermining his marriage. His wife, Mary, has tried to give him strength to break his dependency by encouraging his faith in the Lord.

Jay's death in an auto accident is the catastrophic moment of this plotless play. Driving homeward, possibly under the influence, after a midnight visit to his dying father, Jay meets his end in what appears to be an accident. But on closer analysis as the play unfolds, Jay's death may alternatively be conceived of as an unconscious act of self-punishment for betrayal of his love and responsibility as a husband and father. We never know whether Jay, who had achieved some mastery over his addiction, was drinking on the night of his death, and it is a possibility that his wife must accept and even embrace as she decides how she will remember her beloved husband.

The play is not driven by an intricate plot but rather by the characters' search for meaning in their lives and their discovery that the fullness of life is found in the strength of the family, its community, continuity, and togetherness. The characters contemplate mortality without cliches, avowing that no man is "too big to cry at bein' left alone in a big cold bed"—that is, the grave.[5] The major theme of the play affirms that accident is integral to the life-death-life design, and that all lives seem to be linked together in a continuum that, for the survivor, lessens the sense of the tragic.

The play begins with Rufus announcing his name to the teasing neighborhood boys. His father, Jay, is quick to explain that Rufus is a name to be proud of because it was the name of so many good men of earlier generations of Follets. The naming of offspring after the deceased suggests more than a memorial. It establishes within the person a sense of continuity with past souls, a spiritual source of strength and an intimation of immortality.

Rufus begins to understand the cycle of youth and old age when Jay takes his family to visit the withered, 103-year-old matriarch Great-Great-Granmaw Follet in the Tennessee hills. As a centenarian, Great-Great-Granmaw is anxious to know that when she dies, there will be a continuous progression of births to give immortality to the Follet family. She trembles with excitement when the young Follets gather around her, taking special delight in the presence of her great-great-grandson, Rufus.

Rufus is the only one who sees Great-Great-Granmaw having a urinary accident, so great is her joy when Rufus kisses her. He is aware of his own recent toilet training, the mastery of his infantile incontinence which has given him a sense of pride. He is amazed to see Great-Great-Granmaw's return to infantile incontinence and wonders how it happens and what it means. Great-Great-Granmaw, though she cannot say so, understands where she and little Rufus each stand in the circle of life and death—at his birth, she sent his father, Jay, a postcard announcing that she herself had been reborn.

Firm in his belief that family kinship gives life its ultimate meaning, Jay explains his faith in family as an upward-circling ladder of human continuity leading into the future and backward in time to Adam—what we today could see as an evolving spiral helix of DNA. He contemplates a series of fathers standing on the ladder below, singing to their offspring with the joy of going upward into the future, a fantastic, dynamic image of the continuity of life and time.

When Jay dies, leaving his work as a man and a father unfinished, necessity demands that Mary assume a new role: she must begin to teach her son everything his absent father would have taught him. Each of the meaningful learning experiences in Rufus's short life is poignantly dramatized: his father's teaching him to shake hands like a man; his acceptance into the group by his peers on his father's death; the purchase of a cap, the sign of a man's coming of age; his learning the facts of life from his mother, as she puts his small hand against her swollen belly, filled with life. The experience of feeling the moving limbs of an unborn child, his sibling-to-be, in his mother's womb is profound, coming immediately after seeing his father dead. For the first time, feeling the stirrings of the unborn child in Mary's womb, Rufus realizes the miracle of life, where each of us begins to become what we will be.

Though Mary's unborn child will never know his father as a living person, he will learn who his father was. Jay will remain a power, an invisible link in the continuity of the Folletts' helix.

The title change from Agee's original *A Death in the Family* to *All the Way Home* is a positive way of asserting the major theme of this play. One generation after another spirals into the continuity of family, the power that conquers death.

Anna Christie (1921–1922)
by Eugene O'Neill

A Play in Four Acts. Produced and staged by Arthur Hopkins. Opened on Broadway at the Vanderbilt Theater, November 2, 1921.

The Original Cast

Johnny-the-Priest	James C. Mack
First Longshoreman	G. O. Taylor
Second Longshoreman	John Hanley
A Postman	William Augustin
Chris Christopherson	George Marion
Marthy Owen	Eugenie Blair
Anna Christopherson	Pauline Lord
Mat Burke	Frank Shannon
Johnson	Ole Anderson
Three Sailors	Messrs. Reilly, Hansen, and Kennedy

Anna Christie focuses on the mysterious, primal, unfathomable urges in woman and man that compel them to follow preordained patterns of existence, determined by countless past generations.

The major theme of procreation is given a mystical aura. The Viking god of the Sea, Aegir, is never mentioned by name, but he is the Norse god, personified as that "ole davil sea," that controls the lives of the characters of the play, and those of all the Scandinavian Christophersons and Thor Heyerdahls who identify the sea as the Viking's destiny.

The play opens in Johnny-the-Priest's saloon near South Street in New York City. Anna Christopherson has just arrived in New York from the Midwest, where her father sent her as a young girl, believing she would be safest away from the sea he mistrusts. But on the Minnesota farm where she worked as a household servant, Anna was raped by the family's youngest son. She ran away to St. Paul and worked there as a prostitute, but became ill when the house where she worked was raided by the police and all the women went to jail.

In Minnesota, Anna felt restive and self-destructive—out of her element. Returning to the waterfront, she says she feels comfortable, restored by her sight of the sea, expressing a deep love for the sea-air and the incessant throb and crash of the waves on the shore.

Bathed in the cloud of sea-fog, suggestive of a baptismal sanctification, Anna discovers meaning to her life: she is a sea-woman, subconsciously in love with the sea-god Aegir, destined to be a breeder of sailors, the men whose lives are bound to the sea. Anna's dramatic realization of her reason-for-being provides her with a sense of her worth and the awareness of the duality that roils in her nature: her intense hatred for the land, where men have made her feel worthless, and her love for the sea, where all the elements give validity to her life. To her father's dismay, she declares she'd rather have one drop of ocean than all the farms in the world.

Christopherson warns his daughter against the dangers of the sea-fog, but Anna finds her refuge in it. In the shelter of the fog, her hostility vanishes. She feels renewed, purified, and filled with a capacity to love.

A moment later, Anna sees Mat Burke, a handsome, virile, broad-chested sailor, dramatically and poetically salvaged out of the sea, destined to be her mate. O'Neill commingles the romantic notion of destined love with realistic elements, especially her attraction to Mat's physical manliness, as if Darwin's Natural Selection were a magnetism immediately operative. The power of Mat's unconscious attraction slowly but surely changes Anna's feelings toward men from hate and scorn to love.

Back in Minnesota, sexuality was thrust upon Anna cruelly and too soon, and the result was depravity, promiscuity, and despair. Now, in recognizing and yielding to destiny, Anna seizes the chance to grow naturally into her womanhood and to a life that will be blessed in a loving marriage with the promise of children to become men for the sea.

O'Neill tried to explain the meaning of *Anna Christie* to critics who attacked it for its naturalism. More than a story of individuals, the play makes a philosophical argument: that life is a flowing continuity—demanding the solution of one problem just as another is emerging—suggesting the ebb and flow of the ceaseless ocean tides. But this philosophical and psychological truth escaped many, and eventually, disillusioned, O'Neill dismissed *Anna Christie* as one of his least worthy plays.[6]

He was wrong to do so, for the play is rich in mystical, poetic symbolism and dramatic conflict, even as it conveys the mystery of Nature's power over human beings. O'Neill created Anna and Mat as mystical begetters, links in the eternal chain of sea-generations, governed by the god Aegir. Surging through the play and within Anna herself is Nature's powerful and relentless urge for generation, as insistent and compelling as the ocean waves cresting and breaking into foam on Earth's shores.

Cat on a Hot Tin Roof (1954–1955)
by Tennessee Williams

A Play in Three Acts. Produced by The Playwright's Company. Staged by Elia Kazan. Produced on Broadway at the Morosco Theater, March 24, 1955.

The Original Cast

Lacey	Maxwell Glanville
Sookey	Musa Williams
Margaret	Barbara Bel Geddes
Brick	Ben Gazzara
Mae (Sister Woman)	Madeleine Sherwood

Gooper (Brother Man)	Pat Hingle
Big Mama	Mildred Dunnock
Dixie	Pauline Hahn
Buster	Darryl Richard
Sonny	Seth Edwards
Trixie	Janice Dunn
Big Daddy	Burl Ives
Reverend Tooker	Fred Stewart
Doctor Baugh	R. G. Armstrong
Daisy	Eva Vaughan Smith
Brightie	Brownie McGhee
Small	Sonny Terry

The major theme of *Cat on a Hot Tin Roof* derives from Williams' affirmation that it is the female's instinctive, demanding sexual nature that ensures the continuity of the family. But in this Mississippi Delta household, there is a serious problem with begetting: the male has absented himself from the marital bed. Brick, married to Maggie, is physically and spiritually perplexed by his sexual identity, a dramatic crisis that has driven him to alcoholism.

Before his friend Skipper committed suicide, he phoned Brick and confessed a deep homosexual love for him, giving validity to Maggie's accusation that the two men shared a forbidden intimacy.

Brick, angry with Maggie for her insight and accusation, and believing she is responsible for driving Skipper to his death, begins to drink heavily, trying to block out the fact of Skipper's death and the realization of what that loss truly means to him. Recognizing this, his wife and father plead, command, and taunt Brick into resolving his conflict by accepting the loss of Skipper, urging him to go on living and resume the role of sexual mate to Maggie, who is both beguiling and abrasive in her painful heat.

In Act II, the dramatic interaction between Brick and Big Daddy is a climactic and amazing confessional scene—a psychiatric session with the patient reclining—as intense as Hamlet's intimately probing closet-scene with Gertrude. And just as in *Hamlet*, Williams' bedroom scene is peopled with ghosts from the past.

The playwright carefully describes the master bedroom setting in his "notes for the designer" as he intimates there is a strange, even unique spirituality pervading this particular bedroom. Its ghostly character, William suggests, is one of an intimate relationship, of rare caring and tenderness.

Both the bedroom and the very large bed that Brick and Maggie share here were previously occupied by the plantation's original owners, the homosexuals Jack Straw and Peter Ochello, who took Big Daddy in to live with them.

Though Big Daddy does not admit to any sexual relationship with the pair, he describes their friendship with deep feeling. He demands that Brick examine himself honestly and admit his feelings for Skipper—homosexual or not—without guilt or fear of recriminations, and get on with his life.

Act II ends with the two men, father and son, facing life-and-death issues in one of the greatest moments in modern American drama. Brick, struggling within himself, is unable to come to terms with his sexual dilemma. Big Daddy, trying to stifle his fear, is unable to contemplate his own imminent death from his spreading cancer. The emotional power of pity and terror is overwhelming as each insists that the other face the bitter truth he fears most of all.

Act III reveals the play's major theme, that Big Daddy's dream is that the loved son Brick give him a grandson. Big Daddy's elephant joke cries out *beget*—that Brick must respond to his Maggie in heat to prove himself a man and produce the cherished heir.

In his "Notes," Williams writes that he devised two different conclusions to *Cat on a Hot Tin Roof.* In the first and original ending, Williams offered no revelatory resolution to Brick's homosexual conflict. He felt that the integrity of the play demanded that Brick be who he was and what he was without dramatic evidence of progression toward heterosexual conversion, believing that Brick could not effect such a conversion in his state of spiritual despair.

These ruminations did not sit right with director Elia Kazan, however, who demanded a revised, more culturally acceptable ending.

It was the second ending to the play that was staged in the original New York production and viewed by Pulitzer Prize play jurors. Here, Brick evidences a profound psychological change: he allows Maggie to destroy his liquor bottles, then, finally, surrenders to her sexually. Stroking her husband's cheek, Maggie is gentle in her triumph, but her passion is clear as she declares her love for "the weak, beautiful people who give up with such grace."[7] The line seems more than a hint at Williams' own unwilling but graceful surrender to the triumphant will of director Kazan, who had an eye to a Broadway hit, a play that would satisfy a preponderately heterosexual theater audience.

A self-proclaimed homosexual, Williams was aware of the American Psychological Association's identification of his preference as a psychological disorder. Had he dug in his heels and remained adamant, unwilling to change the ending, the play might never have received the worldwide accolades that it merited, and most surely, like Lillian Hellman's 1934 play *The Children's Hour*, which dealt with lesbianism (and which the Pulitzer panel famously refused to see), it would never have received the Pulitzer. (Incidentally, the American Psychoanalytical Association did not revise its classification of homosexuality—as not a form of psychosis, but a variant sexual orientation—until 1973, eighteen years after the premiere of *Cat on a Hot Tin Roof*.)

Director Kazan's version of *Cat on a Hot Tin Roof* is the culturally acceptable resolution to the conflict and affirms the major theme of generation. Williams' first ending, of course, is less supportive of this major theme, since generation has not been heretofore in the purview of the homosexual. The play Williams originally wrote may instead be seen as a subconscious, Freudian threnody for lost and/or unrequited love: in his suicide, Skipper shows Brick his ultimate devotion—even unto the death, such as Homer's heroes Achilles and Patroclus in the *Iliad*.

Yet, in both versions, the major power of this play is found in the character of Big Daddy, the symbolic embodiment of the father that Tennessee Williams lost—and, from a Freudian perspective, the alter ego the homosexual seeks. Big Daddy's complex character is one of Williams' greatest creations, comparable in stature and conception to a dissolute Falstaff or a possession-obsessed Lear. He is the timeless patriarch concerned with inheritance, this great Mississippi Delta plantation owner no less in need of a son from the bloodline than any Pharaoh of Egypt who surveyed his River Nile kingdom and was concerned with primogeniture.

Or, to make a Biblical comparison, Big Daddy is like a modern Isaac whose two sons are in competition for his blessing and inheritance. The older son, Gooper, has married a cotton queen and fathered many no-neck monster children. He is Tennessee Williams' representation of the heterosexual male with his conventional morality, in many ways a mockery of a man, governed by his conniving wife, and, because of her, destined to be denied the right of primogeniture. Big Daddy, married with children, nevertheless depreciates married life, describing his own loveless, even hateful relationship with Big Mama, valuable only as she served as a breeder. He chooses solidarity not with Gooper, but with Brick.

Williams gives us more than a hint that Big Daddy sees himself in Brick, that Big Daddy's possible bisexuality may underpin his favoritism for Brick. At no time does he condemn or threaten to disinherit Brick for his deviant love. Instead, with fatherly generosity and compassion, Big Daddy sanctions all of Brick's frailty as a passionate man's necessary, animal nature. But, because he knows that his time is running out, that he is dying of cancer, he is passionately stirred to have Brick procreate, hoping in that procreation for an heir. It is only through generation, the prime drive of nature, that the patriarch can feel he has conquered death.

CHAPTER FIVE

The Dysfunctional Family

A Delicate Balance is the only play in the first fifty years of Pulitzer Prize plays that portrays the American family as a hostile, close-bound group of blood-related, loveless individuals, without a family name, but sharing the same roof above their heads. At its premiere in 1967, theater critics struggled to understand the meaning of the play, its questionable moral values, and the bizarre behavior of the characters.

To some critics, the play seemed to echo *Who's Afraid of Virginia Woolf?* in its characters' hurtfulness to self and to those others whom they professed to love. The characters evidenced patterns of psychological instability and confusion in dealing with reality.

A Delicate Balance concerns two dysfunctional families whose members are characterized by instability in interpersonal relationships, with the inconsistent, impulsive, and unstable behavior associated with borderline personality disorder. The borderline's thoughts are constantly alternating between the extremes of idealization and devaluation, between the idea of the worthwhileness and the worthlessness of his or her life experience.

The etiology of this disorder is traced to early childhood abuse and feelings of abandonment. The person so diagnosed can be extremely gifted intellectually and creatively, but this disorder manifests itself in unpredictable behavior and alternating mood swings. All of Albee's players in *A Delicate Balance* seem to be afflicted with borderline personality disorder, unpredictable in their emotional responses, oftentimes confusing and distorting reality. Yet the

Pulitzer committee must have discerned in their very dysfunction a pertinent reflection of American family life.

A Delicate Balance (1966–1967)
by Edward Albee

A Play in Three Acts. Produced by Richard Barr and Clinton Wilder. Staged by Alan Schneider. Opened on Broadway at the Martin Beck Theater, September 22, 1966.

The Original Cast

Agnes	Jessica Tandy
Tobias	Hume Cronyn
Claire	Rosemary Murphy
Harry	Henderson Forsythe
Edna	Carmen Mathews
Julia	Marian Seldes

The time of the play is one weekend—Friday to Monday—in the luxurious living room of the house belonging to Tobias and Agnes. So steely-cold are Agnes and Tobias that it is hard to conceive of their having actually, twice, united carnally to engender offspring— a daughter, Julia, four times married and divorced or abandoned, and a boy, Teddy, who died suddenly. (Whether or not there ever *was* a son Teddy remains forever a mystery, a theme that fascinated Albee and inspired *The Play About the Baby*.) Julia has phoned to say that she is on her way home from the ruins of her untoward fourth marriage.

Albee's surrealistic plot, odd characters, and pseudo-sophisticated dialogue meld together into an implausible fiction. The suburban house in which the action takes place is purported to be real. However, in the real world, there are psychiatrists and well-staffed emergency rooms in hospitals for those who are experiencing psychotic episodes.

In fact, *A Delicate Balance* can be likened to a popular entertainment of the eighteenth century, in which members of high society visited insane asylums to observe the antics of the deluded and mentally deficient. This is a play without a hero. There is no single, likeable protagonist: rather, as in an institution's holding room, there are six mad players, each coming forward at his or her given moment to be the protagonist against the others as antagonists.

The female players are Agnes, the controlling, vitriolic ruler of the house, who wishes she had been born a man; her daughter, the hysterically neurotic Julia; Agnes's hateful sister, the love-starved, unloving, alcoholic Claire; and the intruding neighbor, Edna, in many ways a replica of Agnes. The two men are Tobias and Harry, nearly identical portraits of borderline personalities, stymied even in the attempt to form sentences, and inept in their power to control family struggles.

In the first five minutes of dialogue of Act I, the characters, expressly Agnes, speak openly of their fear of approaching madness. No one makes the practical suggestion that a visit to a psychiatrist is in order. Impending lunacy is spoken of in tones of casual sophistication. And the audience may titter, even laugh aloud as player after player doubts his own sanity.

Disoriented as she is, Agnes reveals that she regards her fear as healthy and sees herself as the fulcrum that keeps her family in some sort of balance. But she is deluded, for there is no balance in this family's battles, fueled by self-indulgence, selfishness, and hate. Each unpleasant family member acts without any concern for wrong or right, bad or good, and each unbalanced character unbalances the others into mental aberration.

The play's major theme is a dark antithesis to the notion of family as a loving and supportive togetherness. Dysfunction is the key word for Albee, who expresses in this play his deepest subconscious thoughts and feelings about scenes recalled from his own life.

In the late 1920s, young Albee was adopted into a wealthy family that did not appreciate his nonconformist nature and attempted to mold him to fit into high society. We can feel the cold, unloving character of that house, not only in Tobias and Agnes's home, but also in a memory flashback that constitutes one of the most interesting of the many bizarre moments of this play. Strangely and incongruously, it is Agnes who recalls several intimate experiences in Tobias' life—from a time long before she had even met him. As if his experience were her own, she describes the life of a youth raised in a dysfunctional, high-society home, where the servants were awake to serve breakfast at whatever hour one came home drunk. Albee suggests here that Agnes has heard Tobias speak so often of his early years that she, schizophrenically, identifies with them as her own.

Albee's upbringing may also inform the play's major metaphor, symbolic of all its relationships: the dysfunctional bond of love that Tobias says he had for seventeen years with his cat. Not unlike a madman in one of Edgar Allan Poe's macabre short stories, Tobias tries laboriously to explain how his love for the cat turned to hatred when he began, schizophrenically, to sense that the animal did not like *him*, because she did not come to sit on his lap as usual.

Perversely, to have his way, Tobias compelled the cat to sit on his lap again and again, holding her down by force, meeting with resistance—finally, of course, provoking the hiss and the scratch. With this as concrete evidence of the animal's dislike for him, Tobias had the animal killed. She must do exactly as Tobias commands or she will not live.

Why having a cat sitting on his lap is so important to Tobias is not explained, but a reason can be readily surmised. Is this possibly a mirroring of the experience the young Albee had with Mrs. Albee and her absolute demand for obedience? Whatever its etiology, Tobias' brutish action reveals his basically unloving nature, proving that despite his protests he never loved the cat at all.

Unloving defines the essential nature of each of the characters in this surrealistic melodrama, even though the concept of love is bandied about, especially by Claire, who, when Tobias confesses his cruelty to his pet, insists that he absolutely loved the cat—that all the members of their family love each other. The measurement of devotion, she says, is in terms of the depths of greed and self-pity.

Of course, Claire's measure is a manifestation of negativity and hate, not love. The long exchange between Tobias and Claire, concerning the character of love, is like much of the illogical dialogue of the play, totally bizarre, as it attempts to confirm the evidence of love in this family where only hatred and madness exist.

More than by love, the family are held together by their dependence on the *house*: the antiseptic marriage of Agnes and Tobias is simply a long-term, house-occupying duality of habit and convenience. For the borderline Julia, the house is a refuge and hideaway from the short, brutish, and nasty marital escapades that bedevil her. For Claire, the house is an asylum where she can drink her life away. For Harry and Edna, the two neighbors who have had a simultaneous psychotic experience but didn't know how to dial 911, Tobias' house is more convenient than driving or taking a cab to the local hospital's emergency room.

For both Tobias and Agnes, the house poses a series of difficult and unanswered questions: Am I my sister's keeper? Are we our daughter's keeper? Are we our neighbors' keeper? Are we equipped to handle people with mental breakdowns? *A Delicate Balance* is not only about bizarre, hateful relationships in a dysfunctional family but also about the limits of friendship—if, indeed, any friendship exists in this play!

Harry and Edna have driven to Tobias and Agnes' house, seeking sanctuary as best friends, both expressing a paranoid fear of the Plague, which they say is unknown, very much like HIV in its earliest appearances. They take possession of Julia's room, filling it with their own clothes and personal effects. Infuriated, Julia storms her room and throws their things into disarray, then bursts into the living room, brandishing a gun and ordering them out of the house.

Miraculously, on Sunday morning, the neighbors' panic has passed and they have packed their things and prepared to depart. Just as surprisingly, Tobias begs the neighbors to stay. But his empty phrases cannot persuade them, and Harry and Edna leave.

The end of the play is drawing near and Albee, presumably wishing his play to have a long run, strives to strike a positive note. Endearingly, Agnes puts her arms around Tobias—the first embrace, or any indication of caring, in the play so far—and breaks the spell of the play's threatening bafflement and despondency with a simple joke.

Now it is time for the curtain. But no!

In a theatrical device of repetition and reversal, suggesting the circularity of life experience, Albee concludes by repeating Agnes' speech from the beginning of the play, in which she muses about her incipient madness. As the day dawns after this long night, Agnes' rhapsody of words serves as a surreal denouement to this drama of demented treachery within a borderline family. "The fear is the wish," according to Freud. And in *A Delicate Balance*, each character openly expresses the fear of going insane. As the play unfolds, examining the past history of the family members, it is obvious mental illness has taken full possession.

The most remarkable thing about *A Delicate Balance* is that it, once and for all, changed the character of the Pulitzer Prize for the drama. In 1917, observing closely the criteria in the Pulitzer will, the prize was given to *Why Marry?* Fifty years later, in 1967, *A Delicate Balance* absolutely negated these criteria, which stressed that the prize-winning play "represent the educational value and power of the stage to raise the standard of good morals, good taste and good manners." But then, some may argue that *A Delicate Balance* ought to be viewed as an educational experience in how *not* to create a home for a family.

PART TWO

Social Protest

CHAPTER SIX

The Rebel Outsider

Harvey and *Picnic* dramatize the behavior and life experience of protagonists who are alienated from society, hostile to authority, uncertain of their own identities, deviant in their sexual mores, and, on the face of it, self-destructive. In many ways the protagonists of these plays resemble the anti-heroes of the Theater of the Absurd, which is grounded in Jean-Paul Sartre's existentialist philosophy stressing the meaninglessness of human life experience, summed up in his pronouncement "Hell is other people."

Both plays' major themes echo an existentialist philosophy, as well as that self-indulgent philosophy of the Beat, the stance of onetime Columbia University students Jack Kerouac and Allen Ginsberg, who named themselves a generation, a community of America's angry young men.

The upper-middle-class society of *Harvey*, and the middle- and lower-middle class society of *Picnic*, are matriarchal in structure. Fathers are portrayed as negative and self-defeating, or are entirely absent from the home. As young males, the protagonists feel unloved and insecure and exist without goals, having known no positive masculine model. The action of the plays may be deemed their subliminal search for that model.

In *Harvey* and *Picnic*, the male protagonists express open hostility toward the female, reject social responsibility, and angrily confront the institution of family. Unlike the plays whose major theme is the need for generation—where family is the prime objective—these two plays show the male avoiding any serious, mature relationship.

In *Harvey*, playwright Mary Chase takes the institutions of family and psychiatry as the butt of her humor. Family is portrayed as inane, petty, and materialistic. Psychiatrists are humorously inept, blindly treating the wrong persons, indifferent to the seriousness of their profession, confused in the ordering of their own private lives, and succumbing to the same psychotic hallucinations as the patients they are engaged to treat.

Landmark psychological studies by Margaret Mead, such as *Male and Female* (1949), and Alfred C. Kinsey's *Sexual Behavior in the Human Female* (1953) found America's gender roles determined by biological and societal factors. Almost like a psychosexual study of a little town in Kansas, William Inge's *Picnic*, in 1953, presents a microcosm that infers the American macrocosm.

Here the family is portrayed as fractured, irreligious, and incapable of teaching any morality to the young. Education is ineffective, constrained by neurotics in the persons of the love-starved teacher Rosemary Sydney and her witless fellow teachers, who seem inept at communicating sound values for living.

With the same passion that motivated the Columbia Beatniks in the zeitgeist of social upheaval after World War II, in their struggle for a place in the sun, the protagonists, Elwood P. Dowd of *Harvey* (1944–1945) and Hal Carter of *Picnic* (1952–1953), search for their own identities and some meaning in their lives. Like the Beatniks, they are rebellious to conventional adult values and life-styles. Dowd and Carter are intent on sensual pleasures, motivated by basic animal and infantile needs, negative to accepted standards of mature conduct in work, play, friendship, and sex. Carter is a Beat-positive fit, assertively angry. Dowd is the other side of the coin, negatively laid back, a Beat seemingly without ego-drive or ego-needs.

Anomie, a word first coined in 1933, is the psychological key word that best describes these Beat rebels who are intent on breaking down and/or rewriting the establishment's standards. The Beatniks' feelings of alienation and lovelessness are directed with undisguised hostility to authority as they indulge in drugs, alcohol, and sex. As they parade their would-be truths and strengths, they do not acknowledge their unconscious fear of inadequacy and impotence.

The playwrights of both *Harvey* and *Picnic* ask the audience to have compassionate understanding of their rebellious protagonists as helpless human beings, rudderless, lonely outsiders, shaped by forces beyond their control, intent on finding love and living their lives to the fullest.

Harvey (1944–1945)
by Mary Coyle Chase

A Play in Three Acts. Produced by Brock Pemberton. Staged by Antoinette Perry. Opened on Broadway at the Forty-eighth Street Theater, November 1, 1944.

The Original Cast

Myrtle Mae Simmons	Jane Van Duser
Veta Louise Simmons	Josephine Hull
Elwood P. Dowd	Frank Fay
Miss Johnson	Eloise Sheldon
Mrs. Ethel Chauvenet	Frederica Going
Ruth Kelly, R.N.	Janet Tyler
Marvin Wilson	Jesse White
Lyman Sanderson, M.D.	Tom Seidel
William R. Chumley	Fred Irving Lewis
Betty Chumley	Dora Clement
Mr. Peeples	Lawrence Hayes
Judge Omar Gaffney	John Kirk
E. J. Lofgren	Robert Gist

Elwood P. Dowd is a forty-seven-year-old bachelor with a substantial inheritance to live on, perfect manners, and a six-foot-tall, lapine drinking companion whom no one else can see. Elwood reports that he first encountered the tall rabbit one early evening leaning against a lamppost, raising his top hat and courteously wishing Elwood "good evening." Now Harvey accompanies him everywhere—to the homes of family friends, to his sister's society teas—but mostly to bars. However, we never see Elwood drunk, or even drinking . . . and we never see Harvey at all.

Like a poltergeist or Pooka, Harvey is said to have magical powers to stop time, to predict the future, and to assume invisibility or
visibility as he sees fit. Though Harvey is an ever mute and invisible creature, the playwright tweaks her audience by autosugges-
tion: thanks to doors opened and closed by unseen hands, objects
mysteriously vanishing and reappearing, and the discovery of a real
top hat with two holes cut out, suggesting an accommodation for
rabbit ears, we are encouraged to imagine the creature, to expect his
materialization at any moment.

At the end of the play, Ms. Chase asks us to believe that some offstage artist has actually seen the rabbit in the furry flesh and painted
an oil portrait of the pals, Dowd and his invisible Harvey. Dowd has
placed the painting over the fireplace in the Dowd library, block-
ing the commanding, dour portrait of Elwood's recently deceased
mother, Marcella Pinney Dowd, whose negative spirit has dominated her household and her son's life.

On a psychological level the dual portrait represents Elwood's
successful attempt to render impotent the controlling superego-in-
fluence of the mother. Elwood was obviously a suppressed alcoholic
when his mother was alive, an effort that demanded concentrated
energy and restraint. Now released from that matriarchal tyranny—
and in possession of her house, which she left to him, "a great home
boy," rather than to her daughter Veta, who lives with him as his
guest—Elwood finds pleasure and consolation in his alcoholism.
Harvey has come as the answer to his prayers—his animal spirit
alter-ego who has given him a new persona, and freedom and license to invite strangers he encounters on the street to come home
with him or go for a drink at Charlie's bar, his favorite hangout.

Elwood seems extremely contented with this state of affairs, but
Veta—another most determined woman, perhaps in the same mold
as her mother—is not. In vain, Veta asks that Elwood voluntarily
commit himself to an institution. She explains the case to psychiatrist Dr. Sanderson: her brother Elwood is damaging the Dowd family's position of respectability in the community and spoiling the
prospect of her daughter's marriage. Veta would be happy, she as-

serts, if Elwood would bring home someone human to resolve his loneliness—but not a rabbit, and not an invisible one.

Misinterpreting Veta's distress, a pair of confounded psychiatrists begin to treat Veta as the patient, and defer to the smiling, affable, courteous Elwood. When finally the confusion of who-is-the-patient is resolved, the psychiatrists zero in on a plan to exorcise the ghostly rabbit with Formula 977, a magic bullet injection promised to transform Elwood into a sober and socially responsible citizen.

The cab driver E.J. Lofgren is one of the several older men who in the play represents the sought-after father-image missing in Elwood's life. Much wiser than the psychiatrists, Lofgren introduces the philosophical notion that resolves the conflict of the play: that every man must have an illusion, and Elwood is entitled to have Harvey as his. He convinces Veta to prevent the injection of Formula 977—for if Elwood were to receive the injection, the cab driver asserts, he'd come to be an obnoxious bastard, like every other human being. Is this playwright Chase's take on human nature? Beyond the fantasy Ms. Chase reveals a deep misanthropy.

According to James Stewart, the actor who played Elwood Dowd in the film version, Mary Chase conceived *Harvey* as a family play, especially suitable for children. The model and inspiration for *Harvey*, originally entitled *The White Rabbit*, Stewart asserts, is modeled on Lewis Carroll's White Rabbit in *Alice in Wonderland*. Yet *Harvey* might more fruitfully call to mind the English Jonathan Swift, a true misanthropist especially lauded for his misread satire about miscreant human nature, *Gulliver's Travels*.

Carroll's scurrying White Rabbit initiates Alice's magical journey into Wonderland; and Harvey spurs the inebriate Elwood into a series of humorous adventures. Ms. Chase's whimsy presents the invisible Harvey and Elwood Dowd, a pair of alcohol-addicted males, as untroubled innocents—which they aren't at all; they're both troubled and subversive, playwright Chase's rebellious unconscious creatures. Just as Jonathan Swift reflects his antipathy to the nature of mankind, so does Ms. Chase in this schizoid fairy tale.

Picnic (1952–1953)
by William Inge

A Play in Three Acts. Produced by the Theater Guild and Joshua Logan. Staged by Joshua Logan. Produced on Broadway at the Music Box Theater, February 19, 1953.

The Original Cast

Helen Potts	Ruth McDevitt
Hal Carter	Ralph Meeker
Millie Owens	Kim Stanley
Bomber	Morris Miller
Madge Owens	Janice Rule
Flo Owens	Peggy Conklin
Rosemary Sydney	Eileen Heckart
Alan Seymour	Paul Newman
Irma Kronkite	Reta Shaw
Christine Schoenwalder	Elizabeth Wilson
Howard Bevans	Arthur O'Connell

Sympathetic to the intense passion of the rebel, *Picnic* is a dramatic portrait of two disoriented, rebellious American youths, Hal Carter and Madge Owens, with deep-rooted identity problems.

Madge is a small-town Kansas beauty from a dysfunctional family. Narcissistically, she assigns great value to her beauty, but she has little intellectual grounding and no viable career goals in mind. Marriage with her boyfriend, Alan Seymour, could provide economic security, but married life in Alan's circle would be a serious emotional challenge for her, given her feelings of inferiority regarding her fractured home, her poor education and her low economic status.

Her mother, Flo, grew up in a loveless household and is raising her two daughters in a fatherless home. Abandoned by her husband, she holds that women are made weak and helpless by a male-dominated society and absolutely humiliated by the very act of sex. She herself has never felt love, she says, and doesn't believe it exists except as an abstraction. But she sees value in a doting husband who can provide well for his wife, and advises Madge to marry Alan now, before her beauty fades. Madge, however, explains to her mother that she doesn't feel sexually attracted to Alan. She dreams of a Hollywood romance with a handsome prince who will see her and be captivated by her beauty—and will thrill her in turn with his masculine good looks.

Her romantic ambition, shallow though it may be, is encouraged by the Owens' neighbor Mrs. Potts. Mrs. Potts confesses to Madge that she suffered her whole lifetime because of one moment of denial, her lack of courage to follow the man she felt she loved. Mrs. Potts personifies the negative component of the play's major theme: she did *not* rebel against her authoritarian parents to find her happiness as she should have, and so she must suffer a life without love.

The image that playwright Inge chooses to signal the arrival of the prince is the train coming into the town station, its whistles overwhelming the quiet of the town with a sense of Fate, of Sirens calling and the promise that the prince will discover Madge and give her a *raison d'être*. Ironically, the prince is a vagabond, Hal Carter.

The dream prince, Hal Carter, the play's main protagonist, is a rebel, like one of the Beat Generation in his sexual libertinism, without being as talented or intellectual as the original Columbia Beats. He played football in college before he failed out academically, and now he lives as a vagabond, hitchhiking around the country, hopping freight trains and finding a day of odd chores anywhere to earn his daily bread.

As the play begins, Carter has ridden the freight to the small Kansas oil-boom town where his onetime college roommate, Alan Seymour, lives, possibly to find a job in Alan's father's oil business.

Like the hobo of anecdote, Hal has offered to clean up old Mrs. Potts' front yard for a meal. Provocatively stripped to the waist, showing well-developed pecs and washboard-ribbed abdominals, he rakes the lawn rubbish and starts a bonfire. Smoke fills the air, charging the atmosphere with the musky smell of burning leaves, like a heady, masculine perfume.

Mrs. Potts' next door neighbors are the Owenses—Flo, the beautiful Madge, and her plain sister, Millie. At first sight, Hal and Madge feel the electric charge of mutual attraction, but Hal learns that his friend Alan is hoping to marry Madge, and he agrees to go to that evening's Labor Day picnic with Millie instead.

For Hal Carter sex is the antidote for loneliness, alienation, and boredom. He is the sensual embodiment of Priapus, the phallic god who emanates virile masculinity. He is blessed with movie-style good looks and says that he has just come from Hollywood, where he had a screen test, but that he left in a hurry when he heard the studio wanted to have all his teeth filed down and capped. (The fear of teeth removal is a sometimes terrifying process to the neurotic mind, equivalent to the fear of castration, according to Freud.) But is this the truth? Is anything that Hal reports true?

Given the predisposition to exaggeration, or out-and-out lying, that we notice as the play progresses, is it possible that Hal was unwilling to assume the strict discipline and responsibility of working as a movie actor? Or maybe the entire Hollywood report is a lie in the same vein as the braggadocio tales he uses to awe his listeners: that he was a deep sea diver off Catalina Island; or that that he made lots of money as a stunt parachutist, jumping out of planes. He magnifies the little gas station owned by his father into a booming oil business and glamorizes his unsuccessful father into a tycoon, before he finally admits that his father works at the lowliest and most poorly paid of all jobs in the oil business—extraction. Hal's feelings of inferiority and failure are so great he is compelled to lie nearly about everything, spouting Bunyanesque, compulsive exaggerations that gloss the painful realities of his life.

Before the crowd leaves for the picnic grounds in the cars that Alan brought, a bacchanalia of drinking and dancing begins. The scene explodes in a confrontation between Hal and the sexually frustrated teacher Rosemary Sydney when Hal refuses to dance with her. The rejected and slightly inebriated Rosemary rails against Hal as Arkansas white trash, predicting that he will lose the job that Alan's father has given him and end his life in the gutter.

The altercation sobers Hal as everyone leaves and he finds himself alone with Madge, sympathetic and stirred by sensual feelings. Moved to talk about the painful experiences of his life, he tells Madge about his disturbed family and the anger that fueled his risky or illicit behavior, like shooting craps, stealing bottles of milk delivered on doorsteps, and running off with a guy's motorcycle, which landed him in reform school at fourteen. Like a Kerouac clone, Hal recalls nostalgically that he felt most free and happy when he was riding that bike on the road.

In his whole life, Hal confesses, he has never been on a picnic, or learned good manners or how to behave in the company of respectable women. In fact, the randy Hal harbors an unconscious hostility toward women, combined with a perverse willingness to be used and abused. This psychological aberration and confusion is derived from Hal's terrible relationship with his mother, who showed him little or no love or caring. After he was released from reform school, he discovered he was no longer welcome in her house, so he went to his father, a weak and unloving alcoholic who now operated a gas filling station and refused to offer any support.

When suddenly the old man died in an alcoholic binge, scraped up from the sidewalk by the police, he had to be buried in Pauper's Row because Hal's mother refused to pay for the funeral. Then, unconscionably, she demanded ownership of the gas station that had been willed to Hal. Indifferent to property or possession, and suffering mixed feelings of anger, hatred and guilt toward his mother, Hal gave over the property and went on the road.

Inge is well schooled in Freudian psychology. The phallic imagery of the filling station with its pump and hose is a significant Freudian icon of masculinity. Hal's relinquishment of the station to his mother is her symbolic emasculation of her son, as she demands and acquires the phallus-power for herself. Hal's emasculation by his mother is a harbinger of a lifetime of setting himself up for emasculation by the demanding female as repetition compulsion. Unaware of the damage his parents inflicted on his ego, Hal relies upon a blind, superficial resiliency to protect him in adulthood.

Act III of *Picnic* is a dramatic masterpiece. The intense emotional relationships of two couples, Rosemary and her boyfriend Howard Bevans, then Hal and Madge, are played out, both pairs having secretly opted for a sexual tryst in lover's lane rather than attend the picnic.

The atmosphere is almost unbearable in its passionate intensity when Rosemary discards her outward show of independence and arrogance, bares her desperate loneliness, and gets down on her knees, begging Howard to marry her. His studied unwillingness and her anguished pleading overwhelm the scene with operatic pathos.

The same tensions reverberate for the soul-searching lovers Hal and Madge.

As the passionate togetherness of their sex passes, each admits to feeling the emptiness and solitariness of anomie, failing to understand that it is not the sex act that binds humans together, but the intangible web of love. Still, Madge begins to feel a powerful, motherly sympathy for Hal, as he reveals his helplessness—everything the macho man hides and denies. Subconsciously summoning up the repressed emotions of love she has always had for her missing father, Madge transfers those tender feelings to Hal, yearning for his love.

Alan enters bent on vengeance, having heard that Madge was with Hal in the Ford in a lovers' trysting place last night, and he has already called the police, accusing Hal of stealing the car, calling forth Hal's memories of the time the police hunted a fourteen-year-old for bike theft. Hal knocks Alan almost senseless to the ground and speaks words to Madge he has never uttered to anyone: "I love you. Come away with me." Madge rebels against her mother's authority and decides to follow her instincts, recalling Mrs. Potts' counsel to follow the dictation of her heart.

Though Inge seems to say love is the essential human commitment, as *Picnic* unfolds, love here seems narrowly to be animal sex without commitment or tenderness. One must rightly question how genuine and mature Hal's love for Madge can be.

Picnic is a drama of harsh realism, with intimations of even more pain to come for the protagonists beyond this play. There is no evidence that Hal has experienced the beginnings of maturation and emotional self-awareness, and his plan to live and work in a sleazy hotel in Tulsa suggests dim prospects for Madge's life.

Picnic disavows conventional standards of sexual morality. It does not portray marriage traditionally as a commitment to constancy in love; however, it does assert the individual's right to choose his or her own way of life. The question the audience asks is: Has Madge thought sufficiently before having made the fateful decision at the end of the play? Is she right to put her entire life at risk for a man she has known for less than forty-eight hours? Does she understand that Hal's life has been a protracted adolescence, that he is an angry, undisciplined, and irresponsible rebel? Is she right to think that her love will help him grow in maturity to become the husband-lover she wants? She has never known a model for a secure marriage. In case she is making a mistake, does she have the courage to survive the way her mother and Mrs. Potts have done—alone?—without a man's love?

Whatever the consequences of Hal or Madge's choices, Inge asserts no one must expect this life is going to be a picnic.

CHAPTER SEVEN

The Self-Sacrificers

In the plays considered here, the idea of self-sacrifice is a person's willingness—for a worthy cause—to die, if necessary, or to deny the self the means to a good life, believing, in both instances, the outcome will reward society. In American history, Nathan Hale is an example of the first, and in world history Mahatma Gandhi embodies the second. In *Why Marry?* and *Men in White*, self-denial is intrinsic to the protagonist's nobility of character as he meets the conflict and reflects the major theme.

In Jesse Lynch William's *Why Marry?* the heroine, Helen Graham, a champion of feminism, with aspirations to be an accredited scientist in her own right, is in love with Doctor Ernest Hamilton, a brilliant bacteriologist, one of the team of American bacteriologists who risked his life in the search for the cure for yellow fever which was an absolute requirement for the building of the Panama Canal. The French engineer de Lessups abandoned the project of the sea-level connection between the Atlantic and the Pacific in 1893, after having suffered the loss of more than 22,000 men to malaria and yellow fever, fatal diseases transmitted by mosquitoes.

President Theodore Roosevelt bought the French equipment and excavation, realizing the necessity of the canal for America's economic growth. He was fully aware that the major problem American construction faced was disease, but he had confidence that medical science would solve the problem. Three American scientists volunteered to be lab-guinea pigs and died after having allowed mosquitoes to infect them. In *Why Marry?*, the character of Ernest Hamilton is understood to be the sole survivor of the experiment, which ultimately yielded useful results. The discovery of an anti-toxin for yellow fever made it possible to open the Panama Canal in August, 1914.

The notion of self-sacrifice in *Men in White* is, in essence, the choice that Dr. George Ferguson must make, surrendering his personal life for the selfless life of the dedicated physician. Inspired by the noble examples of his deceased father and his revered mentor, Dr. Hochberg, Ferguson is torn between his desire to love and to be loved, and his duty to serve society, forced into an unrealistic, either/or choice without the possibility of compromise: the Hippocratic oath or the marriage oath.

Plays of profound social significance, *Why Marry?* and *Men in White* protest double standards in sex. In anti-capitalist terms they present both America's old-moneyed aristocracy and the nouveau riche as selfishly perverse, disinterested in humanitarian efforts. Charitable contributions for scientific research are revealed as offerings of absolution for bad consciences; the benefactor-philanthropist capitalist, who has made his money by taking advantage of widows and orphans, is represented as a crass materialist, who believes that everyone and everything—including entrance to heaven—can be bought for a price. Asserting deeply held ethical principles, *Why Marry?* echoes Shaw's brand of Fabian socialism as it demands society's immediate recognition of its failure in its responsibilities to the worker-scientist it so poorly rewards. *Men in White* reflects the socialism of the Roosevelt New Deal, which exhorts citizens to idealistic action on behalf of humankind.

Why Marry? (1917–1918)
by Jesse Lynch Williams

A Play in Three Acts. Produced by Selwyn & Co. by Arrangement with Roi Cooper Megrue. Staged by Roi Cooper Megrue. Opened at the Astor Theater, December 25, 1917.

The Original Cast

Jean	Lotus Robb
Cousin Theodore	Ernest Lawford
Uncle Everett	Nat C. Goodwin
Helen	Estelle Winwood
The Butler	Richard Pitman
Rex	Harold West
Lucy	Beatrice Beckley
John	Edmund Breese
Ernest	Shelly Hull
The Footman	Walter Goodson

In *Why Marry?* Helen Graham protests against everything that conventional marriage demands, especially the ritual vow of female obedience exacted in the ceremony and enforced in the home. The setting is a sumptuous mansion with beautiful gardens in a high-class Long Island suburb, an easy drive from Wall Street by chauffeured car. The time is a summer weekend, possibly in 1913, before the start of World War I, when it was fashionable and safe to cross the Atlantic from New York to Southampton or LeHavre on a luxury liner.

The owner of the mansion is John Graham, a top-echelon manufacturer and a representative of new wealth in America, married to the socially correct, dotingly obedient, and so far childless Lucy. His two beautiful younger sisters, twenty-nine-year-old Helen and twenty-six-year-old Jean, live with him, and both are very marriageable.

Through the elegant garden of John's manor house, Jean comes running followed by the handsome, multimillionaire playboy Rex Baker, whose father's palatial estate is next door. Rex catches her, and Jean, feigning a struggle against his amorous kisses, blithely asks if he wants to marry her. Startled, Rex stutters a hesitant affirmative. Just at that moment Lucy enters and is happy to hear Jean announce she is engaged to Rex.

Jean sends Rex off to the club to play golf and coyly tells Lucy that she incited Rex to chase her by telling him she believed in that highly unpopular cause among men of their day, women's suffrage. Lucy praises Jean's simple scheme of entrapment but admonishes her that, as everyone knows, Rex is really in love with her older sister Helen—though Lucy herself believes the independent Helen will never attract a husband.

Helen, a scientist who has just returned to America from the Pasteur Institute in Paris, is a model of the dynamic, intellectual New Woman of the twentieth century. In creating her, Jesse Lynch Williams seems to have taken inspiration not only from Marie Curie, who had won Nobel Prize in two different fields by the time *Why Marry?* was written, but also from Victoria Woodhull, one of the most famously and audaciously freethinking women of the late nineteenth century. Woodhull promulgated a woman's right to *free sex*, sex education, suffrage, short skirts, vegetarianism, freedom of movement in society, and easy divorce by simply walking away from an unbearable marriage. In 1872, long before women gained the right to vote, she had already been nominated as the first woman presidential candidate by the Equal Rights Party.

Rex is delighted that Helen, whom he truly loves, has returned to resume her scientific work at his wealthy father's research center, the Baker Institute of Medical Experiment. Yet Lucy's belief that nice men don't like women who go to work or to college, especially to study science, is unshaken. And she chides Helen with news that she is being gossiped about, having stayed one night at the Baker Institute with the handsome and gifted research scientist Ernest Hamilton.

Helen says that night in the lab with Ernest was glorious—scientifically speaking. The product of that evening's work, the Hamilton antitoxin, is a medical breakthrough that has put the Baker Institute in the forefront of international research and promised to win her beloved Ernest the acclaim he deserves.

Unlike Helen, Jean has not been trained for a career and plans to marry. She senses that her biological clock is ticking and wants a home of her own—so much that she would rather marry Rex, whom she admits to Helen that she does not love, than wait for someone else (namely Bob, a young man with whom she has been intimate and who is away at Harvard Law School). Desperate for a change in her life, Jean seems to regret her lack of means for earning a salary on her own. But, as Lucy notes, the marketplace—any kind of professional work—is anathema for any woman in society. Perhaps, Jean tells her sister Helen, who has advised against her engagement, she will come to love Rex after they are married.

Meanwhile, Helen's brother, uncle, and male cousin are considering whether the man she loves can afford to marry and provide for her. With pride Helen points out that the poorly paid scientist Ernest was willing to sacrifice himself in the search for a cure for yellow fever—famously allowing himself to be infected and putting his life at risk. John applauds, avowing that the scientists' discovery of the antitoxin saved the United States twenty million dollars, saved more lives in Panama than were lost in the whole Spanish-American War, and made it possible for the Canal to be built, ending the scourge of yellow fever that for more than a century had spread devastation and death. But the consensus of the group is that scientists do not make their sacrifice for money or glory, but for scientific philanthropy.

John has invited Ernest to the mansion to discuss a possible year's research work at the Pasteur Institute in Paris, a joint venture that will add prestige to the Baker Institute for which John serves as a trustee. In Paris Ernest will work along with Pasteur Institute scientists, and the Baker Institute will pay all his expenses, but he must go alone and leave Helen to manage his laboratory here in New York. John denies her right to go with him because it would create a scandal—unless they marry. There's the issue of this Shavian-styled comedy.

Even unchaperoned and unmarried, Helen says she will go to Paris with the man she loves and do the scientific research for which she has been trained, willingly sacrificing her reputation if necessary. In turn, Ernest declares that he will quit the laboratory and establish a private medical practice on Park Avenue so that he can marry Helen—who responds that she will not marry him if he sacrifices his scientific genius to the demands of social propriety.

John, on the other hand, secure in his marriage and his fortune, is determined that both his sisters will marry—particularly Jean, whose promised connection with the fabulously wealthy Bakers fills him with delight. Even when he learns about Rex Baker's scandalous involvement with a Broadway chorus girl, he pleads with Jean to marry him anyway. Helen is furious that her brother is encouraging an impossible, loveless marriage for his sister with a libertine for the sake of social status; and he rages against her, saying that a woman who gives herself to a man without marriage is no sister of his.

Packed and determined to go with Ernest to Paris unwed, Helen is willing to sacrifice everything for love. But Ernest has postponed departure for one week and requests that the entire family be convened so they can declare their intentions.

The action of Act III takes place on the terrace and garden festooned with baskets of flowers and colorful Japanese lanterns, ordered by Judge Everett who has asked also that the entire family be invited for Sunday supper.

Before all the family are assembled, Rex confesses to having had affairs, but promises that his behavior will change when he and Jean are married. Jean admits to loving another man, but is desperate to leave her brother's house and asks Cousin Theodore the minister to consecrate her union with Rex. When the parson speaks of the white veil as a symbol of the bride's virginity, however, her consciousness of her own sexual past inspires a hysterical reaction, and she ends the blessing abruptly by dashing into the house.

The family arrives for supper and the toasts begin. John introduces Ernest Hamilton as a humanitarian and the greatest scientist in America. The Judge rises and applauds the New Woman, Helen, as the embodiment of all that is noblest in womanhood.

Standing beside them, Judge Everett continues to extol the pair as ideally suited to save the marital institution, that there will never be a more perfect tribute to true marriage than from this fearless pair who are wrongfully accused of trying to destroy it.

When the announcement is made that Cousin Theodore stands ready to join these two together in the sight of God, both Ernest and Helen revolt, crying out that the rector is profaning love, that the church deals with marriage as a sacrament of property, the woman a chattel to be given or sold, the wedding ring an insulting reminder that slaves wore restraining chain rings.

Determined to set the question of marriage and God aright, Judge Everett says that everyone gathered before him knows that in his *heart* Ernest is taking this woman to be his wife, that in the eyes of God they have pledged their love to each other. They agree. Then the Judge with great passion says that, acting with the authority of the law of the State of New York, and in the presence of witnesses before whom they have made their solemn declarations . . . he pronounces them man and wife. Judge Everett has tricked them into marriage!

What is the significance of Judge Everett's claim that respectability has really triumphed at the end of *Why Marry?* Most assuredly it has to do with the fact that in the culture of the time a woman was allowed to have sex only within the purview of marriage. Both unmarried women, Helen and Jean, have made their declaration for sexual love in an approved ritual form of public affirmation and sanctification.

But through his heroine's dialogue, the playwright Williams, echoing Fabian socialist George Bernard Shaw, asserts that marriage rites can no longer be chattel rights and proposes that love between man and woman must be based upon a deep, abiding commitment. Was this an idea whose time had come? It was certainly resonant in Victoria Woodhull's feminist call for "free love" in 1871, and it was sanctioned by the Russian Revolution in 1917. Still, it is noteworthy that Henrik Ibsen's *Doll's House*, a provocative feminist play, is most frequently produced in today's theater––but *Why Marry?*, which proposes "free love" in addition to that same idea of female independence, has rarely been revived. The play celebrates the independent American woman and examines marriage critically, as relevant today as it was in 1917.

Men in White (1933–1934)
by Sidney Kingsley

A Play in Three Acts. Produced by the Group Theater, Sidney Harmon, and James Ullman. Staged by Lee Strasberg. Opened at the Broadhurst Theater, September 26, 1933.

The Original Cast

Dr. Gordon	Luther Adler
Dr. Hochberg	J. Edward Bromberg
Dr. Michaelson	William Challee
Dr. Vitale	Herbert Ratner
Dr. McCabe	Grover Burgess
Dr. Ferguson	Alexander Kirkland
Dr. Wren	Sanford Meisner
Dr. Otis (Shorty)	Bob Lewis
Dr. Levine	Morris Carnovsky
Dr. Bradley (Pete)	William Coy
Dr. Crawford (Mac)	Alan Baxter
Nurse Jamison	Eunice Stoddard
Mr. John Hudson	Art Smith
James Mooney	Gerrit Kraber
Laura Hudson	Margaret Barker
Mr. Smith	Sanford Meisner
Mrs. Smith	Ruth Nelson
Dorothy Smith	Mab Maynard
Barbara Dennin	Phoebe Brand
Dr. Cunningham	Russell Collins
First Nurse	Paula Miller
Nurse Mary Ryan	Dorothy Patten
Orderly	Elia Kazan
Mr. Houghton	Clifford Odets
Mr. Spencer	Lewis Leverett
Mrs. D'Andrea	Mary Virginia Farmer
Second Nurse	Elena Karem

The dedication by the playwright reads, "To the men in medicine who dedicate themselves, with quiet heroism, to man."

At St. George's Hospital the handsome intern Dr. George Ferguson is recognized by the attending chief of surgical staff, Dr. Hochberg, as the most promising of all interns. Dr. Hochberg is a dramatic reincarnation of Hippocrates, the noble and dedicated father of medicine, and he asserts that the true scientist can never be a satisfactory husband, so dedicated must he be to his calling. In this play marriage and medicine ignite the conflicts and demand momentous sacrifices.

Playwright Kingsley compounds the conflicts he poses right from the start by depicting an interfaith marriage in the case of the Jewish Dr. Levine and his Christian wife, Katherine.

When Levine was an intern at St. George's, his wealthy mother objected to their union and shut her son out of her family and her life, mourning him as one deceased. Now a lean, shabbily dressed man, Dr. Levine has come to the hospital to have Katherine x-rayed and her sputum examined for tuberculosis.

Practicing medicine in a poor neighborhood, Levine has been struggling to make a living, and he expresses envy and anger at the corrupt ethical behavior of doctors who want only to have an office on Park Avenue to serve wealthy clients. His liberal view is that just as government provides education for the young, the government should take over health care for the poor. When his wife's illness is identified as tuberculosis, Levine is in despair, for her diagnosis means they must move to a warmer climate, and he will be obliged to start a new practice. For love of Katherine he must make every sacrifice.

Levine's idea of government concern for the health and care of its citizens originated in the Athens city-state, where men like Hippocrates initiated *materia medica*, or pharmacology, and set forth the ethical principles of the profession. In 1916, for the first time in the United States, Congress held hearings on the need for state-run health insurance programs because the average family could not afford the costs of medical and hospital care.

In the despairing years of the depression, the time of *Men in White*, the general public had little earning power and no savings for health services. Hospitals like St. George's were operating with great deficits and depended on contributions from wealthy citizens who would underwrite the costs of building and equipping new wings and wards, and maintaining sections of the hospital's operation so long as their names were carved in stone as philanthropists.

In *Men in White*, real estate tycoon John Hudson promises to be just such a donor. In the largest, most expensive private room in St George's Hospital, Hudson undergoes an examination by Dr.

Whitman, a cardiac specialist. Hudson's daughter Laura is engaged to the intern George Ferguson, but the courtship is troubled: Ferguson has worked his whole life for the opportunity to train under Dr. Hochberg—a commitment that demands nearly all his time and energy. Laura, unlike Helen Graham in *Why Marry?*, insists that he place their relationship above his work at the hospital and set up in practice as a specialist with regular hours.

One fateful evening, after he has had to cancel his plans with Laura, Ferguson phones her to say he has cleared his slate of hospital duty and can meet her after all. She rejects the offer, so Ferguson is studying in his intern-quarters when the student nurse Barbara Dennin comes to pick up the exam notes he promised her when she assisted him that afternoon in attending a young diabetic patient. Ferguson had countermanded an older doctor's order for an insulin injection that would have killed the youngster. (The playwright insinuates that the Park Avenue Dr. Cunningham was not interested in investigating the condition of poor patients, even though he served as a mentor in this teaching hospital.)

Alone with Ferguson in his quarters, Barbara makes clear her admiration and desire for him, and he yields to her temptation. Their failure to use contraception causes the chain of circumstances that end Barbara's life and Laura's romance.

Three months later, in St. George's Medical Board Room, Hudson is named as a new trustee of the hospital. Dr. Hochberg knows that Hudson will readily accept the trusteeship and give generously if the hospital promises to accelerate his son-in-law-to-be Ferguson to associateship immediately so that he can go into private practice and marry Laura.

But Dr. Hochberg believes Ferguson will not accept the associateship, knowing that he is not ready yet. He doesn't know that Laura has told her fiancé she will leave him if he continues his studies under Hochberg, and that Ferguson has decided to follow her wishes.

After Ferguson has broken the news to his mentor, Dr. Hochberg says he wants Ferguson to assist in a surgical procedure on a young nurse, Barbara Dennin, in critical condition with an infection, the result of a botched abortion.

When *Men in White* played on Broadway in 1933 most states had already banned all abortions with the exceptions of pregnancies resulting from rape or incest, or if the fetus was developing abnormally or there was need to save the mother. Abortion is a serious medical procedure that requires stringent attention to antisepsis, and as a nurse Barbara should have been aware of the risk of obtaining an illegal abortion. Yet, as Dr. Wren points out as the team prepares to perform the hysterectomy they hope will save her life, she couldn't have had the abortion at a legitimate hospital, including the one where she worked.

On stage, the operation is enacted in mime, performed like a ballet of white-garbed dancers. The medical teams move around the sheeted gurney with the ghostlike outline of Barbara's body lying still, her legs in stirrups. An amazing scene, overwhelming in its dramatic power!

In anguish, Ferguson feels compelled to sacrifice his happiness with Laura to marry Barbara, whose life he has so badly damaged. When he declares he is going to marry Barbara and go into practice to support her, Dr. Hochberg scoffs at Ferguson's "mid-Victorian idealism," citing as a cautionary tale the ill-fated marriage of Dr. Levine, who is a failure in Colorado and in a recent communication begged Hochberg for a twenty-dollar loan.

But Ferguson is determined and must tell Laura his plan. The passions run high in a dramatic scene in Ferguson's quarters, with Laura's bitter feelings of anger and betrayal, and Ferguson's remorse, repentance, and self-hate.

Suddenly, Hochberg enters with the heartbreaking news that Barbara has died of an embolism. Humbly, he admits that even his forty years of experience could not save her. He tells the despondent Ferguson that the magnitude of what they *don't* know as doctors is not a reason to give up, but rather to fight on for a noble reward that is "richer than simply living." For the last time, the shaken Laura tries to draw her lover away so they can find some solace in each other. But Ferguson knows his place is at Dr. Hochberg's side, striving, even at the expense of personal happiness, to give his best for the relief of suffering humanity.

Originally entitled *Crisis*, Sidney Kingsley's *Men in White* is a naturalistic and realistic drama of social consciousness in the style of Ibsen's *Enemy of the People*, an apt project for the far-left-of-center Group Theater of the 1930s. (In the brilliant original cast of twenty-seven actors, it is interesting to note that the two walk-ons included the great agitprop dramatist Clifford Odets and the brilliant Elia Kazan, director-to-be of Arthur Miller's plays.)

Men in White is the only Pulitzer Prize play that deals with the issue of abortion, though it does not concern itself with the morality of Barbara's right to choose. That right, argued in the Supreme Court's decision of Roe v. Wade, continues to be one of the most divisive political issues in America. In producing this play, which was shockingly explicit and controversial for its time, and selecting it for commendation, the Group Theater and the Pulitzer committee evidenced great courage.

Finally, *Men in White* is the forerunner of the many stage, cinema, and television dramas we have become accustomed to seeing take place in a hospital environment—its emergency rooms and wards offering a dramatic world of limitless possibilities, focusing on the heroic, heartwarming, or tragic lives of doctors and nurses as they confront life-and-death issues that affect us all.

CHAPTER EIGHT

The Nonconformists

Rejecting America's capitalist values, George S. Kaufman and Moss Hart's *You Can't Take It with You* and William Saroyan's *The Time of Your Life* dramatize aspects of socialist philosophy widespread in the 1930s, the years of America's great Depression. In some measure, every member of the audience had been affected personally by the crash of the New York stock market on October 24, 1929. However, some of the rich may have escaped unscathed, dealing solvently in cash. The truly wealthy did not extend themselves "on margin" as did the majority of American investors, snared by greed and hope. Many Americans invested their life savings and then went on to borrow from the banks, only to be wiped out and thrown into debt and despair.

These two social protest plays, disparate in manner and tone, are both bold and unrestrained in their criticism of the moneyed class. Beneath the comedic gloss, both plays communicate a sobering social message: that America has been dealt a near-knockout blow by an economic depression that threatens the American democratic-capitalist way of life, demanding immediate reformation, *or else.*

The protagonists in these two plays are nonconformists, rebels against capitalism, and quick to spot the indifference of the government toward its citizens. But they are not disloyal to America and its principles of freedom. In the 30s, even as they were registering deep dissatisfaction with some of America's basic institutions, Americans were fully aware of the progress and dangers of communism and its ruthless experiment as Stalin and Trotsky initiated their economic and land reforms in a series of Five Year Plans.

You Can't Take It with You strikes at the materialism of Wall Street and the Calvinist work ethic basic to entrepreneur capitalism: the belief that shoulder-to-the-wheel effort will be rewarded by God with tangible, earthly riches. The hero of the play, Grandpa Vanderhof, tells how he walked away from that work ethic, and from Wall Street, too.

Saroyan's *The Time of Your Life* is a reflection of the years of the Depression, dramatizing the Establishment and its laws and enforcers as oppressively fascistic and anti-labor, hostile to the "little man." The playwright strives to prove the sociopolitical philosophy that real truth and beauty are to be found only in society's underdogs and pariahs—the prostitute, the unemployed, and the childlike adult. In a period of widespread economic hardship and deprivation, with the nation's spirit down in the dumps, Saroyan's poetic idealism attempts to dignify the downtrodden and encourage a new respect for America's undervalued middle and lower classes.

You Can't Take It with You (1936–1937)
by Moss Hart and George S. Kaufman

A Play in Three Acts. Produced by Sam H. Harris. Staged by George S. Kaufman. Opened on Broadway at the Booth Theater, December 14, 1936.

The Original Cast

Penelope Sycamore	Josephine Hull
Essie Sycamore	Paula Trueman
Rheba	Ruth Attaway
Paul Sycamore	Frank Wilcox
Mr. De Pinna	Frank Conlan
Ed	George Heller
Donald	Oscar Polk
Martin Vanderhof	Henry Travers
Alice Sycamore	Margot Stevens
Henderson	Hugh Rennie
Tony Kirby	Jess Barker

Boris Kolenkhov	George Tobias
Gay Wellington	Mitzi Hajos
Mr. Kirby	William J. Kelly
Mrs. Kirby	Virginia Hammond
Three Men	George Leach,
	Ralph Holmes,
	and Franklin Heller
Olga	Anna Lubowe

The play takes place in the large living room of Martin Vanderhof's Victorian house, a few blocks away from Columbia University in New York City. The Vanderhof family and house guests are a group of unique, zany individuals who live happily with no anxiety and no duress, following Grandapa Vanderhof's philosophy of enjoying life every minute.

Penny Vanderhof Sycamore, who fancies herself a playwright, asks her daughter Essie and her African-American cook, Rheba, for some creative help. She has writer's block and doesn't know what to do next with her heroine Cynthia, whom, ludicrously, she has brought into a monastery on a visiting day and kept there—still visiting—for six years. Having taken up writing several years ago when a typewriter was delivered in error to her home, Penny composes as inspiration comes and the mood dictates, writing small episodes into her various, unfinished dramatic masterpieces of love, war and sex.

Penny turns next to her husband, Paul Sycamore, for help, but he is himself perplexed by the intricacies of the firework skyrockets he and Mr. De Pinna are devising in the cellar workshop. Ten years ago, Mr. De Pinna, who worked as an iceman, gave up his delivery route to stay with the Vanderhof family, joining Paul in the making of fireworks. He took over a room that had been vacated by a milkman who had died without telling any of the family his real name. On his death certificate Grandpa entered his own name, Martin Vanderhof, Jr.

The Sycamores' elder daughter, Essie, is a would-be ballet dancer, and she is awaiting the arrival of her ballet teacher, the bearlike Mr. Kolenkhov. Even as she practices her ballet steps on pointe, she is simultaneously occupied with making delicious chocolate and coconut candies, called "Love Dreams," which her xylophone-playing husband, Ed Carmichael, packs into candy boxes for door-to-door selling. Ed is also an enthusiastic printer who hand-sets type for epigrams and slogans that he gleans from books in the house library—works of the great authors, including Marx—and proudly includes samples of his press's printouts in Essie's candy boxes.

Essie's younger sister, Alice Vanderhof, the romantic heroine of the play, works as a secretary in the banking firm of Kirby and Son, Ltd., and is the only normal and practical person under the Vanderhof roof.

Martin Vanderhof, Penny's seventy-five-year-old father, "Grandpa" to Alice and her sister, is the lead protagonist of the play; his liberal sociopolitical philosophy guides the story line.

Around this entire household the playwrights have constructed a carefully plotted farce, with hilarious and unexpected turns in the dramatic action. The major theme of nonconformity is played out by each of the play's personalities in their joyous disregard for responsibility, living out their individual, childlike eccentricities.

Amid the various activities that fill the opening scene, Grandpa Vanderhof is just returning home from commencement exercises at Columbia University, which he attends each year to hear speeches he describes as entertainingly banal. Tomorrow he plans to do a little hunting in Westchester to add to the live snake collection in the glass tank gracing a corner of the living room.

When Essie tells Vanderhof that a letter from the U.S. government came to him a few days ago, he is surprised, because no one has written him in the past forty years.

The front doorbell rings, and the caller is Wilbur C. Henderson, a dour, matter-of-fact representative of the Internal Revenue Service in Washington, D.C., who has come to inform Martin Vanderhof that he owes twenty-two years of back income taxes. Vanderhof asks why he should pay for services like the Army and Navy, which he doesn't want, or give salaries to the Congress and the President, whom he doesn't care a fig about.

Suddenly, firebombs explode in the cellar. In a tizzy, Henderson rushes out of the Vanderhof house. At the front door, he passes Tony Kirby, Jr., Alice's handsome boss, recently out of Yale and Cambridge, the son of the banking firm Kirby & Son and her date for the evening.

The beautifully dressed Alice rescues Tony from the bombardment of personal and inappropriate questioning he is facing from her family, and they leave as everyone in the house finds a seat at the dining room table. Grandpa says grace, addressing Divinity with the simplicity of a thank-you note, his words remarkably reminiscent in tone and cadence of the grandfatherly Fireside Chats of President Franklin Delano Roosevelt.

The President's radio broadcasts to the nation from the White House were intended to inspire the disheartened people of America still deep in the despair of a Depression. America's National Recovery Act with its acronymic bureaus was beginning to revive a moribund economy. In contrast is the catastrophic failure of Stalin's Second Five Year Plan as reported to Kolenkhov in a recent letter from Moscow.

Later that night when Alice and Tony return to the house after their date, they realize how deeply in love they are, but Alice has reservations because their respective family values are incompatible. They agree that a week later the Kirbys will come to share an evening, including supper, with Alice's family.

Act II is one of the cleverest farcical contrivances in American drama, itself a theatrical skyrocket, explosive with laughter. The night begins as an ordinary, loony evening at the Vanderhofs'. Alice has reviewed all the preparations for tomorrow night's supper party with the Kirbys, but is confronted by Grandpa, who says that Alice will be giving them a false impression of the family's nonconformist lifestyle.

He needn't worry, however, as the Kirbys are destined to discover the family as it truly is, a houseful of independent spirits, uninhibited and without pretension.

The scene is set: on a table in a corner of the living room is Paul Sycamore's erector set model of the Queen Mary. Kolenkhov is stripped to the waist, boisterously directing Essie, as she dances daintily but dispassionately in her tutu. Ed on the xylophone is furiously banging out discordant music, supposedly the first movement of the sinuous *Scheherezade*. Penny is dressed in an artist's smock and beret, armed with palette and brushes and resolved to finish her oil painting of Mr. De Pinna, who is costumed as a Roman discus thrower and posed on a small platform. Grandpa, having fed flies to his snakes, finds his darts and begins to toss them across the room to the wall dartboard.

At this madcap moment the doorbell rings, and Rheba announces that the Kirbys have arrived—one night early. The mistake is hysterically comic with the Sycamores caught off guard, found out for the nutty nonconformists they are.

Grandpa steps forward to welcome the guests and introduces the Vanderhof menagerie. The problem of supper adds a madcap flurry of excitement as the flustered Penny tells the kitchen helper, Donald, to run down to the A&P to get canned salmon and soup, frankfurters, and a half dozen bottles of beer, none of which the dyspeptic Mr. Kirby can eat.

Everything this evening happens to humiliate and unnerve the banker, who strives in vain to maintain his dignity. Kolenkhov identifies Mr. Kirby as having a fine build for wrestling and, without warning, wrestles him flat onto his back.

Catastrophes happen everywhere. Rheba enters from the kitchen to report that the scrambled eggs went down the sink drain and Donald explains that the frankfurters at the store were moldy so he bought pickled pigs feet instead, but unfortunately Rheba doesn't know how to prepare them.

Offended and abused at every turn, the Kirbys seek to leave, but Tony insists they stay, and to pass the time as the food is being prepared, Penny asks everyone to participate in a parlor game of association. The gist of the game is to write down the very first thought that comes to mind when a word is announced. Penny collects and reads first the responses of her guests, Mr. and Mrs. Kirby, who are both equally humiliated by the inferences made from their answers.

Every response infers a loveless, sexless marriage and the Kirbys begin a domestic quarrel there and then.

They are determined to leave this demeaning evening, but before they can make it to the door, three FBI men storm the living room and declare everyone under arrest. The Department of Justice suspects this house is a Communist cell, printing and distributing fliers that call for an immediate revolution against the United States government.

Rounding up the suspected Communist anarchists, one of the FBI agents has physically pulled Mr. De Pinna out of the cellar, but Mr. De Pinna pleads to be allowed to go down and get his pipe, which he may have dangerously misplaced. Almost before he can say the words, the whole house goes berserk as the cellar, a warehouse for fireworks, explodes, suggesting the start of a Bolshevik revolution. Amidst the flashing light of fireworks and the booming of cherry bombs, everyone in the house is hauled off to the city jail.

The playwrights face a formidable moment. With such a brilliant, zinger-winger ending to Act II, how will they keep this comedy flying?

The morning newspaper reports the Kirbys in the humorously humiliating circumstances of the city jail, and Alice has concluded that any prospect of a liaison with Tony is hopeless. She is packed and ready to leave.

The spirit of Act III sparks alive the moment Kolenkhov appears at the house to announce the arrival of the Grand Duchess Olga Katrina, who has this day off from her waitress job at the Columbus Circle Childs restaurant. The title *You Can't Take It with You* may apply here in particular to the Russian aristocracy who left every possession behind in Mother Russia as they escaped the Bolsheviks. The duchess, separated by the Revolution from her czarist wealth and its concomitant lifestyle and power, optimistically finds joy in the ever-upward-striving style of her new proletarian, American life. Meanwhile, deep within the heart of this play, Kaufman and Hart serve a warning to the *affluent* Americans, including the Kirbys, that in the depths of a Depression, desperate citizens may undertake desperate means for survival, much like what took place during the Russian Revolution of 1917.

The Grand Duchess loves to cook, and her specialty is blintzes, which she would love to make if there were sour cream and pot cheese in the refrigerator. Penny leads the way into the kitchen with the Grand Duchess sweeping majestically behind.

Reconciliation between Alice and Tony comes just in time as Mr. Kirby learns that his materialistic philosophy is wrong, that he has forgotten the simple pleasures of family life. Tony confesses that he deliberately brought his family on the wrong night to see the Vanderhof household unvarnished, as they really were.

And Grandpa wins the philosophical argument with Kirby by saying that if a man is lucky enough to be able to do the thing he loves, he will not suffer sleepless, anxious nights, the pain of indigestion and the inevitable heart attack.

The IRS issue is resolved when the records show that a delinquent milkman, a Martin Vanderhof, Jr., died and was buried eight years ago and that his survivor, Grandpa Vanderhof, Sr., may even be entitled to a refund.

When the Grand Duchess comes from the kitchen to announce that the blintzes are ready, Kirby is flabbergasted to know that czarist royalty is happy to be a waitress in New York City. As she enters with the delicacy, Grandpa again speaks to the Deity with his casual familiarity, asking for a happy marriage for Alice and Tony and good health for all.

"Pennies from Heaven," "The Best Things in Life Are Free," and other popular songs of America in this, the nadir of the Depression, all contain lyrics of hope abounding

You Can't Take It with You helped the American audience escape from its economic worries for three hours, to laugh, possibly with hidden envy, at the courage that Grandpa flaunts in his denial of his social responsibility. But the audience knew this was a fantasy, that if every citizen practiced Grandpa's adolescent have fun philosophy, the end result would inevitably spell chaos for the nation. This does not mean that Mr. Kirby has Grandpa pegged correctly as a Communist, for Grandpa is not radically concerned with overthrowing

America's capitalist status quo. Rather, Grandpa is a fantasy character, much like Rip Van Winkle, another Dutchman who divorced himself from the stresses and strains of real life.

Young Tony Kirby wishes to cast his lot for the unworried life. He reveals his father's hidden past: that Mr. Kirby, senior, the conservative banker, still has the saxophone, a symbol of his nonconformist youth, hidden away in the back of his closet. The character of old man Kirby, who comes to respect the power of Grandpa's philosophy, is cathartic for theatergoers who still have hostile feelings for bankers, having lost their life-savings when banks failed all across the country.

You Can't Take It with You conveys a serious message of social protest against the jungle morality of the capitalist system, and ends with a declaration of faith in America's middle-of-the-road tradition by the young lovers, as Alice Vanderhof agrees at last to marry Tony Kirby.

The Time of Your Life (1939–1940)
by William Saroyan

A Play in Five Acts. Produced by the Theater Guild, in association with Eddie Dowling. Staged by Eddie Dowling and William Saroyan under the supervison of Theresa Helburn and Lawrence Langner. Opened on Broadway at the Booth Theater, October 25, 1939.

The Original Cast

Joe	Eddie Dowling
Tom	Edward Andrews
Kitty Duval	Julie Haydon
Nick	Charles De Sheim
Arab	Houseley Stevens, Sr.
Kit Carson Murphy	Leo Doyle
McCarthy	Tom Tully
Krupp	William Bendix
Harry	Gene Kelly
Wesley	Reginald Beane
Dudley	Curt Conway

Elsie	Cathie Bailey
Lorene	Nene Vibber
Mary L.	Celeste Holme
Willie	Will Lee
Blick	Grover Burgess
Ma	Michelette Burani
Killer	Evelyn Geller
Her Sidekick	Mary Cheffey
A Cop	Randolph Wade
Another Cop	John Farrell
The Sailor	Randolph Wade
Society Lady	Eva Leonard Boyne
Society Gentleman	Ainsworth Arnold
The Drunkard	John Farrell
The Newsboy	Ross Bagdasarian

The Time of Your Life is set in Nick's Pacific Street Saloon, Restaurant and Entertainment Palace at the foot of the Embarcadero on the waterfront in San Francisco, a safe haven for Saroyan's oppressed, poor, and unloved, who all, on this day in October 1939, remember the bitterness of bread lines, Hoover camps, and broken bankers selling apples on street corners.

At a table sits Saroyan's alter ego Joe, the clairvoyant protagonist of the play, who, according to the playwright, is always calm, always eager, always thinking, and always bored. A millionaire, though no one knows where his fortune comes from, he sits in this low-down dive and no one knows why, drinking the most expensive French champagne.

The innocent, unworldly, childlike quality of the people of the play is indicated the moment that Joe calls for Tom, the handsome, thirty-year-old go-fer, to go and buy a couple dollars' worth of wind-up toys for Joe to play with. But before leaving, he must put a nickel into the jukebox and play the Missouri Waltz, Joe's favorite song—sweet, sad, and sentimental.

As Tom is about to go, in comes the unbelievably beautiful Kitty Duval, a young prostitute who lives and works around the corner at the New York Hotel, and at first sight she and Tom fall in love.

Kitty, who has drunk too much champagne, wistfully tells Joe the sad tale of her early years on the Ohio farm with her poor Polish family, when her name was Katerina Koranovsky. In her need to be consoled, she asks Joe to dance, but he refuses, and she is dancing alone when Tom returns from his toy shopping. Joe tells Tom to dance with Kitty, observing that the youth is already deeply in love with her.

For Joe, the ambience of Nick's saloon is absolutely beautiful now, with Tom and Kitty dancing, an array of toys before him on the table, the newcomers Wesley and Harry playing the piano and hoofing it on the stage, the enthusiastic young Willie contending with the pinball machine, and the philosophical Arab sitting at the bar, deep in his memories.

Saroyan describes Nick's saloon as a kind of paradise, a melting pot of ethnicities, where there is kindliness, security, and generosity of spirit, living and letting live as each person follows his own special destiny. Here in this dream-haven there is no conflict, and no evil is allowed to enter, a setting reminiscent of the sacred mead-hall Heorot in *Beowulf.*

Then, just as the monster Grendel infiltrated Heorot, the atmosphere of the saloon turns threatening when the villain Blick, head of the Vice Squad, walks in. Saroyan describes Blick as "a strong man who has no strength, strong only among the weak, a weakling himself who is strong only because he uses his force on the weaker." His character says Blick hurts little people and wants to change the world from something bad to something worse, something ugly.

Seeing no one to arrest at the moment, Blick leaves but warns Nick he will return that evening. Nick's obvious disgust prompts Joe to ask jokingly if he is going to kill Blick. Nick doesn't answer the question directly, but the playwright has foreshadowed assassination.

At the start of Act II, set one hour later in the day, Joe amuses himself by attempting to guess a woman's name from the initials M. L. on her handbag—a harmless pastime, like darts, for boozers. After several guesses, Joe stumbles on Mary, which was his mother's name and also the name of a girl he fell in love with in Mexico City on the day of her marriage to another man.

After listening to this nonsense, Mary asks Joe if he drinks a great deal. He replies that he likes to drink only when he's awake, which is about as much as he likes to breathe. Here, Saroyan, himself addicted to alcohol and depressed in a failed marriage, writes an aria for Joe on his love of drinking. Why drink? he asks himself rhetorically. He drinks because he doesn't like to feel dead most of the time: dead or bored, not knowing what to do with the time of his life.

The policeman Krupp and longshoreman McCarthy, who both work at the docks, come in for a quick beer. One represents the Establishment; the other agitates for workers' rights. But since Krupp has never been obliged to hit McCarthy over the head with a billy club during a protest, the friendship they formed in high school has survived intact.

McCarthy says he doesn't *like* being a common man, that he married a sensitive and cultured woman so that his kids would be "sissies instead of suckers," and now he has a son who wants to be a writer. With seriousness, Saroyan has McCarthy swear he hates the "tribe" who call themselves writers, the users and abusers of language, making all kinds of mischief—basically "the lousiest people in the world." However, believing that rejection turns frustrated artists into dangerous people, he declares that all those lousy writers should be published anyway—and besides, he likes to read.

When asked for his opinion, the Arab, who has been listening intently to McCarthy's tirade, takes his time before offering, "No foundation. All the way down the line. What. What-not. Nothing." Joe expatiates on the Arab's profound reply, saying that the Arab is a prophet, who with the help of one beer is able to fathom the deepest understanding of things, discovering that what and what-not, birth and death, the reasonable and the unreasonable, are one.

Suddenly, Joe asks Tom to go on another shopping trip, to buy an atlas of Europe and a revolver and cartridges. Joe doesn't say why he wants a gun, though earlier Nick spoke casually about killing Blick. As for the atlas, Joe is curious about the geographical location of the village of Pribor in Czechoslovakia, where Sigmund Freud was born. Joe, like Saroyan, is captivated by Freudian concepts of transformation and magical thinking, which is Freud's great discovery in his study of of the wish-fulfillment of dreams. This idea includes the belief that discovering the name of a person or his birthplace may capture that person's intrinsic power, like the captured dwarf-magician in the child's fable *Rumplestiltskin*, or the Hebraic taboo against the naming of the multiple names of Jehovah. While Pribor is irrelevant to anything that happens in *The Time of Your Life*, the play seems to be, in itself, Saroyan's psychoanalytical stream of unconscious free association, an attempt at a "talking cure."

Joe decides to take Tom and Kitty out on the town. When they return, Tom asks what prompts Joe-Saroyan to be so magnanimous, generous, and loving in everything he does. Joe responds with a shadowy history of his personal life, keenly zeroing in on America's warped, capitalist economy and the significance of Christian conscience in the world. (Outside in the street, a Salvation Army band is playing "The Blood of the Lamb," and people are singing and an old sinner is testifying loudly to his sin and subsequent salvation.) He presents Saroyan's basic life philosophy that the rich have stolen their wealth from the poor, who can neither afford it nor protect themselves. "Money is the guiltiest thing in the world," Joe says. "It stinks."

He offers the unloaded gun to Tom and tells him to give it to someone out in the street whom he deems a worthy hold-up man. Tom is taken aback. "You've seen good people who needed guns, haven't you?" Joe insists, but Tom is afraid he'll choose the wrong person, so Joe pockets the gun and instead gives Tom money to buy *Life, Liberty, Time*, and chewing gum, Saroyan's playful catalogue of philosophical *double-entendre*.

He strikes up a conversation with Kit Carson Murphy, Saroyan's zaniest and weirdest character. Dressed like a cowboy, and speaking with the twang of a cow puncher, Kit Carson and his Bunyanesque tall tales spark the play with nonsensical and comic exaggeration.

Kit, who is afraid of the gun, nevertheless pretends to be an expert and advises Joe on shooting technique as he carefully loads bullets into the chamber. He hands it over to Joe, who unloads it again and puts the gun away.

Tom returns and a childish gum-chewing contest begins with Kit as referee. As Tom chews furiously, he tells Joe that he wants to find a job so he can marry Kitty and buy the little dream house she keeps talking about. He doesn't know what kind of job he might be suited for but responds enthusiastically when Joe suggests that he can get a job for Tom immediately as a non-union truck driver. They phone Joe's friend Keith, who owns a trucking company, and Tom gets his first assignment.

When Kitty comes in to look for Tom, Joe explains where he has gone and steps out to look for some poetry books to comfort the lonely girl until her lover returns. Until now, everything occurring on stage has been expositional; Saroyan has held his audience's attention with imaginatively far-fetched and strangely self-contradictory exchanges rather than interpersonal confrontation. But now the patrons of Nick's saloon are about to face a dramatic conflict.

Wesley and Harry, returning to perform in the scheduled evening show, report they witnessed a clash on the waterfront pier between the longshoremen and the police. Nick, who is concerned that the police might use deadly weapons to quell the riot, leaves Harry to tend the bar so he can walk down to the waterfront.

Just then, Blick comes into the saloon and insolently pushes everyone around, stopping all the entertainment. He sees Kitty alone and begins to bully her. When Kit Carson tries to defend Kitty, Blick hauls him outside onto the street, where he knocks him out cold. Joe returns—followed by Tom, who has driven his truck to the saloon—to find Blick humiliating Kitty. When Wesley tells them what has been going on, Blick beats him. Joe commands Tom to take Kitty and drive to San Diego, where they can get married, and the young couple leave hastily.

Saying strangely that he has always wanted to kill somebody, Joe finds the revolver, cocks it, and holds it firmly in front of him, aiming directly at Blick. There is a click when he pulls the trigger, but there is no shot, because the gun isn't loaded.

Nick re-enters with the dockworker, McCarthy, and takes the gun from Joe as he orders Blick out of the saloon.

Suddenly, outside, three shots ring out. Nick runs into the street and reports that Blick is dead, that somebody shot him but none of the cops is moving to find out who did it. Joe slowly gets his hat and coat, but can't tell Nick where he is going or whether he will return. Then Kit Carson enters, and walks over to Joe.

"Somebody just shot a man," Joe remarks. "How do you feel?" Never better, Kit Carson answers. He says he shot a man himself "once," in October 1939, because he didn't like the way the man spoke to the ladies. He recounts that he went up to his room to get his old, pearl-handled revolver and waited in an alley for the man to pass him on Pacific Street where he shot him dead and then threw the revolver into the Bay. Everyone closes around Kit Carson to embrace him, the hero of the saloon.

Without comment, Joe rises, waves good-bye to all, and slowly exits.

The Time of Your Life is William Saroyan's drama about people who reputedly came to Nick's Paradise Saloon in October 1939. But the play truly recalls May 9, 1934, the first day of the West Coast Longshoremen's Strike in San Francisco.

Saroyan's concern for the longshoreman gives everlastingness to that tragic day and the conflict that arose because Roosevelt's National Recovery Act did not consider the shipping industry in restructuring the relationship of shipowners and longshoremen. On May 9, 1934, a thousand policemen came to the docks armed with submachine guns to clear the picket lines to allow strikebreakers to go on board the cargoes to work. In the melee two longshoremen were killed and more than sixty people were injured, prompting the governor to call in the National Guard.

Saroyan's passionate sympathy for the helpless and abused, and his hatred for the authoritarian oppressor, can be traced back to his boyhood and his particular cultural heritage.

Saroyan's father had been a Presbyterian minister in Anatolia, but the tyrannical decrees of the Ottoman government against Armenians demanded their conversion or their death, because of trumped up accusations of political treason implicating Russia and the leaders of the Armenian nation. In 1905 the family emigrated to New Jersey, where William was born in 1908. Three years later, when his father died, William and his brother and sister were placed in an orphanage in California. Their mother, who had found employment in a Fresno cannery, was able to reunite the family five years later. The massacres of the Armenian genocide had begun in Turkey.

Imagine the eight-year-old Saroyan, in an orphanage with his father dead, fearing that the Ottoman intention for Armenian genocide included him. There was no one to protect him, and it was obvious the whole world had turned its back, on these powerless people. The sensitive child was forever haunted by the realization that people could stand by watching the powerful rape, torture, and slaughter the oppressed—and do nothing,

When he was twenty-five years old, the burgeoning writer published *The Broken Wheel* in the Armenian journal *Hairenik*, confessing his rebellious, contradictory and despondent nature:

> The writer is a spiritual anarchist, as in the depths of his soul every man is. He is discontented with everything and everybody. The writer is everybody's best friend and only true enemy—the good and great enemy. He neither walks with the multitude nor cheers with them. The writer who is a writer is a rebel who never stops.[1]

In Nick's Pacific Street Saloon, such a rebel can take refuge from an indifferent and hostile society to discover his own, true identity and find approval for his very being—until Blick, the unreluctant representative of the Establishment, exercises the power of entry. In the momentous killing of Blick—in the blink of an eye, *auf ein augenblick*—Saroyan transforms himself into a legendary righter of wrongs, all in consonance with his magical, transformational, wish-fulfillment thinking. The prostitutes in Nick's saloon are ladies. Grown-up men enjoying wind-up toys and pinball games can prove their power over the machine. Love happens in an instant, as in fairy tales when a kiss transforms a frog into a prince and a hag into a princess. Even the Arab, who might have been a threatening figure for Saroyan, is instead a gentle, harmless poet-philosopher who plays beautiful music on his harmonica. And Blick disappears like the Wicked Witch of the West, dissolving into a puddle and evaporating immediately.

When Saroyan was awarded the Pulitzer Prize, he refused the honor and sent back the check, declaring in subsequent interviews that "wealth cannot patronize art." Saroyan sought to confirm his solidarity with the downtrodden—and hostility toward authority and wealth—by rejecting the prize, and was the only playwright to do so.

CHAPTER NINE

Against Prejudice

American democracy is founded on the principle of "liberty and justice for all," but two Pulitzer Prize plays, Paul Green's *In Abraham's Bosom* and Elmer Rice's *Street Scene*, challenge Americans to apply that principle in their interactions with one another. Although they differ in dramatic treatment, setting, and time, both plays protest the bitter injustices of bigotry and the denial of individual liberty.

Realistic, naturalistic plays, *In Abraham's Bosom* and *Street Scene* attempt the dramatic reconstruction of heartbreaking conflicts in specific segments of American culture. *In Abraham's Bosom* reflects the trials and torments of black freedmen, whose emancipation from slavery was supposedly hard won in the Civil War, but whose freedom was not effectively secured by enforcement of state and federal legislation or by attitudinal changes in the white majority. *Street Scene* recreates the bigotry and immorality in the urban melting pot of New York City, where a large percentage of the twenty million European immigrants who flocked to America between 1890 and 1924 settled in tenement houses of Manhattan, Brooklyn, and the Bronx, providing cheap labor for the low-esteemed and low-paying jobs in services and factories.

Both plays illuminate the troubled lives of the protagonists during these epochs, awakening America's conscience as they presage legislation designed to effect needed reforms for civil rights and punish bigoted hate crimes in America. And both plays decry the anti-liberal forces of the late nineteenth and early twentieth centuries, brutally hostile to blacks and immigrants: the Jim Crow laws in the South after Reconstruction upheld belief in the natural inferiority of blacks, and federal legislation following World War I clearly reflected America's racist fears and prejudices—namely the Immigration Act, which critically limited the admission of people specifically from Eastern Europe and the Mediterranean.

In Abraham's Bosom is a dramatic witness to America's racial prejudice and the cruel separatism that endured until the 1960s, when the federal government began to enact civil rights legislation to terminate the Jim Crow laws and to establish equality in education for African-Americans. The play's protagonist, Abraham McCranie, embodies the battle for the rights granted to all citizens by the Fourteenth Amendment, including African-American' entitlement to quality education as a means of ending their brutal alienation from the mainstream of American culture.

The play begins in North Carolina in 1885 at the end of the Reconstruction period following the Civil War. Oscar Handlin in *Race and Nationality in American Life* describes that period as one that fostered the belligerent mood of the white South and the seemingly impossible dilemma of the freed slave:

> The white South, redeemed, had developed a way of life that maintained and extended the actual inferiority of the blacks. In the last decade of the nineteenth century one device after another had deprived them of the ballot and of political power; their own lack of skill and of capital, as well as discrimination, had confined them to a submerged place in the economy; and the rigid etiquette of segregation made their social inferiority ever clearer. In no aspect of his life could the Negro escape awareness that he was decisively below the white, hopelessly incapable of rising to the same opportunities as his former masters. If ever he lost sight of that fact central to his existence, the ever-present threat of lynching and other forms of violence reminded him of it.[1]

Spanning the years 1885 to 1906, *In Abraham's Bosom* hammers home the difficulty and the danger newly emancipated slaves endured in trying to improve their lives as free people, mocked by promises of an equality that was cruelly denied.

The Ku Klux Klan, who make a ghastly appearance in *In Abraham's Bosom*, surged beyond the American South during World War I in a malignant new incarnation. Indeed, World War I and the 1917 Russian Revolution inspired an era of racial and religious prejudice and vicious hate-mongering throughout the United States and around the world. Economic hardship and the search for political, religious, and individual freedom were bringing great migrations of Europeans to America. But upper-class Americans viewed these newcomers with scorn and suspicion, fearing they brought with them the seeds of communism and revolution. (The Red Scare of those years peaked dramatically in the Massachusetts case of Sacco and Vanzetti, two Italian immigrants labeled communist anarchists and executed in 1927 for a crime they did not commit.) Meanwhile, middle- and lower-class Americans considered these greenhorn intruders unwelcome, glutting the labor market when jobs were hard to find, especially since women, recently enfranchised, were competing in the labor pool.

A virulent anti-Semitism was spreading at home and abroad, abetted by the worldwide distribution of the horrendous calumny *The Protocols of the Elders of Zion*, a forgery describing a nonexistent Jewish plot to achieve world domination. The powerful industrialist Henry Ford and the wildly popular right-wing radio personality Father Charles Coughlin both funded the printing and dissemination of this anti-Semitic propaganda; Ford also supported Coughlin's radio addresses denouncing communists, Jews, and all "Christ-rejecters."

In these two Pulitzer Prize–winning plays, Paul Green and Elmer Rice show all too clearly how grotesque propaganda, economic depression, and the lust for power feed humanity's innate capacity for cruelty, giving the lie to the promise of equality America holds out to the newcomer and to the oppressed.

In Abraham's Bosom (1926–1927)
by Paul Green

A Play in Seven Scenes. Produced by the Provincetown Players. Staged by Jasper Deeter. Opened at the Provincetown Theater, December 30, 1926.

The Original Cast

Abraham McCranie	Julius Bledsoe
Goldie McAllister	Rose McClendon
Muh Mack	Abbe Mitchell
Three Turpentine Hands for the Colonel:	
Bud Gaskins	Frank Wilson
Lije Hunneycutt	Thomas Mosley
Puny Avery	James Dunmore
Douglass McCranie	R. J. Huey
Three Students to Abe:	
Eddie Williams	Melvin Greene
Lanie Horton	Armithine Lattimer
Neilly McNeill	Stanley Greene
Colonel McCranie	L. Rufus Hill
Lonnie McCranie	H. Ben Smith

In Abraham's Bosom chronicles the life and death of Abraham Mc-Cranie, the son of the white plantation owner Colonel McCranie and a black slave. Held suspect by both blacks and whites, Abe tries to find some dignity in his life by striving to get an education and to serve the black community as a teacher.

The first scene takes place in a turpentine forest in eastern North Carolina in the sweltering summer of 1885, twenty-two years after President Lincoln signed the Emancipation Proclamation, setting all slaves forever free and promising that the executive government of the United States would maintain that hard-won freedom. A group of black woodsmen, turpentine farmers, are having dinner after a full morning of chopping into the pine trees and collecting their oozy sap.

McCranie is still out in the woods working as the men call out to him to come and eat his midday meal. Twenty-five-year-old Abe has not had his heart in resin production ever since he witnessed Charlie Sampson being hanged on a telegraph pole and shot by a white posse for allegedly having attacked a white woman. Simpson's body was supposed to hang on the pole for a month, but that same night Abe went to the site, cut down the body, and buried it—much like Antigone in Greek tragedy.

Identifying Abe as the culprit, the posse was determined to hang him from the same pole, but his father, Colonel McCranie, intervened and saved his neck. Charlie Sampson hanging from a tree with a noose around his neck is emblazoned in Abe's mind as the first major symbol of the play, the Ku Klux Klan's prejudiced and vengeful punishment for being born black, and a punishment Abe knows may also fall on him.

The other turpentine workers are well aware that to stand up against a white man in any matter is to risk one's life. To keep to one's work and keep quiet, they say, is the only way to be safe. But Abe has not been playing safe. Recently one of the workers overheard him telling the colonel that he wants to get an education so that he can start a school where he can teach young blacks. Agitating for an opportunity that the white powers are determined not to grant is no way to stay out of trouble; any white man, says a turpentine worker, will tell you that if you give a black man a book, you might just as well shoot him.

Abe enters from the forest, concerned with an arithmetic problem that he has been trying to solve for some hours. Soon Colonel McCranie, carrying his riding whip, enters the clearing too, followed by his white son, Lonnie. When Abe asks the Colonel if he's spoken with the school board about his wish to go to school, the Colonel advises that the time is not yet ripe, but Abe persists. Angry and ashamed to have an ambitious black half-brother determined to create opportunity for his race, Lonnie tells Abe to back off, that the Colonel has already becoming a laughing-stock in the white community for his sake. The argument between the two young men escalates: Lonnie takes his father's whip and brutally lashes Abe, but, being the stronger of the two, Abe grabs Lonnie and hurls him into a muddy thicket.

Even as Abe stands trembling with mixed emotions, the Colonel takes up the whip and beats him cruelly as the youth begs for mercy. "You struck a white man," he thunders, "you struck my son." But then, Abe says beseechingly that he too is the Colonel's son.

The workers are aghast when Lonnie, muddy and in a frenzy, picks up the whip and begins again to thrash Abe, stopped finally by the Colonel, who orders him to go away and bathes Abe's wounds himself with water from the spring. The black witnesses to this injustice restrain each other from speaking out, as they have no power to interfere.

Suddenly Goldie, Abe's sweetheart, comes through the bushes and is horrified to see Abe so badly hurt. The Colonel tells her to take care of the youth and leaves, following Lonnie.

But Abe's fury is intense, confused, filled with contempt and self-hate. He cries out that he wants to kill Lonnie, who beat him like a dog, who made him feel like nothing.

Goldie calms him and tells him she knows a cool place under a tree where she will tend his wounds. The workers are titillated with the anticipation of voyeurs, as the lovers leave for their hideaway and the black chorus sings a passionate spiritual of hope.

> *My feet were wet with sunrise dew,*
> *The morning star was a witness, too.*
> *Away, away up in the Rock of Ages,*
> *In God's bosom will be my pillow.*

The accompanying mouth harp changes to a quick, thumping, libidinous rhythm that puts all the men into a Dionysian frenzy of dancing as they sing, "In Goldie's bosom," setting off raucous laughter as they jostle each other down the hill following Goldie and Abe.

In this passionate first scene, without mincing words or skirting the terrifying prospect of a black man being lynched, playwright

Green establishes the cruel and unjust reality of a Reconstruction-ist South. Throughout the play, the songs, usually written by the playwright, assert the oppressed people's faith in the Lord, that though they may be despised by the powerful whites, they know in their hearts that Divinity is without prejudice and will be their sanctuary.

The next scene opens on a spring day, three years later, in Abe's two-room cabin. The furnishings are dilapidated. Through the single window on the rear wall one can see an expanse of cotton fields. On another wall is a calendar with an illustration of a slave leaving his chains behind him as he walks up a hill toward the sunrise, under the large print caption *We are rising*, an icon of the major theme that the African-American people have cast off chains of slavery and prejudice.

Muh Mack is seated in front of the fireplace rocking a four-day-old infant swathed in blankets. Goldie is lying in a bed, half-covered by a sheet, lamenting that Abe didn't stop Lonnie from cutting down the plum bushes under which her first and second babies were buried, allowing him to plow up the whole cotton field, turning her flesh into the earth.

Abe enters barefoot and dressed in rags, ready to sharpen his hoe with a file, but Goldie warns that filing in the house could bring bad luck, even curse the newborn boy. Abe says they must leave such beliefs behind, and quotes from one of his books that "the Negro is a superstitious person" who imagines evil spirits in the world around him. Yet his confidence in the future those books represent is eroding. In his bitterness he declares that God has indeed cursed him and his household. Can this child survive when his others have died, when the crows and the weather have ruined his crop and the family has no money to live on? God, he now believes, is a white man's God, and there is no God to care for his people.

Goldie tells him to ask the Colonel to help him, but he is still hurting from the humiliation and pain of the Colonel's whipping three years ago.

Muh Mack says Abe's books have destroyed his belief, and she kicks at them, threatening to burn them. Abe pushes her back. Then, suddenly, the Colonel's voice is heard calling from just outside the cabin door. He defends Abe's studious determination and confesses he has come to see the new baby. Muh Mack proudly displays the infant, saying he is as fine and strong as the newborn Abe was when she held him up for the Colonel to see thirty years ago.

Ailing and considering his own mortality, the Colonel has come to deliver a gift to Abe: the survey, title, and deed to this two-room house with its tract of land containing twenty-five acres. The transaction has been signed and recorded in the courthouse, precluding any ownership contest. In addition, the Colonel is making a schoolhouse of the old Quillie House, equipping it with a classroom, and he has appointed two black men to serve with him on the school board to give Abe a chance to prove himself as a teacher.

The Colonel's support of Abe will heighten the hostility of the white community and of his own son, who still resents his half-brother. But the Colonel is disappointed in Lonnie who, it seems to spite the Colonel, has dropped out of college.

His faith restored, Abe prays to God to forgive his blasphemy and vows to raise his child as a new Moses who will bring his people out of bondage.

Untrained but intent on having his students learn, Abe demonstrates in the next scene that he is an overly demanding teacher. In the old Quillie House's one-room schoolhouse only three students have come to class, all the others kept at home by parents who have complained to the school board that Abe loses his temper and has physically punished the Ragland boy.

A school board member arrives to tell Abe that the school is officially closed, handing him the authorized letter handwritten by his brother Lonnie, now head of the board since the Colonel died. Heartbroken and helpless, Abe kneels in prayer.

Fifteen years pass as Abe and his family move around the state, most recently to a furnished room in the poverty-stricken section of Durham, North Carolina. Abe works at the town's power plant, shoveling coal into the furnaces to make electricity.

Goldie is about to go to the store to buy some liver for Abe's supper, but the fifty cents she had in her purse is missing, and she immediately suspects that her son Douglass, who is out, has taken it. Muh Mack says she gave the boy the money and wants to know why the McCranies don't move back to the plantation. Unfortunately, Abe had to sell his house and land to pay the lawyers who fought unsuccessfully to defend him in the case of child abuse brought by the Raglands. But Muh Mack pleads that if they threw themselves at Mr. Lonnie's feet, he would let Abe have his old two-room slave cabin.

No store will extend credit to the McCranies, so Muh Mack makes do with corn bread and a small piece of pork for Abe. As she prepares the meal, she laments the uncontrollable temper that has so often got him into trouble, forcing the family to move from Raleigh to Greensboro to Wilmington to Durham. She knows very soon Abe will get into a fight down at the power plant and they'll all be forced to leave.

Douglass, fifteen, enters, dropping his school books on the floor. When Muh Mack asks him if he has the fifty cents she gave him, he says he bought hot dogs for himself and his school friends. He finds his guitar and plays and sings until Abe comes in, weary and dirty with coal dust, and shouts at him to put the instrument away, calling him "a good-for-nothing."

Abe comes to the table and insists that Douglass, who says he's not hungry, sit with the family as he says grace for the poverty of food set out by Muh Mack.

Abe says he saw Douglass and his "worthless" friends at the hot dog stand and recognized that he was spending money he must have taken from his mother's purse. But money is not the issue, Abe continues brokenheartedly. On the street coming home, he met Douglass's teacher, who informed him that she had to put Douglass back into the third reader, that he doesn't want to learn.

In desperate anger, Abe smashes his fist on the table. Driven by his rage and disappointment at his son, whom he named after the great Frederick Douglass in the hope that he would rise high and lead, he grabs the boy by the collar, lifts him high, and hurls him across the room, where the boy falls on the floor, sobbing.

Abe blames Muh Mack for spoiling Douglass, and she, hurt by his criticism, says she will leave their home. Abe agrees that indeed they will all have to leave, that he has been dismissed from the plant after an argument he had with a white man today.

Goldie and Muh Mack ask to go back to the Colonel's plantation, where the Colonel's will has provided them with a place of refuge. Abe, too, has been longing to return, and to build a foundation for his educational mission in his own birthplace.

Three years later, on a dreary November afternoon in 1906, in the old, two-room slave cabin, Abe is writing a speech he plans to give before a group of black parents in favor of their sponsorship of the Cape Fair Training School, to offer black students basic education, along with manual training and practical arts.

Muh Mack, in a rocking chair by the fireplace, scoffs at Abe's enthusiasm, pointing out that he has spoken so many times to so many groups in so many cities and has accomplished nothing. She complains about his unfatherly feeling toward his son Douglass, whom he has forbidden to come home.

To a skeptical Muh Mack Abe reads the speech, satisfied that it has the power of truth. Indeed, playwright Green has written a great speech that zeroes in on the power of education to create social equality. This same positive theme was presented on August 8, 1963, in a speech by Dr. Martin Luther King Jr. in front of the Lincoln Memorial in Washington, D.C. One hundred years after Lincoln delivered the Emancipation Proclamation, King spoke on behalf of those who still had not realized the full measure of the freedom and opportunity they had been promised so long ago.

As he leaves the house, Abe reminds Muh Mack not to admit Douglass, who has taken up bad habits and bad company. He tells her he'll return by ten o'clock with the school as good as started.

About an hour later on a dark, sandy, country road with towering trees that line the road's dividing forks, Abe, out of breath, staggers out of the shadows. The moon is low and a wind stirs the leaves of the large trees. Shouts of pursuit sound in the distance but soon die away.

A flickering lantern comes onto the road. Lonnie has heard the clamor. Abe tells him how a white-sheeted mob ran off the blacks who had come to hear him and beat him when he tried to deliver his speech. Unsympathetically, Lonnie says Abe was warned to stay in his place—to mind his cotton fields and keep his mouth shut. Claiming that Abe has neglected his crop, Lonnie announces he is re-appropriating the fields and has hired hands coming to pick the crop in the morning. Abe and his family will have to move off the plantation.

In a frenzy, Abe calls Lonnie a thief, and Lonnie counters that he'll kill Abe with his lantern. Abe threatens to hit Lonnie, who swiftly crashes the lantern against Abe's head. Abe forces Lonnie to the ground and chokes him to death, not realizing the tremendous strength in his hands. He goes berserk.

The windblown trees are a posse threatening to capture him. He sees the phantasm of a white posse and, in the midst of them, Charlie Sampson, beaten and bloody, being dragged to the pole where he is lynched. Ghosts flitter in his delirium. He sees a pretty young black woman and a dandified white man walking together into a thicket alongside the road. Recognizing his mother and Colonel Mack, he calls to them for help, but when he follows them and parts the bushes, he realizes, horrified, that he has become a witness at his own conception. He stumbles back, tripping over Lonnie's body, and runs shrieking down the road.

Thirty minutes later in Abe's cabin, Douglass, now nineteen and dressed in cheap, flashy clothes, stands before the fireplace telling Muh Mack about the year he spent on the chain gang, swinging his eight-pound hammer against rocks every day under the broiling sun. Having landed in jail for getting drunk and holding forth on his father's ideas about racial equality, he subsequently stabbed a guard, which extended his time to a year for assault.

Douglass feels he has been rightly punished and has come to believe that his father is wrong—that his place in the world is to do the dirty work for the white oppressors. And, he adds, that's why he drinks—to forget.

But he has his guitar and he'll play Muh Mack's request. The song is the lively "Jonah's Band," and Muh Mack joins in the chorus as the pair sing and dance. Goldie comes in, excited to see Douglass, asking fearfully if the youth has met up with his father. No, Douglass says, Abe has gone to speak at the Quillie House.

Coming from her housekeeping duties at Lonnie's plantation house, Goldie has brought a large hambone that she can fix up with collard greens for supper, but she warns Douglass not to egg his father on. They hear Abe's footsteps and are aghast when he enters unsteadily, his face bruised and his clothes shredded.

Muh Mack collapses in her chair; Goldie sobs violently and buries her face in her hands. Abe blurts out that they have to leave at once. Looking at the wall where the poster of the freed slave hangs, bitterly Abe mutters the motto, *We are rising.*

He tells his family how the Klansmen ran him off—and that he has discovered it was Douglass who betrayed him to them. Brokenly, he confesses that he's done murder and they'll be coming for him. He berates himself, crying out that he is another Cain.

Douglass pleads that he didn't mean any harm, but they can hear the crowd of men coming up the road, and he urges his mother and aunt to come with him. Muh Mack hobbles into the fields behind Douglass. Goldie stays and throws her arms around Abe.

A stone comes smashing through the window, striking the lamp, throwing the room into darkness. Down on his knees, Abe begins to pray to God for forgiveness for his terrible sin, knowing he must suffer torment, envisioning his body being burned to ashes and scattered over the earth.

The leader of the posse calls to Abe to come out, that they can hear him speaking inside, and Abe hears the order to shoot him at sight, like a dog.

Abe steps outside onto the porch. A volley of gunshots rips into his body. The men fire a few more shots, assuring them that he is dead, and they leave, declaring that Lonnie's bloody murder has been avenged and Abraham McCranie will give them no more trouble. Goldie enfolds Abe's lifeless body as the wind blows through the open door of the house, setting the sparks flying from the fireplace.

In Abraham's Bosom can be compared to the story of the Jewish patriarch Abraham in the Old Testament. Abraham, the first Jew, like Colonel McCranie sired two sons: the white-skinned Isaac, whose mother was Sarah, and the dark-skinned Ishmael, whose mother was Sarah's Egyptian handmaiden, Hagar. Backed by the prejudiced, white community, Sarah forced Abraham to send Hagar with her child Ishmael into the desert to fend for herself. Muslims trace their origins back to Abraham, Hagar, and their son Ishmael, who, an angel told Hagar, would grow up to live a life of constant struggle with other men.

The last moments of the Green play can also be considered in the light of the Bible story in which God commands Abraham to sacrifice Isaac to him, but sends an angel to stay his hand at the last moment. In the play. God's miraculous hand is absent as the son Douglass informs the white posse of Abe's education-directed meeting, betraying his father, who becomes the KKK's sacrifice.

Abe McCranie's twentieth-century reincarnation is the great Dr. Martin Luther King Jr., unfortunately also a martyr to the civil rights cause, even in the era of new civil rights legislation intended to open the educational door for African-Americans to prove the equality of the races.

It is interesting to note that this superbly conceived play ran for only 123 performances in New York City, the shortest runs of any of the Pulitzer Prize plays, and there have not been any revivals on or off Broadway in the record. Did the play date quickly, depicting a state of affairs Americans were intent on putting behind them? Or did it represent a truth so painful that audiences were unwilling to face its continuing presence in their world?

Street Scene (1928–1929)
by Elmer L. Rice

A Play in Three Acts. Produced by William A. Brady, Ltd. Staged by Elmer Rice. Opened at The Playhouse, January 10, 1929.

The Original Cast

Abraham Kaplan	Leo Bulgakov
Greta Fiorentino	Eleanor Wesselhoeft
Emma Jones	Beulah Bondi
Olga Olsen	Hilda Bruce
Willie Maurrant	Russell Griffin

Anna Maurrant — Mary Servos
Daniel Buchanan — Conway Washburne
Frank Maurrant — Robert Kelly
George Jones — T. H. Manning
Steve Sankey — Joseph Baird
Agnes Cushing — Jane Corcoran
Carl Olsen — John M. Qualen
Shirley Kaplan — Anna Kostant
Fillippo Fiorentino — George Humbert
Alice Simpson — Emily Hamill
Laura Hildebrand — Frederica Going
Mary Hildebrand — Eileen Smith
Charlie Hildebrand — Alexander Lewis
Samuel Kaplan — Horace Braham
Rose Maurrant — Erin O'Brien-Moore
Harry Easter — Glen Coulter
Mae Jones — Millicent Green
Dick McGann — Joseph Lee
Vincent Jones — Matthew McHugh
Dr. John Wilson — John Crump
Officer Harry Murphy — Edward Downes
A Milkman — Ralph Willard
A Letter-Carrier — Herbert Lindholm
An Ice-Man — Samuel S. Bonnell
Two College Students — Rose Lerner and Astrid Alwynn
A Music Student — Mary Emerson
Marshall James Henry — Ellsworth Jones
Fred Cullen — Jean Sidney
An Old-Clothes Man — Joe Cogert
An Interne — Samuel S. Bonnell
An Ambulance Driver — Anthony Pawley
A Furniture-Mover — Ed A. McHugh
Two Nurse Maids — Astrid Alwynn and Nelly Neil
Policemen — Carl C. Milter, John Kelly, and Anthony Pawley
Two Apartment Hunters — Frances F. Golden and Otto Frederick

Striving for realism, Elmer Rice's *Street Scene* records a day in the life of immigrant and low-income Americans during the summer of 1929, evidencing the insecurity, bigotry, malice, and occasional kindness of the inhabitants of this walkup tenement. The playwright sketches his characters swiftly, cinematically, leaving it to the audience to construct whatever personal history is needed to complete the portraits.

The tenement house is not the symbolic melting pot that melds together all the parts into a harmonious whole. Rather, the tenement is a battle zone setting where disparate families shaped by generations of ignorance and prejudice seem at war with little hope for peace. In this harsh reality of urban life, Rice focuses on the sensational double murder of Steve Sankey and Anna Maurrant by her husband, Frank Maurrant, and the family heartbreak that follows.

The action of Rice's play moves through a host of unrelated, episodic encounters to reveal the signal unkindness of the characters living in the slum housing. With nearly sixty characters, some simply walk-ons to add verisimilitude, the portrait gallery evokes the injustices of oppressors and oppressed, vilifiers and vilified in New York City in the late 1920s.

Just outside the frame of the proscenium, New York City is raucously alive with the background roar of "El" trains, autos, fire-engine and ambulance sirens, the blare of radios and musical instruments, children playing street games, dogs barking and human voices laughing, screaming, hollering, quarreling.

Like Shakespeare's Globe Theater's simultaneous stage, the facade of the brownstone walkup, the front stoop, and the streetfront allows multiple scenes to be enacted at the same time. The ground-floor apartment to the right of the front door leading into the hallway vestibule belongs to Abraham Kaplan, an elderly Russian Jew, visible at a table reading a newspaper; the apartment to the left belongs to Filippo Fiorentino, an Italian musician, married to the stout, blonde German, Greta Fiorentino, who is leaning out of an open front window. The basement apartment belongs to the Swedish janitor Olsen and his wife.

On the stoop, Olga Olsen, Greta Fiorentino, and a bony, middleaged woman named Emma Jones greet each other and exchange complaints about the sweltering heat and its effect on the teething

Olsen baby and on Emma's heat-exhausted dog. Willie Maurrant, a twelve-year old boy, comes down the street on roller skates and shouts up to the second floor for his mother, Anna.

Anna Maurrant, Willie's attractive forty-year-old mother, appears at the open first floor window, and Willie asks her for a dime for an ice cream cone. She wraps the coin in a twist of newspaper and throws it down, and he skates off.

Greta Fiorentino calls up to Anna to come downstairs to the stoop. Emma Jones interposes that Anna doesn't mind her son Willie's rude ways because she's got her mind on other things, in particular Steve Sankey, the milk-bill collector. Olga Olsen says she saw Sankey going into the Maurrants' apartment today, the second time this week. On this circumstantial evidence, judgment has been sealed. The significant players on the front stoop are like a Greek chorus as they prepare the audience for the inevitable calamity.

Carl Olsen's offstage voice calls for his wife Olga to assist with the cranky baby, and she hurries down the stairs to the janitor's apartment.

Emma Jones observes that foreigners like the Olsens know nothing about bringing up babies, but she is immediately checkmated by the indignant Greta Fiorentino. Tactfully, Emma Jones narrows her criticism, saying she wasn't talking about the "Joimans" or the Irish, but about the Swedes and the "Polacks" and the Jews.

On the second floor right, Daniel Buchanan opens his front window and greets the women below. His pregnant wife is suffering in the heat, which puts the women onto a discussion of pregnancy and childbirth as Frank Maurrant enters the scene.

Frank announces to his wife that he is going to Stamford, Connecticut, tomorrow to do the lighting for a stage play having its tryout there. He is angry with Anna when he learns that Willie and Rose are not at home and that Rose is working late at the real estate office. The other women sympathize with Anna as she gives voice to the positive major theme of the play, that people ought to be more tolerant of each other and live together in peace, and that a kind word now and then would make life more bearable.

At this moment Steve Sankey enters the scene. The playwright's stage directions are explicit: Emma Jones and Greta Fiorentino exchange looks, and Anna Maurrant and Sankey avoid looking at each other. Sankey says he is going to the drugstore to buy ginger ale for his wife and his two little girls.

Miss Agnes Cushing, a spinster in her mid-fifties, comes down the front steps, on her way to buy some ice cream for her bedridden, seventy-two-year-old mother. After a few more minutes of conversation, Anna Maurrant declares she is going to look for Willie, and walks off in the same direction as Sankey did a few minutes earlier.

The moment Anna is gone, the gossips explode with excitement, wondering whether her husband Frank is wise to what's going on behind his back. Breathlessly, Miss Cushing rushes in carrying her ice cream, bursting to tell the women that she just saw the reckless Mrs. Maurrant and Mr. Sankey together in the doorway of a warehouse in the next block, his hand on her shoulder. But when Frank Maurrant enters, they cover for Anna, saying that she has gone to look for their son—that children Willie's age need a lot of looking after.

In her first-floor window, Shirley Kaplan appears carrying a glass of hot, steaming tea for her father, who agreeably puts down his Yiddish newspaper when he determines it contains nothing but bad news, "deevorce, skendal, and moiders."

In this mix of native origins, another foreign accent is heard when presently the American-Italian Filippo Fiorentino comes in with his violin tucked under his left arm, balancing five ice-cream cones in his right hand. He has brought treats for everyone.

A social worker with the Charities, Miss Alice Simpson, castigates Mrs. Laura Hildebrand for using the grocery money the Charities gave her to take her children to the movies. She goes upstairs with Mrs. Hildebrand as Mrs. Maurrant returns to the stoop, where the neighbors are speculating that Laura Hildebrand's husband ran off with another woman and left his poor family destitute.

Fiorentino presses money on Mrs. Hildebrand, who is on the point of being evicted, and Kaplan speaks up in her defense. When Frank Maurrant says her predicament isn't the landlord's fault,

Kaplan declares that capitalist ownership of private property puts the masses at the mercy of property-owning classes.

Nonsense, Frank Maurrant responds. As a "woikin' man" and a dues-paying member of the Stage Hand's Union for twenty-two years, he says he has security. Filippo Fiorentino is similarly sanguine about the Musician's Union, though Shirley Kaplan complains about the weakness of the Teacher's Union.

When Kaplan continues with his polemic against capitalist exploitation, that America is ripe for a revolution by the working class, the Joneses protest vehemently against the teaching of godless Communist ideas to America's children.

Maurrant adds belligerently that if a foreigner is not happy here in America, he should go back to wherever he came from, because in America we don't want foreigners telling us what to do. He believes that the morals of the times reflect a lack of respect for law and order, and for God. Anna says that people are just trying to get something out of life, some happiness.

Maurrant's rejoinder is foreboding: he asks what Anna means by trying to get something—something they oughtn't to have? His argument with Kaplan escalates to name-calling and threatens to become violent.

With deep sensitivity, Anna speaks the play's psychological message against prejudice, saying she can't understand why people are always hurting each other, holding grudges, saying unkind things. Again Maurrant mockingly questions what his wife means.

Twenty-one-year-old Sam Kaplan enters reading a book. Filippo says he saw Sam in the front row at the concert earlier that evening, and a discussion of music preferences ensues. Sam, a sensitive esthete, says he loves classical music that touches his soul. Filippo casts his vote for Italian opera, and soon Mrs. Fiorentino is playing Puccini on the piano as Filippo and Anna waltz.

Suddenly Steve Sankey appears carrying a paper bag from which the neck of a ginger ale bottle protrudes. The dancers are whirling on the sidewalk and he stops to watch. Sitting high on the stoop, Maurrant sees him and rises. The moment Anna sees Sankey, she stops dancing and goes up the stairs. Sankey remarks that it's a hot night for dancing and wishes everyone good night.

In response to her husband's questioning, Anna identifies Sankey as the milk-bill collector who lives down the block somewhere.

Then Willie runs in sobbing, his clothes torn. He reports he was in a fight with the bully Joe Connolly, who said something to him that made him mad, but when urged to tell what Connolly said, he doesn't answer. The Maurrants exchange a look of recognition that the mean gossip about Willie's mother is widespread.

Maurrant says he's going to Callahan's for a drink and that Rose had better be home when he comes back or else. Anna goes upstairs to her apartment to wait.

As soon as both Maurrants are gone, Emma clucks with the delight of a harpy on having seen the dramatic triangle: the adulterous lovers and the cuckolded husband all together. Filippo says that Willie got into a fight because Connolly said his mother was a whore, and Emma says that Connolly was right.

Sam Kaplan, who overhears this defamation, likens the group to a pack of destructive wolves and rushes into the house. Mrs. Fiorentino observes that he must be in love with the Maurrant girl, Rose—an interfaith alliance Emma looks on with alarm.

It is late and, saying good night, the tenants go to their respective apartments as Rose Maurrant, the play's protagonist, enters with Harry Easter, the handsome, well-dressed young manager of the real estate office where Rose works.

Rose refuses Easter when he asks if he can go upstairs. Boldly, Easter grabs and kisses her, and she breaks away, saying it isn't right because he's a married man. As Rose parries Easter's advances, the front door opens and closes constantly, whether it is Mrs. Olsen checking the lock on the door or Emma Jones going out to walk her dog.

It is with the greatest effort that Rose extricates herself from Easter's clutches, and most opportunely too, because at that moment she sees her father coming. Quickly Easter says good night and exits.

Rose explains to her father that Mr. Easter took her out for dinner and dancing after work, but she leaves unanswered his question about Easter's marital status, which raises her father's anger as
he says that no married men are going to come nosing around his
family.

Suddenly Daniel Buchanan comes dashing out of the vestibule,
his coat and trousers over his pajamas. He has to call Doctor Wilson
to tell him that his wife is beginning her labor. Rose offers to call
from the drugstore so Buchanan can go back upstairs to his wife.
Maurrant follows Buchanan back into the house as Rose runs off to
make the calls, meeting Mae Jones and Dick McGann as she exits.

Mae, a shopgirl, and her date, Dick, are both about twenty-one,
noisy, randy, and very drunk. Before the pair goes stumbling off,
Rose re-enters, and Mae asks her how the milkman is doing. Rose
is deeply mortified by Mae's question, and by the advances of Mae's
older brother Vincent, a taxi driver off shift who has observed the
embarrassing exchange. When Rose tries to pass Vincent to go up
the stairs, he blocks her way. Putting his arm around her, he says
he'd like to take her out for a ride in his hack. She fights to free
herself as he passes his hands over her body and pulls her hard to
him.

Just at this moment, Sam Kaplan who has come to the window,
jumps out onto the stoop to confront the tall, muscular Vincent.
With his big hand flat against Sam's face, Vincent sends him sprawl-
ing backwards down the stairs onto the pavement.

Rose says that she'll call her father down if Vincent touches Sam
again, and Vincent laughs at the threat.

Suddenly Vincent sees his mother coming toward the house
with Queenie, her dog. Vincent explains that he was having a little
friendly argument with "Ikey Finkelstein" because he didn't like his
saying good evening to his girlfriend. Vincent's mother tells him to
go upstairs and notes aloud that Rose has plenty of admirers, "but I
guess you come by it natural."

Angrily, Sam swears he will kill Vincent, but Rose calms and com-
forts him. Trepidously but trustingly, she asks if Sam thinks there is
any truth to the slander directed against her mother. Sam recalls the

ugly gossiping that offended him and says that they are living in a tenement with nasty people, as vicious as sewer rats.

A scream from the Buchanan's apartment! A new life is about to be born. Sam philosophizes on the cruelty of humanity, and the meaninglessness of life itself.

But Rose will not be depressed, saying that this morning after an anxious and sleepless night, she walked through the park to work and was uplifted when she saw the lilac bushes in full bloom, remembering the Whitman poem she and Sam had read together.

Again, from above, Buchanan calls to Rose to phone the doctor because his wife is breaking water, but just then Dr. Wilson himself, a seedy, older man in a crumpled Panama hat and carrying a doctor's black bag, arrives.

In his undershirt Maurrant appears in his front window, calling Rose to come up, and he warns he doesn't want to call her again.

Sam asks to kiss Rose and clasps her tight as she offers her lips. A moment later she is at her open window up above, and with another good night, wafts him a kiss and pulls the shade down. Sitting on the stoop, Sam listens to the late night sounds of Manhattan: another scream from the Buchanan's apartment; deep snoring from the Fiorentinos' apartment; a boat whistle from the East River; a clock begins to strike twelve.

Sam raises his clenched fist to heaven, then sits down on the stairs, lowering his head into his hands in despair.

What meaning does life have without love and friendship? Did Elmer Rice, born Elmer Reizenstein, a Jewish boy like Sam, believe that by changing his name he could ever get away from the destructive power of prejudice?

At the end of Act I, all the major characters have made their appearance, and will continue to behave true to their nature, exerting the power of their life force—for good and ill—into the tapestry of Rice's *Street Scene*. Essentially a pessimist like the English philosopher Thomas Hobbes, Rice envisions human nature as indelibly prejudiced, self-centered, nasty, brutish, and glorying in exercising power over others. Like Hobbes's *Leviathan*, the socio-philosophical treatise whose monster is the symbol of society, the tenement is

Rice's symbol of the urban environment, the hostile state of nature, meaning a state of war, "where all are against all." Rice's characters in *Street Scene* create a cruel, Hobbesian image of life as the shadow of the tragic, double murder begins to figure in the dramatic design.

Anna Maurrant and her lover Steve Sankey are found together by Frank Maurrant in the trap he has set. Maurrant, who never intended to go to Stamford, knew full well who Sankey was even when he asked his identity on the stoop. Maurrant is single-minded in his drive for power over what he believes are his possessions; the Hobbesian sovereign authority claims absolute ownership and command of his wife and children.

At the end of the play, with her mother dead and her father going to prison for life, with no possibility of remaining in the tenement flat, Rose suffers the consequences of her parents' sins. She communicates the playwright's dramatic truth at the end of the play in response to Sam Kaplan's declaration that he loves her and they belong together. Rose answers that belonging to someone in togetherness is a form of dependency that is unfair to all persons involved—that if her father had been self-sufficient belonging to himself and not acting possessively, thinking to *own* her mother, this tragedy would never have happened.

Rose tells Sam that she doesn't want to belong to anyone but herself—that she will find love when and if the time comes, but that loving and belonging are not the same thing. In love with Rose, Sam wants to give up everything, including his hopes of law school and a good career, to go with her to the suburbs to start a whole new life together. But Rose foresees Sam's vision as an impossible future for both of them, that circumstances could arise that would change their feelings for each other and destroy their chances for a lifetime of happiness.

Rice provides more realism to conclude the play: from the Fiorentino apartment comes the sound of Dvorak's *Humoresque*, played by one of Filippo's students on a scratchy violin. A group of children offstage begin to sing the roundelay "The Farmer in the Dell." A couple, prospective renters, enter to examine the vacant apartment in the tenement, a new cast of characters entering the war zone.

As a socially concerned playwright and a political liberal, in *Street Scene* Rice asks for the elimination of the melting pot ghetto, the tenement house where hatreds simmer and fester. He proposes that people need space to breathe, time to think, away from the harsh and harried city that fosters hatred rather than tolerance.

This is a concluding scenario far different from that of the roseate America envisioned by the English novelist Israel Zangwill in his *The Melting Pot*: "America is the place where Celt and Latin, Slav and Teuton, Greek and Syrian, Black and Yellow, Jew and Gentile, the palm and the pine, the pole and the equator, the crescent and the cross would together build The Republic of Man and the Kingdom of God."[2]

For Rice, the tenement house is a hateful Tower of Babel, its inhabitants self-involved, indifferent, and hurtful to one another, motivated by negative or destructive intent. Everywhere the conflict is personal: husband against wife, Christian against Jew, rich against poor, ignorant against educated. American togetherness in the tenement environment is a cruel, relentless economic and ethical struggle. As a social protest play, *Street Scene* does not yield an easy solution to the dramatic themes it explores: how to find happiness in life and one's proper place in American society.

CHAPTER TEN

Against War

Protesting war, political oppression, racial prejudice, and genocide on a global scale, four outstanding Pulitzer Prize plays assert the value of human life and human rights: Robert Sherwood's two plays *Idiot's Delight* and *There Shall Be No Night*, Frances Goodrich and Albert Hackett's *The Diary of Anne Frank*, and Richard Rodgers, Oscar Hammerstein II, and Joshua Logan's *South Pacific*. Each of these plays reflects America's political, social, and philosophical faith in the brotherhood of man and the belief that war is not the acceptable norm for the human condition. In these plays the brutal cacophonies of hateful "isms"—Nazism, Fascism, Communism, and Nipponism— trumpet the horrors of the decade 1935 to 1945.

In the United States the political sensibility of the period was dominated by three-term President Franklin Delano Roosevelt. In his memorable "Quarantine Speech," addressed to the nation on October 5, 1937, he described the condition of European-Asian aggression as a spreading epidemic of world lawlessness.[1] War rampaged in a bloody frenzy in Africa, Europe, and Asia, but the Congressional Neutrality Acts kept the U.S. uninvolved.

In Spain, from 1936 to 1939, the Fascist power of General Francisco Franco triumphed in a bloody internecine war that destroyed the Loyalists' hope for a republican government.

In Italy, the warlord Mussolini with his army of Blackshirts was beginning his projected resurrection of the Roman empire by invading Ethiopia.

In Germany, Hitler, in defiance of the Versailles Treaty and the League of Nations, marched his horde of Brownshirts into the neutralized Rhineland, on the first leg of a journey he had promised would lead to world conquest by a *pure* Germanic race, revenge for Germany's humiliation at the end of World War I, and the extermination of the Jewish people in Europe.

In Asia, the Incident at Marco Polo Bridge was Japan's open declaration of war on China, and its armies swept through that country as the first step of Japan's plan for conquest of land, resources, and markets, the political conception of a Nippon Empire to encompass the Eastern hemisphere, Australia, New Zealand, and all the islands of the Pacific.

On December 7, 1941, in a sneak attack on Pearl Harbor, the Japanese set out to destroy the U.S. Pacific Fleet to prevent it from intervening in their seizure of the oil reserves of the Dutch East Indies. The toll was devastating: eight United States battleships were bombed and sunk in the Harbor, hundreds of aircraft on the ground were destroyed, and more than three thousand U.S. servicemen were killed or wounded.

President Roosevelt and Congress declared war on Japan. Three days later, Germany and Italy declared war on the United States. The tyranny of the Axis powers had to be defeated. America's involvement had become inevitable.

Four Pulitzer Prize plays, *Idiot's Delight, There Shall Be No Night, The Diary of Anne Frank*, and *South Pacific*, communicate the doctrine of Roosevelt's famous speech: "America hates war. All Americans hate war. America hopes for peace." These plays reflect the hostility of the people of the world at war, vividly dramatizing the suffering and death of individuals who were caught in the conflict.

Many philosophical and ethical questions are posed in these plays: Does God consider life on this Earth an absurdity? Are human beings insignificant and expendable little toys for His playful pastime? Is human nature essentially good or evil? Does the expression "brotherhood of man" mean anything? Is God dead? They reflect the tumult of a civilization rocked to its foundations, seeking a reason and a way to move forward.

Idiot's Delight (1935–1936)
by Robert Emmet Sherwood

A Play in Three Acts. Produced by The Theater Guild, Inc. Staged by Bretaigne Windust. Opened on Broadway at the Shubert Theater, March 24, 1936.

The Original Cast

Dumptsy	George Meader
Signor Palota	Stephen Sandes
Donald Vavadel	Barry Thomson
Pittaluga	S. Thomas Gomez
Auguste	Edgar Barrier
Captain Locicero	Edward Raquiello
Dr. Waldsee	Sydney Greenstreet
Mr. Cherry	Bretaigne Windust
Mrs. Cherry	Jean Macintyre
Harry Van	Alfred Lunt
Shirley	Jacqueline Paige
Beulah	Connie Crowell
Edna	Frances Foley
Francine	Etna Ross
Elaine	Marjorie Baglin
Bebe	Ruth Timmons
First Officer	Alan Hewitt
Second Officer	Winston Ross
Third Officer	Gilmore Bush
Fourth Officer	Tomasso Tittoni
Quillery	Richard Whorf
Signor Rossi	Le Roi Operti
Signora Rossi	Ernestine De Becker
Major	Murray O'Neill
Anna	Una Val
Irene	Lynn Fontanne
Achille Weber	Francis Compton
Musicians	Gerald Kunz, Max Rich, and Joseph Knopf

The major symbol of *Idiot's Delight* is the setting of the play itself on Monte Gabriele, named after God's messenger, the Archangel

Gabriel. The fictional hotel, set high in the Italian Alps, overlooks the nations that historically seem to be constantly at war with each other.

At Armageddon, according to the Book of Revelations in the New Testament, Archangel Gabriel blows the trumpet announcing the end of the world and the advent of the terrors of Judgment Day.

In the real world of the mid-1930s, the playwright, who knew the evils of war intimately, having been gassed and wounded years earlier in the Canadian Black Watch in World War I is appalled to hear the heavy artillery rolling in Europe once again, threatening a calamitous conflict barely two decades after World War I, which was falsely advertised as the war to end all wars.

Idiot's Delight's cast of players includes the lead protagonist, Harry Van, an American showman and hoofer on tour with Les Blondes, his troupe of six talented females. At the hotel he finds Irene, an enigmatic Russian beauty; Doctor Waldersee, a German cancer researcher; Quillery, an arch Communist, Captain Locicero, an arch Fascist; and Achille Weber, an international arms dealer. This collection of unique archetypes of various antagonistic societal and political perspectives comes together on Monte Gabriele, the collected assemblage a literary device as old as the Tabard Inne in Chaucer's *Canterbury Tales*.

Except for the American representative, Harry Van, Sherwood's portraits are more stereotypes than individually distinctive human beings. Despite the gravity of the subject matter and the bitter ending, the playwright tells us it is a comedy, and it is the focus of that awkward conjunction that presents the major difficulty of the play.

The dramatic action plays out a ruthless and cunning gamesmanship: "Cat and Mouse"—Captain Locicero, the Fascist, has Quillery, the Communist, killed when he denounces Fascism; "Caught in the Web"—Harry and his troupe Les Blondes are trapped unwittingly in an international, deadly confrontation; "Unknown Identity"—Irene, the moving power of the play, is a mysterious beauty who after first meeting Harry vanished from his life for a decade; "Love to Hate"—Doctor Waldersee's noble Hippocratic love for humanity reverses to a murderous intent as he plans to create deadly chemicals of

extermination; "Doublecross"—Achille Weber, the munitions merchant, ruthlessly abandons his mistress Irene to her doom; and the
endgame, "Kill the Little People," played by all nations as they secure
the deadliest weapons possible from Achille Weber.

The title of the play *Idiot's Delight* suggests a string game, like
Cat's Cradle, a time-waster like Solitaire. Sherwood suggests that
an existentialist God, a solitary, lonely old beard, plays with human
lives in this time-wasting game that has no meaning and no end.
Sherwood's depiction of the advent of Armageddon demonstrates
the idiocy of the endless, senseless game that men have played from
time immemorial: kill or be killed.

The leading protagonist, Harry Van, representing an easygoing,
fair-minded America, is the biggest loser in all the games. To Harry
life is like a Hollywood movie, a diversion to make the suckers feel
good, like the phony mind-reading act he once produced in Omaha,
Nebraska, in 1925, when he first met the beautiful Irene.

Now, ten years later at the elegant Hotel Monte Gabriel, high in
the Alps where the boundaries of Switzerland, Austria, and Italy
converge, he meets Irene in a too-remarkable coincidence that aims
to prove that destiny plays the very same capricious, meaningless
game as God's "Idiot's Delight."

As Act I begins, Pittaluga, the owner-manager of the Hotel Monte
Gabriel, is testy with everyone because the hotel has so few guests,
and argues bitterly with the young American Don Navadel, the hotel's social director, whose connections Pittaluga was counting on
to lure his wealthy friends away from popular hotels in Chamonix
and St. Moritz.

Suddenly the wailing of sirens is heard from the Italian bomber
air base at the foot of the mountain, signaling that combat planes
are about to take off. Captain Locicero, the senior officer of the air
base, enters the lounge and explains that the sirens are announcing
a practice drill to see how quickly bombers can be up in the air for
defense if need be.

Dr. Waldersee, an elderly German, enters to ask the Captain when
the Italian train will cross the border into Switzerland, for he must
get back immediately to his laboratory in Zurich to supervise his

ongoing research for a cure for cancer. The Italian government has stopped all trains from leaving the country. The Captain says that when word comes from Rome, the frontier will be opened.

The Cherrys, a pair of devil-may-care English honeymooners, come into the lounge, happy to learn that there's dancing and entertainment every evening.

New guests have arrived, and the first one to come in is Harry Van, a second-rate showman who has had a colorful career as a booking agent, a barker, a hoofer, and a crooner. He has just arrived by train en route to Geneva with his troupe of six showgirls, a featured live act that has just finished playing the Balkan circuit.

The Captain checks all seven American passports and informs the troupe that the train will not go to Switzerland tonight; in fact, if hostilities between Italy and France begin, the train many never go. Ogling Les Blondes appreciatively, he adds that he hopes they will remain at the hotel indefinitely.

Harry is seemingly unaware that at this moment Europe is on the brink of World War II, egged on by Mussolini's adventurism in Ethiopia. He tells Quillery that he's traveling with his bevy of beautiful girls from New York, a song-and-dance show that was a hit in Monte Carlo and Zagreb. Quillery says he was on that train with them from Zagreb, where he had gone to attend a Labor Congress convened to try to prevent Europe from plunging into another war. But, Quillery says, Mussolini seems determined to conquer the world, and world conquest is an addiction that grabs all tyrants.

Harry responds to the idea of the power of addiction, making a personal confession about his onetime bondage to cocaine. It is an addiction that inflated his poor ego to self-importance—like the delusions of grandeur that have beguiled the dictator Mussolini. It is interesting to note that Sherwood, in establishing Harry's persona, reveals the addiction that he himself shook off earlier in his life.

Suddenly Donald, the social director, enters escorting the newly arrived Irene, a blonde Russian beauty, through the lounge to the windows to look at the majestic mountain view. When she sees big bombers taxiing out of hangars onto the large airfield down below, she recalls her experience as a flier to the hotel guests: once, to save her life, she was forced to make a parachute jump over the jungle in Indochina.

The sirens blare! Achille Weber, the international munitions dealer, joins Irene, who asks if the sirens mean that war is imminent. No, Weber replies. He is sure war will not happen because he has been extremely successful in munitions sales; all the enemies are too well prepared, and so, too afraid of each other. Weber's reply is tongue-in-cheek; he knows his wares are expendable items, purchased to be used.

The moment Harry spies Irene, he is struck with the belief that she is the same beautiful Russian woman with whom he spent a passionate evening ten years before in Omaha, Nebraska. Inspired by the memory of one fantastic night of love a decade ago, he goes to the piano and plays a Russian song, "Kak Strana" (How Strange), a theatrically sentimental sounding of his heartstrings.

Suddenly the Captain enters to inform Weber that war has been declared between Italy and France and that Nazi Germany has mobilized in support of Fascist Italy. Naively, Irene asks Weber, as though he were a diviner, how his analysis could have failed. Weber replies that spontaneous combustion of dictatorial egos triggered the hostilities.

This evening, the guests of the hotel are in confusion. To quiet all fears, Harry Van presents his Les Blondes act for the evening's entertainment. Quillery, the arch-Communist, says angrily that Harry's banal entertainment is a travesty as Fascist bombs are dropping on Paris, killing thousands. The Italian Fascist military arrest Quillery and drag him out of the lounge as he cries out that he will not be silenced.

As though nothing unusual has happened, the orchestra plays a dance tune, and all the hotel guests move onto the dance floor. Harry asks Irene to dance.

In a verbally sophisticated pas de deux, Harry and Irene move nimbly across the dubious terrain of her past life. Is Irene a compulsive liar? Was she actually wounded by a bayonet in her desperate escape from the Bolsheviks? Is she really an aristocratic relative of the Czar? Or does her tale elevate her to a new rank as Baroness Munchausen?

No matter. More than anything, even the possibility of a European conflict, Harry is interested in the answer to the single question: is she the red-haired beauty, touring as part of a mandolin-playing song-and-dance team, who spent an unforgettably erotic night with him at the Governor Bryan Hotel in Omaha, Nebraska in 1925? He swears that the femme fatale he met that night indelibly impressed her very essence upon his brain, and for the past ten years he has lived with that deep infatuation.

Irene demurs, almost coquettishly, and claims he is like all Americans: ingenuous, sentimental, and idealistic. Harry responds with a saint's innocence or a schoolboy's, saying his mind is sound psychologically, that he has known millions of people intimately and he believes in the goodness of human nature, never having met more than one man out of a hundred that he didn't like.

The conversation concludes because Weber enters, interrupting the dancers to inform Irene that it is time to go to bed. She leaves, and Harry, still hanging in doubt, goes to the piano to play once again "Kak Strana"—"How Strange."

The next morning, the guests are informed that the Blackshirts shot Quillery to death this morning. Despair and fear hang heavy in the lounge as the assembled guests consider the possible entry of England into war on France's side against Italy and Germany. They are relieved, at least, to hear from the Captain that Rome has scheduled the train for Switzerland to leave at four o'clock this afternoon.

The doctor reveals that he has changed his destination: instead of going to his lab in Austria, to seek the cure for cancer and perhaps the Nobel Prize, he is going to a laboratory in Germany to devise chemical warfare for the Nazis.

The Captain distributes the passports, and all are in order, except for Irene's. The Captain indicates to Weber that despite the problem of her papers, in deference to him they will allow her passage. But Weber—in an unpredicted and inexplicable reversal—says she is not traveling with him and her papers are none of his affair. In that case, the Captain says, she will have to be detained, and Weber says one must do what it is necessary to do.

When Irene learns that she is not allowed to leave Italy, she knows at once that she has been double-crossed by Weber because last night she repudiated him as a seller of weapons of mass destruction, responsible for the massacre of helpless, innocent people. Harry has no power to help her with the authorities. Irene must remain on Monte Gabriele, most likely to die if and when French bombers arrive to blast the air base below.

Harry is determined not to lose Irene again, and together they drink champagne as the sounds of approaching French bombers roar through the night, and bombs begin to burst in air—a fury of light and sound as Armageddon approaches, asserting the Lunts' theatrical *Liebestod* as together they sing "Onward Christian Soldiers."

In *Idiot's Delight* there are two salesmen: the hero, Harry Van, selling entertainment, and the villain Achille Weber, selling weapons of mass destruction. The nations of Europe torn between the forces of Communism and Fascism are the marketplace for their wares and services. Harry Van is concerned with the scant bookings for his traveling showcase of beautiful girls. Achille Weber is the well received supplier of deadly munitions to any nation that will pay his price.

As the antagonist, Weber plays "Kill the Little People" and undermines the security of nation after nation, constantly increasing each country's inventory of ever more deadly war materials. The protagonist, Harry Van, playing most often behind a clown's mask, is at heart a softie and an idealist, even though worldly-wise, prepared to give his life for the cause of love.

There are so many things to disbelieve in the story line, first that Harry would have cherished the memory of his one-night stand with Irene for ten long years. It is incredible that Irene rediscovers her faith in humanity by way of loving the simple and good-hearted Harry. It is far-fetched to believe that his credo—that the meek will inherit the earth, adopted from the Sermon on the Mount—gives them strength in their last moments of life on Monte Gabrielle. It is hard to believe that Irene, after so many years as Achille Weber's mistress, becomes the moralist for the little people and defies Achille to his face as a deathmonger.

The playwright should have accepted the challenge of writing the scene in which Irene and Achille break up. Possibly he could have devised some reason to make Irene's death dramatically meaningful at the end of the play. As it is, her dying is simply circumstantial, not heroic.

The bombs are bursting outside the huge windows and Harry asks Irene if she remembers *Hell's Angels*, starring Jean Harlow, a film by Howard Hughes that ends in the same kind of fiery disaster. For Van, his dying is as unreal as a Hollywood flick. But war is real and obscene. Seeing this 1935 play a few years later, in 1939, when Poland was actually invaded by the Nazis, would have jarred, not delighted any audience's sensibilities with its admixture of the reality of battle death and the make-believe of theater.

But the Lunts carried it off. Romantically, Harry professes to see love as salvation and God as love. In his *Liebestod* with Irene, Harry believes he has proved his love and at the same time freed Irene, ending the humiliation and persecution she had been forced to live with. Still, in the end, Achille Weber and his evil ilk triumph in the slaughterhouse game of "Glorious War."

The climax comes with an ironic cruelty, recalling Mussolini's macabre description of the beauty of war, of the powerful excitement that thrills the heart on seeing the spurting fountain of blood or the bomb shattering the too-proud, armored tank: "War alone brings to its highest tension all human energy and puts the stamp of nobility upon the peoples who have the courage to meet it." [2]

Playwright Sherwood, in spite of all his religious protestations, surmises that God Himself may be playing games, or piqued by nations who are arming for war, turning their backs on God and His love for humanity. He also insinuates that God may not even exist, that He may have died or simply become too senile to pay any more attention to His creation. Or, lastly, the playwright conjectures, it may be God's indifference that will allow chaos to destroy the Earth.

Just as in Shakespeare's history plays, historical inaccuracy does not nullify the urbane charm of the play or the pacifist intention of the playwright. Reflecting the mood of an America baffled by the pessimism of post–World War I existentialism and beaten down by a worldwide economic Depression, *Idiot's Delight* is more than a slick pseudo-romantic comedy. Its gravity comes from Sherwood's serious antiwar feelings, and from the bitter irony of his prescient scenario.

There Shall Be No Night (1940–1941)
by Robert E. Sherwood

A Play in Three Acts. Produced by The Playwright's Company, in Association with The Theater Guild, Inc. Staged by Alfred Lunt. Opened at the Alvin Theater, April 29, 1940

The Original Cast

Dr. Kaarlo Valkonen	Alfred Lunt
Miranda Valkonen	Lynn Fontanne
Dave Corween	Richard Whorf
Uncle Waldemar	Sydney Greenstreet
Gus Shuman	Brooks West
Erik Valkonen	Montgomery Clift
Kaatri Alquist	Elizabeth Fraser
Dr. Ziemssen	Maurice Colbourne
Major Rutkowski	Edward Raquello
Joe Burnett	Charles Ansley
Ben Gichner	Thomas Gomez
Frank Olmstead	William Le Massena
Sergeant Gosden	Claude Horton
Lempi	Phyllis Thaxter
Ilma	Charva Chester
Photographers	Ralph Nelson and Robert Downing

The major theme of Sherwood's *There Shall Be No Night* is as discordant as that of *Idiot's Delight*: War is evil. Has God deserted the innocent and the just, allowing war and its attendant evil to flourish and overwhelm?

The play calls on Divinity to protect the little nations that have done no harm and are too weak to protect themselves from the cancerous spread of Nazism. It asks America to be alerted and prepared for the inevitable onset of the disease as it spreads around the world.

Sherwood's preface boldly states his intent in *There Shall Be No Night*:

> I decided to raise my voice in protest against the hysterical escapism, the Pontius Pilate retreat from decision, which dominated American thinking and, despite all the warnings of the President of the United States and the Secretary of State, pointed our foreign policy toward suicidal isolationism.[3]

The play is set against a sequence of historical events: the Nazi war machine has swallowed the defenseless nations of Central Europe one by one: Austria in March 1938; the Sudetenland in September 1938; and, in repudiation of the Munich Pact, Czechoslovakia in March 1939.

Then the impossible, the totally unexpected occurs! In August 1939, a treaty is enacted between Germany and her arch-arch-enemy, the Soviet Union, dividing the eastern European spheres of influence between their two powers, thereby allowing the Nazi infection to spread further eastward toward the Soviet Union.

In September 1939, Poland is taken, and in December 1939, Finland succumbs.

There Shall Be No Night encompasses the tragic year on the European continent from March 1938 to December 1939, the time of the Russian and German invasions of Finland and Norway. The impact of the spread of Nazism is reported by Dave Corween, a character probably modeled after CBS's assigned news reporter W. L. White, whose on-the-spot radio reporting vitally informed a vitally concerned America.

The hero of the play is a world-renowned neurologist, the Nobel Prize–winning scientist Dr. Kaarlo Valkonen. In the beginning of the play, as a Pulitzer Prize laureate, he is interviewed by Corween in an international broadcast from his native Finland. He sums up his faith in God and humanity with the vision of St. John that provides the title: that God manifests in humanity as Intellect and that Reason promises peace.

Dr. Valkonen's neurological theory holds that the human vision of life and truth has become distorted, allowing irrationality and inhumanity to overwhelm all reason and faith. Nazism is the epidemic of the irrational that threatens to degenerate human beings into ruthless, witless creatures, transforming civilization into a lawless jungle.

There Shall Be No Night holds high the humanity of Finland and America as the two democratic nations courageously opposed to the brutish forces of evil. The first major symbols of the play are three portraits of Americans that hang on the walls of the Valkonens' living room.

Dr. Valkonen's beautiful wife Miranda is a native American, born in New Bedford, Massachusetts, and these portraits are of her forebears, reflecting more than a hundred years of the American experience, delineating the outstanding qualities in American character that Alexis de Tocqueville discovered and recorded in his great *Democracy in America.*

The first portrait is that of Miranda's highly honored great-grandfather Eustis, an American naval hero of the War of 1812. He exemplifies the heroic American who will fight for the right to be free—against the imperious British fleet, against brigand pirates in the Mediterranean, and against the British with Jackson at the Battle of New Orleans.

In writing about Eustis's life, Sherwood looks to inspire the Americans of this day to emulate the resolve that hero evidenced in that war when a bully Britain seized and impressed American seamen into British naval service. Sherwood seems also to suggest that great-grandfather Eustis was at the Battle of Lake Erie standing beside Admiral Perry when he sent the courageous message to President Harrison as the British attacked: "We have met the enemy and they are ours."

The second portrait is of Miranda's grandfather, a cunning businessman who bought his way out of serving in the Civil War for
three hundred dollars, became a carpetbagger after the war, made a
fortune selling shoddy uniforms, and married the beautiful daughter of a ruined Southern aristocrat.

The third is Miranda's father, typical of the self-indulgent youth
of the turn of the century, systematically squandering every penny
he inherited, becoming the glamorous idol of every head waiter
in every fashionable restaurant in the dazzling capitals of Europe.
Miranda traveled with him and watched him live out his *carpe diem*
philosophy.

But now, the playwright asks, what of Miranda's character? She
tells Coween that she was traveling with her father when she first
met Kaarlo in St. Petersburg. He was a medical officer there, and
when he came to America to study after the Revolution, they met
again and married. When Valkonen wished to return to Finland, she
lovingly stayed by his side.

With dual allegiance, Miranda feels her heart and mind belong
equally to both countries, as does their son Erik, who takes pride in
his dual heritage. But she believes that Erik will be guided to love
Finland more because he is in love with a beautiful and plucky Finnish girl, Kaatri.

In the Valkonen living room Corween sets up the radio-transmis-
sion system for the doctor's address to America. The power of his
moral philosophy is evidenced in the speech that Valkonen reads
into the microphone, condemning Hitler and the Nazis as barbar-
ians determined to enslave the free people of the world. A research
neurologist, Valkonen infers that the disease of insanity has infected the entire German nation, causing its mass degeneration to the
brute. He proposes that each person, and especially each German,
strive to know himself for all the good and virtuous powers within
him. How he is to do this Valkonen does not explain.

The speech is broadcast across America, heard in New Bedford
where Miranda's relatives live. (It is interesting to note that on
the basis of Sherwood's excellent ability to write such passionate
speeches, the playwright was engaged to write many of the speeches

that President Franklin Delano Roosevelt delivered to the American people).

The theme of Dr. Valkonen's radio address that an insanity seems to be spreading around the world is seconded as Dave Corween lists the political upheavals, conflicts, and wars he has covered recently in places like Manchukuo, Ethiopia, Spain, China, Austria, and Czechoslovakia.

Corween, Kaarlo, and his son Erik, who is now an enlisted soldier in the Finnish army ski-patrol, discuss Hitler's takeover of nations whose lines of defense were easily demolished. Finland relies on the strength of its Mannerheim Line, its major defense against an enemy's invasion. When Corween asks about their feelings toward the Soviet Union, Erik says that his father likes the Russians, having worked with the great behaviorist Dr. Pavlov.

Corween says the Nazis have succeeded in terrifying the world with the Bolshevik menace, but in Moscow he found that Russians want to be left alone and in peace. Kaarlo agrees based on his service as a doctor in the Russian army, saying he thinks Russians are like Italians—charming, hating to fight, and not knowing how to hate.

A neighbor, Dr. Ziemssen, the German Consul General, comes to tell Dr. Volkonen that his speech was heard by shortwave in Berlin and that Germans are well accustomed to hearing people maligning them, as Mr. Corween does regularly in his overseas newscasts. But Ziemssen protests that the Finns need not fear the Germans, who know the Mannerheim Line is impregnable and therefore will not so much as attempt an attack.

Erik recalls that the Czechs, too, believed they had substantial defenses against invasion. Dr. Ziemssen reassures Erik that the Finns are more intelligent than the Czechs. And luckily they have no Western allies to betray them. Ziemssen's remarks are directed to Corween, who was at Munich when the English Prime Minister Neville Chamberlain bargained the Czech's Sudetenland's annexation to Hitler in exchange for his promise to keep the "peace in our time." He ridicules the British and the Americans as gullible and stupid, no match for the brilliant German mind.

As Ziemssen censures the American character, Erik rallies to its defense, saying that it was the Americans who taught the whole world that democracy was worth fighting for. Nor will Erik accept his fiancée Kaatri's scathing criticism of today's Americans as soft and self-indulgent because their lives are too easy.

Though there is some wisdom in Kaatri's assessment of America's isolationist walls of security—the broad expanses of the Atlantic and Pacific Oceans—the dramatist warns that these will soon prove as indefensible as the Mannerheim Line, illuminating the validity of Roosevelt's Quarantine Speech, which took as its keynote the false security of the isolationist doctrine.

As Ziemssen predicts, the war begins with the Russians, rather than the Germans, bombing and attacking the Mannerheim Line. Blackout curtains shroud all the windows of the living room, as Russian bombers have been dropping bombs on sections of Helsinki.

Corween comes to advise Kaarlo and Miranda to leave the country for America, saying that passage has been arranged for them, but Kaarlo refuses the offer, seeing his responsibility to stay and fight against the invaders. Erik announces he must report for duty.

Suddenly Ziemssen comes in to say that he has been recalled to Berlin and advises the Valkonens to leave Finland, that the little Finnish army of two hundred thousand is no match against the ten million Russians. However, Ziemssen explains that Finland will not be ruled from St. Petersburg, but from Berlin, that the Russians are serving the Nazis as planned, and when their service is completed the Communists will be purged like excrement. The German plan is to enslave all of Scandinavia as it has Poland, a country that will never rise again.

Astounded by Ziemssen's frankness, Volkonen asks where one can go to escape enslavement by the Nazis. Nowhere, Ziemssen replies, adding that the Western hemisphere—the United States, Canada, Mexico, and all of South America—are to be conquered, the whole world to come under German domination. Destiny, he believes, has ordained this triumph of the "master race."

Volkonen immediately tells Miranda that she must leave Finland, but she refuses to go without him, and he is resolved to stay and fight for his country.

It is New Year's Day, 1940. Kaarlo, a colonel in the medical corps of the Finnish Army, is in full uniform, getting ready to go the city of Viipuri to visit the hospital at the Mannerheim Line where many are wounded and dying.

Corween enters, together with a young Polish officer, Major Rutkowski, and three Americans. Joe Burnett is an aviator; Ben Gichner and Frank Olmstead are in the American Ambulance Corps, attached to the Red Cross; and all have voluntarily come to aid Finland.

Kaatri is very concerned that she has not heard from Erik since his first letter two weeks ago and reveals that she is pregnant with his child but intends to get an abortion. Miranda and Kaarlo convince her to go to term, expressing great joy in the prospect of a new baby.

From his hotel room, Corween reports the terrible news to America that the Russians have destroyed the Mannerheim Line as well as the city of Viipuri, causing untold numbers of casualties. Miranda comes to ask Corween to lend her fifty dollars in American currency since Finnish currency is now worthless on the foreign exchange, and she promises to repay the loan. She has managed to get secret passage for Kaatri to Norway and then to the States. A few days ago she and Erik were married—in the hospital, just before he died. Miranda wants her grandchild to be born in America, her link with the future, her hope for survival.

She has no knowledge of Valkonen's whereabouts, but believes that he is close to the Russian border in eastern Finland, where bombing by Russian planes has been intense.

Finding a country schoolhouse, Kaarlo Valkonen tells the American Red Cross drivers Ben Gichner and Frank Olmstead they should set up one of the classrooms as a temporary field ambulance station to which they can bring the wounded.

To Valkonen's joy he sees painted along the ceiling, all around the room, the beginning lines of the epic poem *Kalevala*, one of Finland's sacred cultural traditions.

The long heroic poem recounts the courage of Finnish heroes who set out to retrieve from their enemies the magic mill that grinds out meal and gold supportive of the Finns' homeland. Kaarlo believes that Finnish children learn their basic morality from this national epic just as American children learn the basis of democracy in the great lines of Jefferson's Declaration of Independence:

> We hold these truths to be self-evident, that all men are created equal, that they are endowed by their Creator with certain unalienable rights, that among these are Life, Liberty and the Pursuit of Happiness.

With news reports of deeper Russian invasion of eastern Finland, driving across the frozen ice of Viipuri Bay, it is a matter of hours before the enemy will be shelling the schoolhouse, and Major Rutowski leaves to ascertain whether the Russians have cut off the railroad line that might allow reinforcements to come to Viipuri to support their effort to withstand the Russian onslaught.

Frank Olmstead is reading a copy of Valkonen's book, which he bought when he first met the Nobel Prize winner in Helsinki. He asks the author why there is a non-scientific ending to his scientific work, a declaration that humans are evolving spiritually, eliminating the beast within them by the constant development of intellect and reason.

Here Sherwood recapitulates the major theme of the play that war is a contagious disease that has infected humanity from time immemorial. But the playwright is hopeful that in spite of the oppressiveness of the evil forces sweeping the world, the humanity of American ideals will survive and goodness will ultimately triumph.

Dramatically, Valkonen quotes the mysterious predictions of the Book of Revelations as his prime source for belief:

> And they shall see his face, and his name shall be in their foreheads. And there shall be no night there and they need no candle, neither light of the sun; for the Lord giveth them light; and they shall reign forever and ever.

BOOM! Suddenly Russian weaponry is heard close by. Despite the ongoing blasts, Valkonen continues to speak, ending with the hope that one day humanity will become genuinely sane.

At that moment, the American flier, Joe Burnett, appears. His plane was brought down by Russian artillery, but he managed to make a landing behind the Finnish lines. On the highway he met Major Rutkowski, who told him to come to the schoolhouse.

Burnett tells Kaarlo that before Erik died in the hospital, he and Kaatri were married and that she is in Norway on her way to Massachusetts. Valkonen withdraws into the next room to write a letter of farewell to Miranda. The group of resistance martyrs leave the classroom to fight the enemy.

The final scenes of the play tend to be unrealistic and melodramatic. Back in Helsinki, unable to able to persuade Miranda and Uncle Waldemar to leave with him for Norway, Corween promises he will deliver to Kaatri the package of memorabilia of Valkonen's life, including autographed pictures of fellow scientists, the Nobel gold medal, and the farewell letter that he wrote in the schoolhouse. In imitation of her great forbears, Miranda has loaded her rifle, determined to meet the horde of Russians or Nazis head-on and in the end burn the house down to the ground, a Finnish tradition of defiance like the Chinese scorched-earth policy.

But now comes the playwright's problem: how to let the audience know what Valkomen wrote in his farewell letter! The cinema allows the camera to scan the letter, or a voice-over can read it as the lens focuses on actors' faces for reactions. For a playwright the technique of having a character read a long letter aloud is most awkward since it stops the forward action of the play and states what the audience has most likely already gleaned emotionally to be its contents.

However, Sherwood is intent on two objectives: passionately communicating the driving force of the play, the morality that motivates Valkonen's self-sacrifice, and, at the same time, proving that he can write as moving an address as Pericles did in his funeral oration in 490 B.C.E., honoring the soldiers who died fighting barbarism for a noble cause: protecting democracy.

Miranda reads, reiterating Valkonen's belief in Christ and the mysterious truth of His resurrection, citing the fact that the greatest leaders of humankind—Christ, Socrates, Lincoln—all were put to death in unforgettable circumstances that guaranteed the everlastingness of their lives as symbols of humanity's potential greatness.

The play ends on a note of dire expectancy as Uncle Waldemar plays a Finnish folk tune on the piano and Miranda, with rifle at her side, awaits the arrival of the enemy.

The brutality and irrationality of Communism, Nazism, and Fascism are about to destroy everything that is good and beautiful at the end of both of Sherwood's antiwar plays, *There Shall Be No Night* and *Idiot's Delight*. In both, the playwright incorporates his philosophy that we are evolving from base savages, the war-diseased and contagious lowest form of human life, into moral creatures.

The Diary of Anne Frank (1955–1956)
by Albert Hackett and Frances Goodrich

A Play in Two Acts. Based on the book *Anne Frank: The Diary of a Young Girl*. Produced by Kermit Bloomgarden. Staged by Garson Kanin. Opened at the Cort Theater, October 5, 1955.

The Original Cast

Mr. Frank	Joseph Schildkraut
Miep	Gloria Jones
Mrs. Van Daan	Dennie Moore
Mr. Van Daan	Lou Jacobi
Peter Van Daan	David Levin
Mrs. Frank	Gusti Huber
Margot Frank	Eva Rubinstein
Anne Frank	Susan Strasberg
Mr. Kraler	Clinton Sundberg
Mr. Dussel	Jack Gifford

Anne Frank must be ranked among the most valorous of women in the twentieth century. Her diary stands as a living testament of courage under fire, of protest against religious intolerance, and of the monstrosity of the Nazis' inhumanity.

The Diary of Anne Frank, a play adapted from the published work *The Diary of a Young Girl*, translates to the stage the experiences of several Jewish families who, from 1942 to 1944, remained in hiding from the Nazi SS who rounded up Jews in every country of Europe to be sent to slaughter at the German death camps. The play does not deal with American life as the Pulitzer will required, but it does affirm America's compassionate concern for human rights everywhere as it sets out to dramatize Anne Frank's more than two years in hiding.

"Dear Diary," the play begins, as Anne writes in the book her father gave her on her thirteenth birthday. "Diary" is to be her dearest, most trusted friend, as she has no other soul with whom to share her innermost thoughts. In an effort tantamount to self-analysis, Anne wants to tell Diary about herself, recording what she thinks about and how she truly feels, without reservation, with full confidence in Diary's faithfulness.

In an ingenuous and unpremeditated text, Anne reveals her adolescent emotional and intellectual self. In its pages she records thoughts, actions, and interactions with the other persons in the attic, revealing clear stages in her emotional maturation. She courageously confronts herself in the search for truth and understanding. In simple, clear-sighted prose she expresses the joy of being alive, with all the dilemmas of an adolescent and all the longings. She breathes life—like a novelist—into a collection of fallible human beings who are forced to live together in the cramped quarters of the Secret Annex in fear of the Nazi Germans' death camps.

The playwrights, Goodrich and Hackett, begin at the narrative's end and flash back to the beginning to tell the story in a cinematic technique. The time is 1945 immediately after World War II, the Allies having defeated the Germans. As the lights come up, the distant sounds of a carillon and ship whistles in Amsterdam's harbor fade out and Otto Frank, Anne's father and a survivor of the death camp Auschwitz, opens the door and climbs the stairs to revisit the tiny rooms of the attic where he and seven other Jews hid for more than two years. The attic rooms are in disarray, an abandoned site.

Miep Gies, a Dutch girl who works in the warehouse office on a lower floor, has found Anne's diary. Mr. Frank is overwhelmed emotionally as Miep, his trustworthy secretary for many years, hands him the very book he gave Anne on her thirteenth birthday; he sits on a couch and begins to read aloud.

Suddenly, over his voice, we hear a young girl say her name is Anne Frank, born thirteen years ago in Germany on this very day— June 12, 1929—and that her family, her father and mother and sister Margot, had to leave Germany for Holland when Hitler came to power because her family is Jewish.

But then in 1940 the Germans overran Holland, and Jews were commanded by law to wear the identifying yellow star. Her father was forced to re-register his spice importing business in his partner's name, as businesses registered to Jewish owners were being confiscated by the German-controlled state. When his elder daughter, Margot, was summoned to report to a work camp, Otto Frank took his family into hiding in the top-floor attic of his office building. Another family joined them: Mr. and Mrs. Van Daan and their sixteen-year-old son Peter.

Now, backwards in time to July 1942.

The scene is the same attic as it was furnished when the Franks first came to hide.

Mr. Kraler, who for some years has been employed by Mr. Frank, is now registered as owner of the spice importing business. He, like Miep, is considered a loyal friend. As they are accomplices against the Nazi tyranny in control of Amsterdam by sheltering and providing food to Jews, both are guilty of a criminal offense that will summarily send them to a death camp.

They instruct the two families, the Franks and the Van Daans, of the absolute requirements for silence and immobility during the daylight hours so as not to attract the attention of any of the workers in the floors below.

Anne begins to write in her journal that she looks forward to their incarceration ending soon, so she will be able to resume her normal life. The record of the events of each day—the laughter, the tears, the fears, the petty arguments of frustrated, frightened people, huddled together in cramped quarters—and Anne's thoughts about the meaning of their lives—all these are the reflections of a teenager who once knew freedom, went happily to school, visited her girlfriends, and rode her bike. The imprisonment does not dampen Anne's hopeful dreams of a successful career as a writer, of finding love, and of becoming a mother.

Anguished days and nights pass with petty inconveniences and annoyances, with boredom and inertia, with palpable fears in the compulsory silence as Nazi sirens sound outside in the streets confirming the terror of possible discovery and the tortured termination of life.

But Anne lives with the continuous hope for survival. She works hard under her father's tutelage in Latin and algebra, and asks Miep constantly for the latest news when she brings rations—always hoping to hear that the Allies have landed.

As a teenager, enthusiastic and curious about the intimate lives of the adults she must share her time with, Anne provokes all kinds of reactions. Her mother constantly finds fault with her inappropriate actions and words, comparing her unfavorably with Margot. Mrs. Van Daan half-willingly allows Anne to try on her gorgeous fur coat and becomes furious when Anne spills milk on it. Mr. Van Daan finds Anne a spoiled brat, much too garrulous and much too inquisitive.

With the advent of Mr. Dussel, a Jewish dentist who has been allowed by Mr. Frank to find refuge in the attic, their fears are confirmed: Dussel tells them of Jews being sent to the death camp at Mauthausen, quite different from the optimistic reports that Miep and Mr. Kraler have been giving them, obviously trying to help keep their hopes and courage high. Anne is deeply struck when she learns that her best friend Jopie DeWaals and her family have been taken from their home by the SS and sent to a death camp.

Anne records that *sharing* is the key word for the occupants of the secret Annex. The use of the WC is communally established with only evening flushings. Anne is required to share her small quarters with Mr. Dussel, who seems an unappreciative guest since he lets her know that he finds nothing right about her—her appearance, her character, or her manners.

The Annex is crowded, but Anne feels alone, since there is no one to whom she can confide her inmost feelings. She finds companionship vicariously in the many books she reads, and in her secret diary, the recipient of all her social, psychological, and philosophical musings.

Months pass and Anne is tormented by nightmares. One night she awakes screaming that the Green Police are taking her away as they did her friend. Mr. Dussel is alarmed her screams will bring the Gestapo, and her mother tries compassionately to make light of her fears, promising to stay with her until she falls back to sleep. But Anne rejects her mother's best efforts, prompting tears of helplessness from Mrs. Frank. Both parents are deeply concerned with the anxiety that torments their sensitive child, but it is Mr. Frank whose empathy touches Anne more deeply, and it is to him that she declares her love.

On the first night of Hanukkah in December 1942, everyone is gathered at the table and Mr. Frank recites the Hebrew prayer that offers thanks to God that one has survived to celebrate the holiday of the Miracle of Lights. Anne brightens up the ironic proceedings by distributing thoughtful homemade presents to everyone, and the celebrants sing joyful, traditional Hanukkah songs.

Suddenly, from the floors below comes a loud crash. Everyone freezes and Mr. Frank blows out the candles. Peter attempts to put out the overhead lamp, loses his balance, and knocks the iron shade to the floor with a loud thud. The watch dog in the lower floor begins to bark, and they all realize that whoever is in the building must know that floors above are occupied. Mr. Frank suspects a thief and fearlessly goes below to explore.

It was a thief, Mr. Frank believes, because the cash box and a radio are missing, and the intruder was in such haste to get away that he left the street door open. But now someone knows the attic is inhabited. The families panic but decide they must stay in their refuge, and at the start of Act II—on January 1, 1944—have been in hiding for one year, five months, and twenty-five days.

For Anne, life in the attic seems to be at a standstill, but something important is happening. The Van Daans still argue with each other over petty things, and her mother still doesn't understand her. But a miracle is taking place, and every time it has happened—the sweet, painful secret of menarche—she knows the mysterious promise of being a woman.

When Miep says she is going to a New Year's party with her fiance, Dirk, Anne is all eagerness to know what she will wear, and what they will have to eat, and everything else—the questions of a lonely and deprived young woman.

Mr. Kraler asks to talk in private with Mr. Frank, who gives him permission to speak openly. Hesitantly, Mr. Kraler recounts an incident the day before with a worker named Carl. Some weeks ago Carl asked Mr. Kraler whether Mr. Frank was safe in Switzerland, as rumor had it. Then, yesterday, he came to Mr. Kraler's office with invoices to be paid, but kept staring at the bookcases that hide the entrance door to the attic, saying that he remembered there was a door there.

Without waiting for his response, Mr. Kraler continues, Carl said he wanted more money, twenty guilders more each week. Mr. Kraler says he feels it is the demand of a blackmailer and it has to be paid.

Everyone agrees. According to Mr. Frank, it is probable that Carl was the thief on that Hanukkah night. He cannot be fired; he must be paid. At least if the blackmailer is profiting from the arrangement, he will not want to bring it to an end by alerting the Gestapo to the families' presence.

After Mr. Kraler leaves, the mood is one of absolute despair, but Mrs. Frank says stoically that they are all safe in their hideout, unlike the thousands of people in concentration camps. This is no consolation to Anne, who says poignantly that all the grownups have had their chance to live and to make the world a better place and they have failed—but she and Peter are young and haven't had the chance, and are trying to hold on to some ideals as those very ideals are being destroyed. Peter admires Anne for speaking up so boldly and from her heart—expressing, for both of them, their adolescent innocence and lost hope.

The situation worsens, with food rations cut drastically because the people who sell Miep the counterfeit ration books have been arrested, and Mr. Kraler has been admitted into the hospital with ulcers. But Anne finds hope in the news that the Americans have landed on the southern tip of Italy, the knowledge that spring is coming, and the discovery that Peter understands her and feels the same way about life as she does.

Anne pays a visit to Peter's room, a first date that is happy and sad and charming as the two young teenagers come together to find common ground for understanding and love. They reflect upon their past and sensitively explore the changes in attitude to each other that they've felt, and the possibility of their friendship continuing when they are back in society. Anne is ecstatic knowing that she and Peter can express their deepest feelings to each other. His misplaced kiss on her cheek sends her into seventh heaven and she fairly floats about the entire attic kissing everyone, including the unlovable Mrs. Van Daan, who reads the kiss as a confirmation of her most profane thoughts about Anne's promiscuity.

Anne's recounting of Mr. Van Daan's pilfering a piece of bread in the middle of the night is one of the play's most provocative and dramatic confrontations, and serves along with the secret Annex as an icon of the play's major theme, the innate human drive to survive. The emotional tension of the scene, compounded by nearly two years of anxiety, calls forth all the latent meanness of the occupants of the hideaway. Relentless in her anger, Mrs. Frank demands that the Van Daans leave at once, and gives Mrs. Van Daan money for Miep to find a new place for them. But when Peter says that he must go with his parents, Anne cries out that the Van Daans must stay, that Mr. Van Daan can have her food, that the Van Daans will be caught if they go out. For love, Anne will make any sacrifice.

Suddenly, Miep arrives with news that ends all contentions. The B.B.C. has just announced that the Allied invasion in France has begun, that four thousand ships—British, American, French, Dutch, Polish, and Norwegian—have landed on the Normandy shores in what Churchill and General Eisenhower have called D-Day.

Amazingly, a celebration begins with Anne, Pete, and Margot singing the Dutch national anthem and parading around the room with Peter banging out a march rhythm on a frying pan.

Mr. Van Daan tells how ashamed he is and asks forgiveness for stealing the bread from the children. Anne, too, asks her mother's forgiveness for having treated her so unkindly. In her heart Anne prays that the Allies come to Holland fast.

Mr. Frank opens a bottle of cognac and pours shots for Mr. Van Daan and himself and they toast *L'Chaim*, "to life," a salute, a wish, and a bitter irony.

It is July 2, 1944, and Anne considers the significance of her fifteenth birthday, determined to be a writer when she grows up, and, like the authors she has been reading, to go on living even after her death.

A few weeks later, on a Friday, a normal workday, they have not heard the sound of workers moving about below. There are no sounds at all until suddenly, in Mr. Kraler's office, a telephone begins to ring—and rings incessantly. Where is everyone? Why doesn't someone answer? Has Mr. Kraler died? Is Miep calling from outside to tell them something, perhaps a warning? A sense of dread clouds the attic.

The fears of the worst scenario begin to undermine the courage of each of the Van Daans, setting tempers spinning out of control with words of recrimination. Whose fault is it that they are in this predicament? Mr. Van Daan could have arranged emigration to England or Switzerland. But no, Mrs. Van Daan couldn't leave her possessions, her magnificent Biedermeyer furniture. In contrast to their outspoken savagery, Anne and Peter sit together considering stoically the beauty of the blue sky they see through the skylight.

Peter confesses the pain of his helplessness, knowing they await an inevitable doom. He has no belief in religion or God and becomes impatient with Anne as she speaks of faith, of the goodness of people who have been so loving to them, and of the dearness of knowing Peter. She tries to console Peter in his despair by saying they are not the only people who have had to suffer, and she looks to her own maturational life for a metaphor for consolation: that the world is going through a phase of growing, of change. The stage they live in now is characterized by an absolute ruthlessness that may last for hundreds of years, but some day that will change and become beautiful, because in spite of everything they've suffered, she believes that human beings are good at heart.

Suddenly there is the sound of a car's brakes squealing to a halt outside the building, followed by another. In the attic they are as immobile as statues, fearing the worst, seeking an inner quietude—in vain—as the telephone begins to ring again, a punctuating threat. Then silence. Mr. Frank starts down the steps as the others watch. The ringing begins again and stops, and the sound of a door being crashed in booms below, followed by the clamping of heavy boots on the stairs, louder and louder. Men's voices shout in German, commanding that the door be opened. The door is shattered. The light falls upon Anne, standing with satchel in hand—no longer a schoolgirl, but a mature woman who knows what her fate is to be and faces it trembling, trying to believe in God's protection.

Herded like cattle to the slaughterhouse, the Jews have no alternative.

In the darkened theater, Anne's voice says they have been given five minutes to get everything packed, but she will leave the diary, hoping that Miep or Mr. Kraler will find it and guard it, because someday . . . her voice trails off into silence.

In November 1945, in the abandoned attic, Mr. Frank reports to Mr. Kraler and Miep that after being liberated from Auschwitz, he searched for his family only to learn that he was the sole survivor. But he found a woman in Rotterdam who had been in Bergen-Belsen with Anne and told him of her last days in that camp where she was exterminated.

The last words of the play are theatrically uplifting and unrealistically noble, as Anne's loudspeaker voice says that she still believes people are truly good at heart. In taking this quote out of context and using it to end Anne's story, playwrights Goodrich and Hackett give the words a new and unlikely meaning: a Christlike "Forgive them, for they know not what they do." Can we tell ourselves with certainty that this young girl, who longed for the opportunity to live her life in freedom, forgave her killers in the end?

A great irony in this history deals with the fact of two diaries: one that represents the zenith of being human and moral, the other, the absolute nadir, man as an inhuman, murderous beast.

Approximately twelve years before Anne began her diary in her attic prison in Amsterdam, not far away in the Landsberg fortress, in southern Germany, sentenced to five years for treason against the Reich, Adolph Hitler wrote his diary: *Mein Kampf: Four and a Half Years' Struggle Against Lies, Stupidity, and Cowardice.*

Anne's diary portrays a young woman in love with life; positive and caring about people; concerned with self-improvement; looking forward to marriage, a family, and a creative career. Hitler's is a seething cauldron filled with hate, anger, and recriminations against the world in general and against the Jews in particular, promising to exterminate them first from Germany and then from the world. Hitler's Final Solution ordained Anne's death five years before she was born, as well as the deaths of millions of others.

Anne Frank probably never read *Mein Kampf,* or heard Hitler speaking to the German nation of the peace that would follow the destruction of the Jewish people. If she had, would she still have written her ingenuous words of trust in humanity's secret heart?

Playwrights Goodrich and Hackett have dramatized Anne's diary with an eye to Broadway, intending to appeal to all audiences, young and old. While they strove to be as true to the book as possible, they knew that if the play was to have appeal, it must end with an upbeat message. Therefore they made Anne's optimism the final and essential message of the play, with no express evidence of the absolute evil she and her family faced.

Yet the play succeeds in giving another life to Anne's emotional and intellectual consciousness. The play has been translated into many languages and performed on the main stages of the world from Tokyo to Toronto to Johannesburg, from Sydney to Stockholm to Berlin. It is a lasting and compelling achievement, confirming to audiences around the world that Anne's death was not in vain.

South Pacific (1949–1950)
by Richard Rodgers, Oscar Hammerstein II, and Joshua Logan

A Play in Two Acts. Based on James A. Michener's Tales of the South Pacific. Music by Richard Rodgers and Oscar Hammerstein II. Produced by Richard Rodgers and Oscar Hammerstein II in Association with Leland Hayward and Joshua Logan. Staged by Joshua Logan. Opened at the Majestic Theater, April 7, 1949.

The Original Cast

Ngana	Barbara Luna
Jerome	Michael De Leon
	or Noel De Leon
Henry	Richard Silvera
Ensign Nellie Forbush	Mary Martin
Emile De Becque	Ezio Pinza
Bloody Mary	Juanita Hall
Bloody Mary's Assistant	Musa Williams
Abner	Archie Savage
Stewpot	Henry Slate
Luther Billis	Myron McCormick
Professor	Fred Sadoff
Lt. Joseph Cable, U.S.M.C.	William Tabbert
Capt. George Brackett, U.S.N.	Martin Wolfson
Cmdr. William Harbison, U.S.N.	Harvey Stephens
Yeoman Herbert Quale	Alan Gilbert
Sgt. Kenneth Johnson	Thomas Gleason
Seabee Richard West	Dickinson Eastham
Seabee Morton Wise	Henry Michel
Seaman Tom O'Brien	Bill Dwyer
Radio Operator Bob McCaffrey	Bill McGuire
Marine Cpl. Hamilton Steeves	Jim Hawthorne
Staff Sgt. Thomas Hassinger	Jack Fontan
Seaman James Hayes	Beau Tilden
Lt. Genevieve Marshall	Jacqueline Fisher
Ensign Dinah Murphy	Roslyn Lowe
Ensign Janet MacGregor	Sandra Deel
Ensign Cora MacRae	Pat Northrop
Ensign Lisa Minelli	Gloria Meli
Ensign Connie Walewska	Mardi Bayne

Ensign Pamela Whitmore	Evelyn Colby
Ensign Bessie Noonan	Helena Schurgot
Liat	Betta St. John
Marcel, Henry's Assistant	Richard Loo
Lt. Buzz Adams	Don Fellows
Islanders, Sailors,	
Marines, Officers:	Mary Ann Reeve, Chin Yu,

Alex Nicol, Eugene Smith,
Richard Loo, and William Ferguson

From the terrace of Emile de Becque's island plantation house, one can look out, over the bay and the open sea beyond, to the distant island of Bali Ha'i with its twin volcanic mountains.

Two Eurasian children, Ngana, a girl about eleven, and Jerome, a boy about eight, are frolicking about on the terrace, singing a simple French song that tells of the happiness one may find in life if one loves: "Dites-Moi Pourquoi La Vie Est Belle."

As unrealistic as a painted backdrop of a golden-sand beach with huge, cresting ocean waves, *South Pacific* is a love-at-first-sight romance adapted from James Michener's Pulitzer Prize–winning novel, *Tales of the South Pacific*. The song sung by little Ngana and Jerome asks an ironic question, "Why is life so beautiful and gay?" The answer comes: "That one loves and is loved." And love happens in the most unexpected quarters—even "across a crowded room," according to the song that the rich French expatriate De Becque sings on first sighting the beautiful Nellie Forbush, U.S. Ensign from Arkansas.

The major metaphor in the play is the escapist magical island of Bali Ha'i, far removed from the rest of the world. The play identifies it as a hedonist paradise without any of the inimical prejudices and taboos of Western civilization. The native culture is sensual and un-inhibited, though primitive as it is represented by the playwrights' anthropological theatricalities—grass skirts, naked breasts, shrunken heads, and weird fertility rites.

On Bali Ha'i, the handsome hero, United States Marine Lieutenant Joseph Cable, meets and falls in love with Liat, the beautiful,

seventeen-year-old Tonkinese daughter of Bloody Mary, a Polynesian version of Little Buttercup in H.M.S. Pinafore, selling her South
Sea island trinkets and baubles.

The scene is ur-Gauguin with washes of tropical color as Cable
sings his adoration to the lovely primitive Liat. Both are ecstatic
in their sensual love on this paradise island. But Cable knows that
back in his hometown of Philadelphia his relationship with Liat will
be condemned. Similarly, Nellie cannot bring herself to marry Emil
because his former wife, the mother of his children, was Polynesian,
and she believes their relationship was wrong.

The major theme examines the conflicts of racial prejudice in
the love relationships of both couples—Cable and Liat, and Nellie
and Emil. The social protest against race-hatred zeroes in on education by parents and institutions: in one's early, formative years the
child is taught to hate and fear. The playwright's as well as Cable's
antidote is simply to love.

Despite the serious implications of a bloody war with the Japanese and the clash of disparate East and West cultures, *South Pacific*
is a happy, romantic musical with sex and love vibrant in the tropical air. Indeed, sex is the all-important subject in this outpost of the
U.S. Navy that sailors, Marines, and Seabees think about, dream
about, talk about, and sing about.

Captain Bracket, old iron belly, is a caricature of a naval officer
in charge of an U.S.-occupied island in wartime. He introduces the
Thanksgiving Day show that humorously celebrates the military
male's sexual frustration in the chorus of "There Is Nothing Like a
Dame."

The heroine, Nellie Forbush, combines the patriotic seriousness
of a Marine ensign with the seductiveness of one of the drawings of
wartime pinup girls that appeared regularly in *Esquire*, a lusty man's
magazine. Nelly's surname Forbush suggests a joke about female
genital hair for a bunch of horny guys. And unconscious intimations of an actual sexual encounter are suggested in Nelly's main
solo about "washing that man right out of my hair"—as on stage,
Nellie, in a shower, shampoos provocatively.

Nellie's inculcated Midwestern bigotry is transformed when she discovers that De Becque long ago heroically risked his life for France, just as now he is voluntarily risking his life in the American war effort. She repudiates her mother's narrow-minded, Little Rock bigotry and recognizes her deep love for De Becque, who proves his courage when he volunteers as a citizen to undertake the dangerous military reconnaissance mission with Lieutenant Cable to ascertain the movement of the Japanese fleet as it passes through the channel on neighboring Marie Louise Island.

When Cable dies in the venture, De Becque completes the mission that, according to the play, initiates America's South Pacific offensive, the island-to-island war that was to defeat the Japanese. The mission to Marie Louise Island with the subsequent rout of the Japanese fleet suggests the Battle of the Coral Sea that first began to turn back the Japanese in the real-life conflict.

Nellie is held up as living proof that racial prejudice and discrimination are learned rather than innate. The play ends on a note of hope that the Eurasian children will be well loved by stepmother-to-be Nellie De Becque, prepared socially and psychologically to enter Western culture whether in France or in America. But there is no suggestion of any wider application of the lesson Nellie learns, such as Dr. Martin Luther King's demand for equal opportunities for non-whites in America.

Staged in 1949–50, not quite five years after VJ Day, August 15, 1945, and the atomic bomb dropped on Nagasaki, *South Pacific* expresses no real rancor or prejudice against the Japanese for their dastardly blow at Pearl Harbor on December 7, 1941. The play, however, does suggest that there will be a continued American presence in those Pacific islands liberated from the Japanese occupation. The Philippines were given a token independence in 1946, and in 1954 SEATO, the South East Asia Treaty Organization, which includes Australia and New Zealand, promised to protect Asia. In 1959 Hawaii was invited into U.S. statehood.

The gruesomeness of war in the South Pacific is never dealt with realistically in this play. Yet *South Pacific* is the only Pulitzer Prize play that attempts to show American armed forces in active combat in the Pacific theater in World War II. Despite the singing and dancing and the escapism of Bali Ha'i, the play honors the American fighting men and women, dedicated to American values, and prepared to give their lives to what they believed was a just war.

PART THREE

Political Heroes

CHAPTER ELEVEN

The Charismatic Historical Hero

The making of a political hero who reflects the essential character of America and shapes American politics is the major theme of two Pulitzer Prize plays. Each hero, beset by unresolved personal problems in his private life, moves into public life to contend within the political arena, hoping that he will have the courage, clear-headedness, and charisma to influence fittingly "the judgment of the great tribunal of the American people."[1]

These two plays, each based on the character of real heroes in American history, are *Abe Lincoln in Illinois* and *Fiorello!* They dramatize the Sturm und Drang experiences that temper their titular heroes for the political challenges of their lives. Max Weber, in *The Theory of Social and Economic Organization*, considers the political hero as essentially a "charismatic authority" whose successful opposition to traditional authority is based on intangible personal appeal. Weber judges the hero as responding to a Divine "call in the most emphatic sense of the word, a mission or a spiritual duty."[2] In *Abe Lincoln in Illinois* and *Fiorello!* the spiritual quality of the hero takes precedence over the political issues, bringing new dimensions to America's hero worship.

The tall, gaunt Abraham Lincoln and the short, hefty Fiorello La Guardia are distinctive personalities with whom Americans can easily identify. The rail-splitter, even in the 1840s, was often identified in the popular mind with the tall, star-spangled Uncle Sam cartoon. The images of Lincoln and Uncle Sam seem to have merged into one, representative of America's spiritual leadership, to resolve the threat of a divided Union.

In the person of Fiorello (Little Flower) La Guardia, the American public could put aside the widely held stereotypes of Italian-Americans as gangsters like Al Capone, or anarchists like Sacco and Vanzetti, or buffoons like Jimmy "Shnozzola" Durante. Here and now, America would come to respect the patriotism and dual ethnicity of the Little Flower, New York City's ninety-ninth mayor and a crusader for justice for the "little man" and for government integrity. In the play and in the history of the city of New York, Fiorello La Guardia stands as a defender of the American liberal tradition. As Lincoln is destined to preserve the Union, so La Guardia is called to save New York City from political corruption. *Abe Lincoln in Illinois* is a classical and rhetorical play, threaded with history and spiritual Americana; *Fiorello!* is spunky and urbane, a big, brassy, tuneful Broadway musical.

Abe Lincoln in Illinois (1938–1939)
by Robert E. Sherwood

A Play in Three Acts. Produced by the Playwright Company. Staged by Elmer Rice. Opened on Broadway at the Plymouth Theater, October 15, 1938.

The Original Cast

Mentor Graham	Frank Andrews
Abe Lincoln	Raymond Massey
Ann Rutledge	Adele Longmire
Judith	Iris Whitney
Ben Mattling	George Christie
Judge Bowling Green	Arthur Griffin
Ninian Edwards	Lewis Martin
Joshua Speed	Calvin Thomas
Trum Cogdal	Harry Levian
Jack Armstrong	Howard da Silva
Bab	Everett Charlton
Feargus	David Clarke

Jasp	Kevin McCarthy
Seth Gale	Herbert Rudley
Nancy Green	Lillian Foster
William Herndon	Wendell K. Phillips
Elizabeth Edwards	May Collins
Mary Todd	Muriel Kirkland
The Edwards' Maid	Dorothy Allan
Jimmy Gale	Howard Sherman
Aggie Gale	Marion Rooney
Gobey	Hubert Brown
Stephen A. Douglas	Albert Phillips
Willie Lincoln	Lex Parrish
Tad Lincoln	Lloyd Barry
Robert Lincoln	John Payne
The Lincolns' Maid	Iris Whitney
Crimmin	Frank Tweddell
Barrick	John Gerard
Sturveson	John F. Tracey
Jed	Harry Levian
Phil	Kevin McCarthy
Kavanagh	Glen Coulter
Ogleby	John Triggs
Donner	David Clarke
Cavalry Captain	Everett Charlton

The historical facts of *Abe Lincoln in Illinois* evidence his early developmental years as a humanist and a politician , from the 1830s to his election as the sixteenth President in 1861. The play dramatizes his early loss of Ann Rutledge and his marriage to Mary Todd, and his epiphenomenal call from the western frontier to Washington to save the Union. It reflects the way Lincoln was molded by the significant people in his life who recognized his uniqueness: Mentor Graham, the schoolteacher, who instructs him in rhetoric and philosophy; Ninian Edwards, Joshua Speed, and Judge Bowling Green, who encourage him to become the Illinois Whig assemblyman; Mary Todd, his future wife, who divines his innate potential to be president and encourages him to undertake the responsibility of his destiny; and last, and most important, the fictional character, young Jimmy Gale, who causes him to hear the call of the God to Whom Lincoln had studiously closed his eyes.

"The Substance of Abe Lincoln in Illinois" is Sherwood's beautifully written supplementary series of twelve essays, appended to the first edition published by Charles Scribner in 1937, corresponding to each of the twelve scenes of the play. Here Sherwood asserts that the play is not about Lincoln's achievement, but rather it is:

> a play about the solidification of Lincoln himself—a long, uncertain process, affected by influences some of which came from within his own reasoning mind, some from his surrounding circumstances, some from sources which we cannot comprehend. As many as possible of these influences are indicated in this play; the rest are left to the imagination of the audience, because they are beyond mine.[3]

Sherwood cites his sources as a biographer is obliged to do, but he adds that as a playwright he is concerned with feelings, not facts, and so has given himself full license to utilize his imagination to bring the life from the various printed pages of his sources to bring a dramatic creation onto the stage. Because of the absence of dramatic obstacles and the overabundance of information, in several scenes the playwright's efforts are not entirely successful.

Scene 1. (1833) Mentor Graham, the beloved schoolteacher, has taken in a boarder, the young Lincoln, rejected by an unfeeling stepfather. Teaching him the principles of language skills, Shakespeare, and surveying, Mentor writes that Lincoln is the most companionable person anyone would ever want to meet. And yet it seems that a strange morbidity lives in the youth, struggling against the life force within him. Lincoln tells Mentor that he is afraid, that when he went to New Orleans, he feared people might kill him. He said he could see that in the look in their eyes they had murder in their hearts, similar to that look his stepfather had. On one occasion, Graham even found it necessary to dissuade the youth from committing suicide!

Scene 2. (1834) Ninian Edwards, the son of the governor of Illinois, comes to New Salem to gather support for his candidacy to the Illinois State Assembly to rein in President Andrew Jackson's stand on issues like the National Bank, the annexation of Texas, and abolitionism—all to bring the Whigs back into power. Following a scuffle in a saloon that bolsters the "fighting-man" image of Lincoln, young Abe commiserates with Ann, whose fiance has written her that he is not coming back to New Salem to marry her. When Lincoln himself proposes marriage, Ann says she is appreciative of his offer and calls him a *good Christian gentleman*, to which Abe answers he is not. Which of the three words is he denying?

Scene 3. (1835) Bowling Green, his wife Nancy, and Joshua Speed discuss Lincoln's love-relationship to Ann. Abe enters and announces Ann's death in a way that seems to confirm what they have conjectured: that he loves Ann more than anything or anyone he's ever known. He intends to kill himself and join Ann in death. Directed by Bowling, Abe goes upstairs to sleep it off in his bedroom.

Scene 4. (1840) William "Billy" Herndon is Abraham Lincoln's partner in a busy law office on the second floor of the Court House in Springfield, Illinois. Bowling Green and Joshua Speed visit Lincoln to find out if he is interested in running for Congress and discover to their chagrin that he wants to avoid the legal limelight and the political contest and is willing to serve only on the Electoral College. Lincoln gives no reason for his shrinking-violet stance. When Ninian Edwards comes in, he invites Lincoln to his home to meet his sister-in-law, Mary Todd, a young, single lady who has just arrived from Kentucky.

Scene 5. (1840) In their elegant parlor, Ninian Edwards and his wife Elizabeth discuss the problem that Lincoln presents as a seemingly disinterested party to the vivacious Mary Todd, daughter of the president of the Bank of Kentucky and a descendant of a long line of English gentlemen. They are astounded when Mary says that Lincoln is the man she is going to marry, because they believe she will never be happy with a man so indecipherable, even though he seems to hide no part of his simple soul from anyone.

Mary confesses she is unlike her sister Elizabeth, who is happy to have married an established, wealthy scion of Springfield society. She wants the challenge of taking the multi-talented but rough-hewn Lincoln, a man of questionable lineage, to reshape him, and is willing to share his destiny even though it may mean insecurity and poverty. Despite Elizabeth's warning that they are ill-suited to each other, Mary has determined that Abraham Lincoln is fated to be her husband.

Scene 6. (1841) In a dramatic reversal—on New Year's Day, the date set for the Lincoln-Todd wedding—Lincoln writes a letter asking Mary Todd for release from his plighted troth to her. He considers Mary's grand idea of becoming the First Lady of the nation delusional and does not want to be whipped and driven upward in social or political spheres. Billy Herndon, well inebriated, charges Lincoln not to abandon Mary, and to be grateful that he has an ambitious woman at his side to help him do what his conscience and the Fates demand.

It may be that his political leadership will end the misery of two million black slaves and prevent slavery from spreading like a disease into the Western territories that are about to become states of the Union. But the Constitution guarantees property rights, Lincoln answers, voicing the slaveholder's basic legal argument. Slaves are deemed property by law. Herndon rebuts that Lincoln knows in his heart that God in Heaven demands he fulfill his obligation to Him, to his fellow human beings, and to his own immortal soul. But Lincoln rushes out in a panic, beyond the reach of friends or the voice of reason.

Scene 7. (1842) Two years have passed, and it is a clear, moonlit night on a prairie near New Salem. In this fictional scene the playwright presents the major theme: Lincoln is the hero designated by God to prevent the extension of slavery into the pristine West and to champion the eradication of that disease entirely from the American continent.

Having set out three months before by covered wagon from their home in Maryland, Seth Gale and his wife Aggie and ailing seven-year-old son Jimmy are camped near New Salem on their way to join a wagon train in Kansas heading out for Oregon. An old friend of Lincoln's from Illinois, Gale had kept in touch with his friend by mail after moving east to Maryland. Rough Jack Armstrong is the first to meet the westbound homesteaders and has gone to find Lincoln and a doctor to aid the fever-stricken boy.

Traveling with the Gales is the freed black slave Gobey, whose freedom would be nullified if the Gales entered into any of the neighboring slave states. According to Lincoln, this goes against the dictum of the Declaration of Independence that all men are created equal and free to enjoy liberty in the United States. Abe recalls that Mentor Graham once said America could end up being carved into slave and non-slave countries like the nations of Europe, and that the Revolutionary War and the dream of a United States would be invalidated.

Seth Gale sees his son Jimmy as the next generation of Americans who will fight for the same causes that inspired Washington and the Founding Fathers and asks Lincoln to say a prayer—another excellent example of Sherwood's power to write moving and religious-oriented speeches. The impromptu prayer asks the Lord Jesus who died upon the cross to spare the life of Jimmy Gale. His dangerous illness is equated with the illness gripping the young American nation, which must be brought back to healthful wholeness if it is to survive as a vital entity.

The miracle happens: Jimmy recovers. In awe, Lincoln believes his prayers have been answered. He declares that by his newfound faith, he is ready to answer the call to serve, now believing he has been summoned by Divinity to save the Union. Still, he has a premonition of impending tragedy, and his sadness fills the shadows of the scene. The thankful Gales and the freed Gobey bless Lincoln as he goes off to fetch a doctor who lives close by.

Scene 8. (1842, a few days after Scene 7.) Lincoln arrives at the Edwards home to see Mary Todd. He apologizes for having jilted her on their wedding day and asks if she could forgive him enough to marry him. He explains that on the prairie he had a life-changing experience, that he was strongly tempted to go West with the Gales but came to understand that his destiny was in the East with her as his wife to guide and inspire him. He promises that he will never desert her, but will devote himself to doing what is right as God will give him the power to see that right. Mary is effusive in her declaration of love for her husband-to-be.

Scene 9. (1858) On a speakers' platform in an Illinois town, Judge Stephen A. Douglas and Abraham Lincoln debate significant political issues that affect the lives of all Americans. This scene is representative of the oratorical skills of both men. Douglas claims the plight of the factory worker in the North is as wretched as that of the black slave in the South, and that Lincoln erroneously claims the Declaration of Independence applies to the black man. The Supreme Court's recent findings in the Dred Scott case— that blacks are inferior in their nature and may be accounted a property—*prove* that Lincoln is wrong. By his assertions, Lincoln is discounting the Supreme authority of this land and inflaming the nation toward civil war, setting brother against brother.

Lincoln protests that the Supreme Court's decision in the Dred Scott case is erroneous, prejudicial, and dangerous. The Declaration of Independence does not say all men are created equal *except* for blacks, or Catholics, or Jews, or the poor. One race cannot enslave another, and one state cannot shut its eyes to the unconscionable immorality of slavery sanctioned by another state if the United States of America is to remain united. A house divided against itself cannot stand. Split into free states and slave states, America will not endure.

Scene 10. (1880) Eighteen years of marriage have passed and the setting is the parlor of the Edwards house, where the Lincolns are now living. Abraham is surrounded by his three living sons: Tad, a seven-year-old, on his lap; Willie, aged nine, sitting alongside him on the sofa; and Robert, seventeen, a student at Harvard home for a holiday. His close friend Joshua Speed is a house guest, and all are engrossed in Lincoln's telling how on the prairie he found a doctor to bring young Jimmy Gale back to health and how successful and happy Jim is, now a grown man on his farm in Oregon.

Lincoln is expecting the arrival of a delegation of three men from the East: Crimmins, a political leader; Sturveson, a wealthy manufacturer from Philadelphia; and a Reverend Dr. Barrick from Boston. They are coming to evaluate his fitness as a Republican candidate for president of the United States. Humorously, Lincoln goes on to tell his surprised wife Mary that the visitors probably want to see if they live in a log cabin and keep livestock in the house.

Lincoln welcomes the entourage and responds to their inquiries into his beliefs about religion, economics, and national affairs—including slavery. They recall his excellent defense in one of the Douglas-Lincoln debates that the North's factories allowed workers the right to strike, an absolute impossibility for slaves. Lincoln says that he believes in the democratic system that gives hope for progress and improvements in the lives of employer and employee alike.

He has been labeled an atheist and declares he has refused to become a church member because he has found no church that suits his form of worship. But he says he will join that church that enforces the Lord's laws of Leviticus 19:18: "Thou shalt love the Lord thy God with all thy heart and with all thy soul and with all thy mind, and thou shalt love thy neighbor as thyself."

The three investigators take Lincoln's sincerity for shrewdness and believe he can win the election by "currying favor with the mob." When their candidate is safely in the White House, they muse, this slickest and most circumspect of politicians will surely see the expedience of submitting to their control.

Scene 11. (1860) It is the evening of Election Day, November 6, 1860, and at the noisy and crowded Lincoln campaign headquarters in the Illinois State House, the Lincolns and their eldest son, together with Ninian Edwards and Joshua Speed, are studying the large map of the United States with red flag pins indicating a win for Lincoln, white marking a state in doubt, and blue for states lost to Breckenridge and Bell. In the excitement of the race, suddenly Mary becomes paranoid and cries out irrationally that Abe hates her and wants her to go home—that he and all his friends wish she had never come into his life.

In a frenzy, Abe curses Mary for making a spectacle of herself and says that she must never again express publicly the mad thoughts she has uttered so often in the privacy of their home. Confused and helpless, Mary laments that on this night, with her husband poised to win the presidency, the dream of her existence, everything joyous has collapsed, shattered by his curse. As she leaves in tears, Lincoln tells Robert to see that she gets home safely.

The final tallies start arriving, and it becomes evident that the glum-looking Lincoln has won the election. Captain Kavanagh has been appointed his bodyguard to protect him against the threats to his life in the event that he should be the winner.

Scene 12. On February 11, 1881, a crowd of civilians facing a group of soldiers with fixed bayonets fill the Springfield railroad station waiting for President-elect Abraham Lincoln and Mrs. Lincoln to board the last car of the chartered train that will carry them to Washington for the inauguration. The bodyguard, Kavanagh, has been on the job for the past three months and hears that people in Richmond are placing two-to-one bets that Lincoln will not be alive to take the oath of office on March 4. Indeed, the southern states are in great turmoil about this Presidency.

Soon the entire Lincoln family enters and climbs onto the train. The crowd clamors for a speech of farewell, and Lincoln responds with a touching expression of appreciation for all the kindness the people of Illinois have shown him. He knows it is a grave responsibility that he must assume in Washington, and commits himself to the preservation of the promise that all people are free to pursue happiness as they see fitting. He believes the Union can only be held together by the ideals of the Declaration of Independence that created the American democracy, and he is determined that the dire dictum "this too shall pass away" shall not be the fate of this great nation.

As the band strikes up "The Battle Hymn of the Republic," the crowd sings and cheers, and the train, decorated with star-spangled bunting, powers up steam. Then, with whistles blowing, it carries the Lincolns away from Springfield.

In his well-wrought, lengthy essay "The Substance of Abe Lincoln in Illinois," an addendum to this published play, Sherwood cites the scholarship sources he tapped for the dramatic action, scene by scene. But he is remiss in failing to present significant features of Lincoln's psychological portrait to discover the etiology of his melancholia.

His brooding nature may be attributed to his having suffered deep trauma after two untimely encounters with death. When he was six years old, his mother died, poisoned by milk of a cow that had eaten toxic white snakeroot grass; then, in his twenties, his beloved Ann Rutledge died of a fever.

Commenting on his gloomy nature, Mary Todd says Lincoln seems to have had a poem engraved in his mind, an obsession with a life of sorrow, a notion that he is moving along a rugged pathway of life to some terrible doom. Perhaps she was thinking of Thomas Gray's popular poem "Elegy Written in a Country Church-yard," warning that "The paths of glory lead but to the grave."

Or is there another possible reason, some self- awareness that obsessed him? One that dampened, even contended with his innate ambition, which was driven by a superior intelligence and sensitivity?

Sherwood opts not to deal with the issues of Lincoln's considered illegitimate origins, his unusual surname, and intimations of homosexual tendencies.

After the assassination, William Herndon, Lincoln's law partner, did intensive research, questioning everyone who knew the martyred President when he lived in Illinois. He produced *The Life of Lincoln*, an unexpurgated study of reminiscences that all together paint a compelling portrait of the young man as others saw him and were affected by him.

There is no baptismal record associated with Lincoln's birth. It is held that Lincoln's biological father was an Abraham Enloe and that Nancy Hanks was impregnated by this married man who saw fit to have her wed to Thomas Lincoln to give the boy a family name. Still today Lincoln's genealogy remains in doubt. Interestingly, in English and American tradition, Abraham is not a common baptismal name in the white community.

In Herndon's book there is an amazing account of Lincoln's long-term relationship with William Greene, with whom he first worked as a clerk in a general store in New Salem in 1831. Greene and Lincoln slept together in a double bed for four years.

Herndon also fleetingly records that Lincoln slept with his life-long friend Joshua Speed, as well as A.Y. Ellis, a merchant in New Salem, and that in Washington his bodyguard Captain Derickson slept in the same bed with him in his cottage when Mrs. Lincoln was absent.

Interestingly, Lincoln's letters to male friends always end with salutations of love, whereas his letters to his wife do not. And so, inasmuch as the attempt to account for Lincoln's morbidity attributed to his mother's and Ann Rutledge's deaths is not convincing, the case may be made for his suffering emotionally from his awareness of his bisexuality.

Sherwood obviously disregarded by choice any of these citations in Herndon's *Life of Lincoln*, worshipfully unwilling to introduce anything that might be deemed negative in the persona of this country's greatest president. There is no proof that these sexual innuendos or allegations have any validity; the conclusions that one draws must surely reflect the prejudicial character of the interpreter.

On February 22, 1861, on his inaugural journey to Washington, Lincoln stopped at Constitution Hall in Philadelphia, where the Declaration of Independence was signed. Here he spoke impromptu:

> I am filled with deep emotion at finding myself standing here, in this place, where were collected together the wisdom, the patriotism, the devotion to principle, from which sprang the institutions under which we live . . . I have never had a feeling politically that did not spring from the sentiments embodied in the Declaration of Independence . . . which gave liberty, not alone to the people of this country, but, I hope, to the world, for all future time. . . . Now, my friends, can this country be saved upon that basis? I may say, in advance, that there will be no bloodshed unless it be forced upon the Government, and then it will be compelled to act in self-defence.
>
> My friends, this is wholly an unexpected speech . . . I have said nothing but what I am willing to live by and, if it be the pleasure of Almighty God, die by.[4]

Throughout history there has been a myth-making tendency, accompanying the apotheosis of the assassinated hero, the martyr to a cause. Sherwood's play presents Lincoln prepared by destiny to save the Union and to die for that cause on Good Friday, April 14, 1865, shot by John Wilkes Booth as he sits with his wife in the Presidential box at Ford's Theater, watching a comedy. Though Sherwood acknowledges that Lincoln belonged to no church, he protests that he was a true Christian, willing to sacrifice his life to preserve the integrity of the United States of America. Lincoln never belonged to any Christian church, though his ethical sense underscored his every action. It is likely that rather than feeling called by God, as Sherwood suggests, he was motivated by his belief in the Bill of Rights and the Constitution.

Fiorello! (1959–1960)
by Jerome Weidman and George Abbott

A Play in Two Acts. Music by Jerry Bock. Lyrics by Sheldon Harnick. Staged by George Abbott. Produced by Robert E. Griffith and Harold C. Prince. Opened on Broadway at the Broadhurst Theater, November 23, 1959.

The Original Cast

Announcer	Del Horstmann
Fiorello	Tom Bosley
Neil	Bob Holiday
Morris	Nathaniel Frey
Mrs. Pomerantz	Helen Verbit
Mr. Lopez	H. F. Green
Mr. Zappatella	David Collyer
Dora	Pat Stanley
Marie	Patricia Wilson
Ben	Howard da Silva
Ed Peterson	Del Hostmann
Second Player	Stanley Simmonds
Third Player	Michael Quinn
Fourth Player	Ron Husman
Fifth Player	David London
Sixth Player	Julian Patrick
Seedy Man	Joseph Toner
First Heckler	Bob Bernard
Second Heckler	Michael Scrittorale

Third Heckler	Jim Maher
Fourth Heckler	Joseph Toner
Nina	Pat Turner
Floyd	Mark Dawson
Sophie	Lynn Ross
Thea Almerigatti	Ellen Hanley
Secretary	Mara Landi
Senator	Frederic Downs
Commissioner	Michael Quinn
Frankie Scarpini	Michael Scrittorale
Mitzi	Eileen Rodgers
Florence	Deedy Irwin
Reporter	Julian Patrick
First Man	Scott Hunter
Second Man	Michael Scrittoralle
Tough Man	David London
Derby	Bob Bernard
Frantic	Stanley Simmonds
Judge Carter	Joseph Toner

Fiorello! is sung full-throated in a bravado major key. The musical triumphantly soars as the chorus describes its diminutive political hero with the rousing "On the Side of the Angels," presenting this Italian-Jewish-American politician as the champion of the underdog and the poor. La Guardia fights political and economic corruption wherever he finds it, intent upon improving the lives of the economically depressed, the exploited, and the hopeful immigrants who constitute the millions of citizens of America's greatest metropolis. Lovably avuncular, Fiorello is a man for and of the people, fused out of the ethnic melting pot of the City.

The symbolic prologue supplies the clue to the substance, structure, and sentiment of the book by Weidman and Abbott, summing up La Guardia's personality. Fiorello is reading the funnies. He announces himself to be on the side of the good guys, the protector of little Shirley Shorthand, the comic strip heroine whose adventures he is recounting, box by box, over radio station WNYC to a strikebound, and therefore paperless, Sunday New York City. The bad guy is Alderman P. T. Pickel, Shirley's fierce-looking and dangerous boss, whose gang figures largely in the book of this musical. Vivid as the illustrations in a comic book, Fiorello La Guardia has all of the bravery and goodness, if none of the Herculean looks, of Superman himself.

The characters of *Fiorello!* are, indeed, two-dimensional, and the telegraph-style, terse, and emphatic dialogue calls for comic-strip balloons. Each scene carries the story line further, like the sequences of boxes in a cartoon strip .

Operating without self-interest, Fiorello La Guardia fights gangsterism, motivated by his sense of fairness and humanitarianism. Only at one moment does his defiant stand against political corruption reflect a personal component: he attributes his father's death in the Spanish-American War to dishonest contractors who, without oversight, supplied poisoned foods for army personnel.

Act I immediately picks up the positive, good-natured tone of the Prologue, setting the scene in La Guardia's law office, headquarters of the good guys. Morris, La Guardia's aide, informs the audience, in rhyme, of the office's sanctity, proclaiming that this hero serves endless justice to the friendless. There are many petitioners seeking justice, declaring their admiration in broken English. They know Fiorello will help them with free legal services because he's got a heart that beats on the side of the angels, the anthem of the first musical number.

Dora has come to La Guardia's office to ask him to undo what she claims is an injustice. Her friend Thea, the leader of their cause, has been arrested on trumped-up charges. Marie, Fiorello's competent and adoring secretary, promises that her boss will surely help. The police have arrested Thea, falsely claiming that she was soliciting, wiggling her hips provocatively. The beautiful Thea is indeed the organizer of the peaceful march, the first strike in the city by women needleworkers.

Mr. Schirmer, the slimy owner of the sweatshop The Nifty Shirt Waist Corporation, has reneged on his promise to give the women a raise if they worked through the busy season. Perhaps with money under the table, the sweatshop owners have enlisted the city authorities and the police to prevent a strike, even a peaceful picketing march.

Who will fight the grubby sweatshop operators and rein in the New York City cops and ward heelers to see that justice is done? Like Superman, Fiorello appears to take on every crook and fraudster in City Hall.

But how to do it? How does one get into the political swim tank and avoid being devoured by the sharks? Fiorello has heard that the Fourteenth District is in search of a candidate to run for Congress and so, intent on being that candidate, he must hustle down to talk with one of the big bosses who run the city.

The Ben Marino Association Clubhouse on West Third Street is New York City's Republican political headquarters. Here, stereotypically shady politicos describe their self-interested involvement in the game of urban politics in a song that equates politics metaphorically with the rough, ruthless, and for-keeps game of poker.

Without any prospects, Ben is scouting around for a candidate for Congress to run on the Republican ticket for the Fourteenth District's Twelfth Ward, and Fiorello offers himself. Since Marino has no other reasonable choice, he accepts the cocky little fellow as a candidate.

Meanwhile, on the street outside the garment sweatshop, a band of peaceful women picketers march and sing "Unfair," carrying placards complaining that they are dreadfully underpaid. The five and a half cents per hour they earn as sewing machine slaves in this Lower East Side sweatshop keeps them all below the poverty line.

A group of paid hecklers interfere, taunting the women with demeaning jibes. Floyd, the cop on the beat assigned to keep the peace, is riled when one of the women gives him a strike placard to hold. Floyd warns the women that he will pull them in if they don't stop causing a commotion. Undaunted, the women call him a Tammany grafter, employed, like the hecklers, by that underworld political machine. Floyd says he's going to take the leader, Nina, to the station on charges of sexual solicitation, because he saw her wiggling her hips.

Like a firehorse responding to the firebell, La Guardia charges in to protect the Constitutional rights of the shirtwaist machine operators and warns that he'll slap a writ of interdiction on anyone who dares to interfere. Officer Floyd is cowed and retreats apologetically, saying he's only doing his duty.

Nonsense, says, Fiorello. A cop has sworn an oath to uphold the integrity of his office and it is obvious here that the sweatshop has bought protection. Everyone had better know, announces the scrappy lawyer, that he is going to bring all of them down.

In a sudden impulse, Fiorello asks Marie if she's free to have dinner with him this evening. The lovesick girl is overwhelmed with ecstasy at the invitation by her idol. But suddenly, the needleworkers enter triumphantly with Thea Almerigatti, who has been released on bond bail. For Fiorello it is love at first sight!

Here is Thea, a gorgeous, courageous Italian girl, hailing from Trieste, a city Fiorello has lived in and loves. They speak in Italian, finding a common heartbeat. But then she tells him her sadness that the Austrian army is attacking Trieste, because the Austro-Hungarian Empire wants the Adriatic seaport. World War I is about to happen.

Captivated by Thea's ethnicity, beauty, wit, and charm, Fiorello invites her for dinner and phones to break his dinner date with Marie.

We next witness a rally on a New York City street corner to elect Fiorello to the U.S. Congress. The first speaker on the platform is Neil, Ben Marino's protégé. He characterizes Fiorello with a string of banal superlatives that say nothing. But then Thea addresses the crowd from the platform attesting to Fiorello's courage in fighting for the right of factory girls to strike for higher wages. The crowd is excited as Fiorello himself mounts the podium and declares that he is dedicated to cleaning up the corruption of the city and getting rid of the obnoxious smell of Tammany Hall.

Ben Marino and his political hacks are in shock when La Guardia actually wins the seat to Congress, and without their help, which means no patronage, no office handouts, no division of the spoils.

On the rooftop of a tenement house in Greenwich Village, patrolman Floyd is making love to Dora, one of the sewing machine strikers, when he should be covering his beat. He tells Dora that Congressman La Guardia is disliked in Washington, because he's talking up a storm for America's entry into World War I and trying to enforce a draft resolution in Congress.

Marie is determined to go to Washington with Ben Marino to talk La Guardia out of his war-hawk stance. But Fiorello says he can't be silent when he knows France and England can't win the war against the German Kaiser without America, and to show his genuine faith in the mission, he has himself enlisted in the American Expeditionary Force.

Out on a street in front of the Ben Marino Club in New York City, there is a sendoff for Fiorello as he goes into the Army. Fiorello enters dressed in a flier's uniform and is escorting Thea, whom he has asked to marry him, if she will have him. Thea has already asked her priest, unsure whether a good Italian-Catholic girl could marry an Italian-Jewish-Episcopalian, and she promises she will wait for him to come back from war.

A silver screen is lowered and the Pathé News rooster crows triumphantly as the movie news reports La Guardia's experiences in the A.E.F., from his induction to his experience as a pilot of a fighter plane in aerial combat shooting down a German bomber, and finally the Armistice and his return to New York harbor and the Statue of Liberty.

As Fiorello comes down the gangplank from the troop ship, with crowds cheering, he gives Thea the key to the city of Trieste, she says she will marry him, and the couple embrace as the chorus sings the heartwarming strains of "Home Again."

Ten years later, in 1928, Fiorello is scheduled to speak at a rally in Italian Harlem, making his bid for mayor of New York against the incumbent mayor, the popular Jimmy Walker, ruler of Tammany Hall. Dora drops by Thea and Fiorello's apartment unexpectedly with news of her husband Floyd's being awarded the city's garbage disposal contract for lower Manhattan, evidence that he is deeply involved in Tammany's political machinery. He has bought Dora a swanky penthouse apartment, and she says how thrilled she is to be meeting New York City bigwigs like Jimmy Hines and Al Smith.

In the dialogue exchange, Dora learns that today Thea visited the doctor, who advised rest for her run-down condition—though there are clear intimations that she is seriously ill with tuberculosis. After Dora leaves, Thea sings a nostalgic song recalling her courtship with the man she will love until the end of her life.

Meanwhile, at Floyd and Dora McDuff's new penthouse apartment the butler has set up the bar in anticipation of a meeting with a lot of crooked Tammany politicians, including Jimmy Hines and the notorious gangster Frank Scarpini.

A New York City Judge, a commissioner, and a politician enter and exchange information about the illegal rigging and fixing that is taking place in the city's courts and business offices.

Corruption is rampant among elected officials. Gangsters are allowed to operate against society's greater good.

Fiorello is a champion who will defend society against the outlaws, establish order for the general welfare, and protect the poor and underprivileged against all injustice. There is no difference between the greed of the politicians and the gangsters; all live by deceit, fraud, and theft. La Guardia is the watchdog they all fear.

Suddenly, in comes the main item of the business meeting: Miss Mitzi Travers, who, with her dancing entourage of bouncing beauties, begins to entertain with the song "Gentleman Jimmy," whose lyrics define Walker as believing in everyone's right to live the way he wants. Put into practice, his live and let live philosophy makes New York City as lawless as the Wild West.

Back in Fiorello's office, Ben Marino prophesies that Fiorello will lose the race because he has been unwilling to play ball with the Tammany politicos. Dramatically, Fiorello, the champion for justice, stands alone, beset on all sides by naysayers and enemies.

Then comes the anvil blow: Fiorello receives a phone call from Thea's doctor, advising him that she has only a short time to live.

While Fiorello is on the phone, Dora arrives and speaks to Marie privately, admitting that she is torn by indecision. She wants to be loyal to her husband Floyd, but she is profoundly grateful for all that Fiorello has done for her, and discloses the criminal Scarpini's plot to kill Fiorello at the rally that very night.

With the greatest urgency, Marie tells Fiorello everything that Dora has related: that after the fire alarm signal is sounded, a baby carriage loaded with paving blocks will be thrown down from the rooftop to kill Fiorello standing on the podium. Swiftly, the "Little Flower" responds to the challenge, directing Morris to allow no one—not even a cop—to pull the fire alarm, and organizing a squad of men to safeguard the rooftop so that no baby carriage is there to be used as a lethal weapon.

On the corner of 105th Street and Madison Avenue the rally gets under way, with the sound of Fiorello's voice and an occasional cheer from the crowd indicating that he is on the speaker's platform.

Suddenly a frantic man comes rushing onto the rooftop, calling, "Fire! Fire! The building is burning!" Neil wrestles with him, saying the building will have to burn, that no alarm will be sounded until La Guardia finishes his speech. A group of thugs enter as reinforcement to the frantic man, but Neil stops them by saying he could identify them in court as criminals if there is any trouble.

At this moment, Morris joins Neil to tell him that he's just received a message that Thea has died. They hear the last words of La Guardia's speech, followed by the roar of a cheering crowd, and both men go down to meet Fiorello to give him the tragic news.

The moment they leave the fire alarm box unguarded, the thugs pull the alarm and produce a baby carriage loaded with bricks, which comes down from the rooftop onto the speaker's platform.

Miraculously, Fiorello manages to escape unharmed, only dirtied by the shower of dirt and dust that falls with the bricks. Fiorello is furious with Neil and Morris for their failure to protect him, until he learns why they abandoned their post.

Fiorello is nearly destroyed by the loss of Thea, which is followed immediately by his losing the mayoralty race to Gentleman Jimmy.

Four years pass, and the honest Judge Seabury recommends Fiorello as candidate for a Republican-Fusion ticket for the upcoming mayoralty election, again to oppose the seemingly invincible Democratic Mayor Jimmy Walker.

Fiorello and the Republican leader Ben Marino are hopeful that this election will spell the end of Tammany Hall. The evidence of corruption is infallible, and surely Fiorello will win.On this triumphant note, La Guardia finally discovers that Marie is his best friend and he asks her to marry him, the very question she has been longing to hear for fifteen years. Joyously, Marie breaks into a reprise of "I'll Marry the Very Next Man," joined by the chorus of men who shift to the musical's finale, the upbeat anthem, "We Want La Guardia."

Fiorello! is a lively Broadway musical that scans the mountain peaks of La Guardia's political career without exploring the deep valleys of heartbreak that shaped his kindness. As Jerome Weidman portrays him in the musical's book, plucky is the word for the indefatigable American hero, whose defeats served only to embolden him.

A vocal and dynamic defender of justice for the American people, Fiorello (Little Flower) Enrico La Guardia was born in New York City in 1887 to an agnostic father, Achille Luigi Carlo La Guardia, and a Jewish mother, Irene Cohen, who hailed from Trieste, Austria-Hungary, where the couple met and were married in a civil ceremony.

An educated musicologist, Achille served in the 11th Infantry in Fort Whipple, Arizona, as solo cornetist, composer, and sometimes bandmaster. He wanted to be renowned like his idol, John Phillip Sousa.

When the *U.S.S. Maine* was blown up in Havana Harbor, the 11th Infantry was transferred to Florida in preparation for assignment to Cuba. Weakened by malaria, Achille was nearly killed by eating some U.S. Army rations of tainted meat and was forthwith discharged with a pension of eight dollars a month.

Achille took his family to Trieste to live with his widowed mother-in-law, but in researching a hotel business enterprise in his compromised physical condition, he suffered a fatal heart attack and died on October 21, 1904.

Though devastated by his father's death, Fiorello recouped pragmatically and hustled to secure a position in the United States Consular Service offices in Budapest, Trieste, and Fiume. This prepared him for work, from 1907 to 1910, in the U.S. Immigration Service at Ellis Island, New York, where he was translator and interpreter, speaking many languages including Italian, German, Yiddish, and Croatian. With his gift for languages, concern for humanitarian service, and boundless energy, Fiorello studied law at New York University and passed the bar in 1910.

And here is where the musical *Fiorello!* begins.

Like a bloodhound investigating every hint of corruption emanating from mayor Walker's gangster-dominated Tammany, La Guardia set out to bring the offenders to the bar of justice and made a name for himself. In 1933, La Guardia ran for mayor against Jimmy Walker—for the second time—and this time won. Over three successive terms in the mayor's office, New Yorkers came to admire the energy and ethos of this little fighter.

To survive as a Broadway musical, there has to be romance of some sort, and playwright Weidman obliges by dramatizing Fiorello's less-than-passionate courtship and marriage to Thea, and his even less romantic union with the Penelope-faithful Marie, who waited for years on the fringe before the widower Fiorello thought to wed again. No children were born of either marriage, but Fiorello and Marie did adopt children to round out a family circle to occupy Gracie Mansion.

Fiorello! is a Broadway paean of praise for one of the greatest mayors of New York City who wanted to toss his ten-gallon hat into the presidential ring but died early of pancreatic cancer. Weidman's book tells the success story of an American hero, a champion for honest government whose driving force sought the power to make justice prevail.

CHAPTER TWELVE

The Fictional Political Hero

The three Pulitzer Prize plays that create fictional political heroes are *Of Thee I Sing*, *Both Your Houses*, and *State of the Union*. They exemplify the American hope of finding a hero who will establish a national harmony in a time of economic discord, legislate prudently for the general welfare, and champion democratic justice. Each of these plays reflects actual crises in American history, and provides a fictional hero who opposes self-interested forces in Washington that threaten to undermine the American democratic political structure.

The hero of *Of Thee I Sing* is J. P. Wintergreen, a handsome, youthful president, very unlike Herbert Hoover in the White House in 1932. Wintergreen's winning campaign platform is Love, virile and revolutionary. The musical is a fantastic song-and-dance escapade of wish-fulfillment in which the big, bad wolf, Depression, explodes in a puff of smoke.

More realistically concerned with political and economic issues of the Depression, the fictional congressman Alan McClean of *Both Your Houses* is labeled a muckraker by wrong-doing, greedy politicians. He discovers corruption on Capitol Hill and champions the cause of Congressional oversight and thrift.

In 1946, more than a decade later, *State of the Union* dramatized the conflicts faced by the would-be president Grant Matthews, a successful corporate executive whose know-how and drive directed America's airplane production line to help win World War II. Now in peacetime Matthews hopes to continue to direct capital and labor amicably to maintain prosperity in the nation.

Common to these three political Pulitzer Prize plays is the character of Washington, D.C., itself, presented as a community of con artists, drunk with the power entrusted to them, disregarding the promises they made to their constituents. These scoundrels remain in office year after year, continuing their unresolved debates over silent money and lobbying and appropriations bills, tariffs and outsourcing, illegal immigration and national security.

Like old fish, political longevity breeds an aroma of corruption.

The major theme of all the political Pulitzer Prize plays is a call to arms to Americans to understand the character of political leadership in Washington. Their major dramatic action is the search for the honest, moral individual whose convictions will serve in the making of an American political hero.

Of Thee I Sing (1931–1932)

A Play in Two Acts. Book by George S. Kaufman and Morrie Ryskind Music by George Gershwin. Lyrics by Ira Gershwin. Produced by Sam H. Harris. Staged by George S. Kaufman. Opened on Broadway at the Music Box Theater, December 26, 1931.

The Original Cast

Louis Lippman	Sam Mann
Francis X. Gilhooley	Harold Moffet
Maid	Vivian Barry
Matthew Arnold Fulton	Dudley Clemens
Senator Robert E. Lyons	George E. Mack
Senator Carver Jones	Edward H. Robins
Alexander Throttlebottom	Victor Moore
John P. Wintergreen	William Gaxton
Sam Jenkins	George Murphy
Diana Devereaux	Grace Brinkley
Mary Turner	Lois Moran
Miss Benson	June O'Dea
Vladimir Vidovitch	Tom Draak

Yussef Yussevitch	Sulo Hevonpaa
The Chief Justice	Ralph Biggs
Scrubwoman	Leslie Bingham
The French Ambassador	Florenz Ames
Senate Clerk	Martin Leroy
Guide	Ralph Riggs

Of Thee I Sing, the first musical to be awarded the Pulitzer Prize, with its satirically political book, brilliant musical score, and wittily sophisticated lyrics, reflects the patriotic attitudes of a resilient America in the depths of the Depression. Though the hero sings the title's love song to his beloved wife, Mary Turner, the audience understands the play's message of love for America: *My country, 'tis of thee, sweet land of liberty, of thee I sing.*

Reminiscent of the ancient Greek comedies by Aristophanes, *Of Thee I Sing* uses barbed and playful satire to poke fun at American politicians. In this extravaganza, Love—often sacred, but most of the time profane—is the presidential political platform presented as the philosophical and fun foundation for American life.

John P. Wintergreen, nominated as the hero of promise by a group of political pundits, runs for President and, to promote national enthusiasm for his candidacy, decides to hold a bathing-suit beauty contest whose winner will be his bride and the White House's First Lady.

The idea of a beauty contest is as old as Paris and Aphrodite and the golden apple. In America, at the turn of the century, Flo Ziegfield enhanced the vaudeville stage with his Follies, parading bevies of beauties provocatively gowned. From Ziegfield's idea came the Miss America Pageant, which originated in 1921 on the Boardwalk of Atlantic City, expressly to bring crowds there over the Labor Day weekend. Contestants in one-piece bathing suits strutted before the set of judges who selected the most beautifully featured, graceful, and curvaceous. Many American women were up in arms, calling this public display of flesh demeaning to womanhood, a half-step above prostitution.

In the opening number of *Of Thee I Sing*, Wintergreen is named as the people's choice for President because he loves everyone,

including the Irish (represented by the wisecracking Francis X. Gilhooley) and the Jews (represented by the wisecracking Louis Lippman). The Irish and the Jews, the most recently arrived immigrant
groups, were the most feared and shunned by America's Protestant
society.

Lippman and Gilhooley are a pair of vaudeville standup comics
like Sid Caesar and Fred Allen. Clowns like these can trace their an-
cestry back to the buffoons of the Roman comedies of Plautus and
Terence. Victor Moore, who was the original Alexander Throttlebottom, was one of theater's goofiest deadpan clowns.

With much sophomoric sexual innuendo set in a racy vaudeville
spoof, the playwrights establish John P. Wintergreen's presidential
platform as Love . The politicos in their hotel room ask the cham-
bermaid what everyone wants most in the world. Love is her answer.
And so they seize on this banal concept as a political platform and
couple it with even greater foolishness: a Miss America pageant,
and Wintergreen for a husband as a prize.

On the Atlantic City Boardwalk twenty-four gorgeous young
women in bathing suits dance and parade around to impress the
judges. The judges find for the curvaceous, Southern-drawling Diana Devereaux as the most beautiful.

However, as Fate would have it, Wintergreen loses his heart to
Mary Turner, his very pretty secretary, the very moment he tastes
the delicious homemade corn muffin she gives him from her lunch
box. Not only can this excellent secretary bake great muffins, she
can cook, sew, and make lace curtains. By comparison, Diana Devereaux can't do anything but look gorgeous and wiggle her natural
endowments. The Wonder Woman is Mary Turner, fully equipped
with feminine charm, intelligence, and domestic know-how.

A comedy vaudeville skit, especially one with gorgeous girls,
must always have a horny clown, extravagant in his thoughts and
gestures, but humorously impotent in his actual performance. This
numskull is the vice presidential nominee Alexander Throttlebottom, by profession a hermit, whom nobody knows or recognizes.
His name tells it all: he is a recreation of the foolish tinker Bottom
of *A Midsummer Night's Dream*. In keeping with the tradition of all

previous vice presidencies, he is ordered to disappear, become invisible, go back to his hermit's cave, because nobody wants to know the Vice President.

A silver screen descends and the movie news of the day reports the results of the national ballot couched in ridiculous news items, like the humor magazines *Judge* or *Mad Comics*. It announces that Wintergreen is the winner in the presidential election.

With decorous pomp and circumstance Wintergreen is sworn in as President by the Supreme Court Chief Justice with the Supreme Court in attendance. Immediately after the inaugural oath, Wintergreen takes the marital oath with Mary Turner in a filmed wedding ceremony, shutting out forever the winner of the national contest, the designated First Lady, Diana Devereaux.

The nation is in an uproar that Wintergreen has played unfairly until Mary and Wintergreen publicly declare their deep, mutual love.

The French ambassador demands that Wintergreen annul his marriage to Mary and marry Diana or face impeachment for having jilted her. All the politicos begin calling for Wintergreen's impeachment or immediate resignation.

Meanwhile Throttlebottom is roaming around the Capitol unrecognized and totally unaware of what's expected of him, even ignorant of his significant role in the Senate.

All opposition to Wintergreen is silenced when Mary announces her pregnancy. President John P. Wintergreen and Mary are the proud parents of twins, a boy and a girl, and America rejoices as Love pays off and all the Wintergreens will live happily in the White House until the end of the presidential term.

Diana Devereaux's claim against Wintergreen is fully resolved when she decides to marry Vice President Throttlebottom, rounding out the musical's link with *A Midsummer Night's Dream* by repeating Titania's love-fascination with the ass Bottom. (Titania is another name for Diana, the moon goddess.) And Diana Devereaux's lineage is traced back humorously as the illegitimate daughter of an illegitimate son of an illegitimate nephew of Napoleon. So much for French morality!

Written in the nadir of the Depression, *Of Thee I Sing* closes its eyes to what President Herbert Hoover in his *Challenge to Liberty* indicates are the serious problems that have plunged America into economic disorder:

> The lingering effects of the stupendous destruction of the war; the economic dislocations of the peace; the vast speculation founded on the increasing effort to avoid payment of both private and public debt through inflation and manipulation of currencies; the efforts to make some other nation pay governmental debts; the explosive fuel of nationalism; the unassimilated scientific discoveries and inventions; all these have brought the Great Depression, with its vast unemployment and untold misery. Stupendous problems have been thrust upon us for which our social system is blamed.[1]

Hoover disclaimed all responsibility for the Wall Street Market crash.

The satirical lance *Of Thee I Sing* aims to prick and deflate the windbag politicos in Washington. The musical is an entertainment and a cathartic, dispelling the real anger directed toward President Hoover and the Republican government that failed to warn of the dangers in the inflationary economy or come to provide economic support after October 1929. It castigates the unethical money lenders and bankers, and the money-hungry munitions makers who marketed World War I, as now the nations of the world have sunk deep into debt and despair.

Despite the spoofing and dramatized ineptness of the executive branch, the play is an appeal for moral leadership, for relief of poverty by providing work, and for a guarantee of basic democratic principles. As soon as Wintergreen is President, he undertakes to resolve the Depression, "the greatest economic calamity in the history of the American people."[2] The economic misery Americans are suffering is humorously mirrored in the White House when Mary tells Wintergreen to ask for an increase in salary from the Congress because of the outrageous cost of maintaining the White House.

But the President is afraid that if he dares to speak up to the money-people, he'll be laid off.

Wintergreen sings his optimistic message based on his Presidential platform: Prosperity is knocking at Depression's door, and "Love Is Sweeping the Country." But the audience is aware of the reality, that poverty, hunger, and homelessness are depressing the majority of Americans. Thanks to the laissez-faire attitudes of the Coolidge and Hoover Presidencies, the government has set no regulatory policy for big business, allowing the burgeoning of monopolies and hindering the organization of unions to protect the worker.

Below the surface, Wintergreen's platform likewise avoids serious attention to economic reform . The subtext assures citizens that it is okay to be poor, because the sun and the moon belong to everyone, and love and sex compensate for the loss of material pleasures of mansions and yachts, and everyone knows that only love makes life worth living.

The second issue of Wintergreen's presidential resolve focuses on America's foreign policy, in particular its relationship to France.

In the first two decades of the twentieth century, Americans fell in love with Paris, the city of lights, the most admired city in the world, the shining center for the world's creative arts and the disciplines of scientific research. "I love Paris" was the theme of many popular songs. There American artists flocked to share the spirit of freedom with expatriates Gertrude Stein and Ernest Hemingway. Even the brothers Gershwin expressed their love of Paris in music and song.

But *Of Thee I Sing* takes a critical position on politics, reproving France for its unpaid ten-year-old World War I debt. The play suggests that there is a substantial bankruptcy in the French gold treasury, as well as in the French treasury of Love.

When the French ambassador fights Diana's cause, citing her lineage as French, the humorous discovery of the line of illegitimacies becomes a salacious commentary on sexual promiscuity in France. Diana then becomes a foil to the red, white, and true-blue Mary Turner, and in this play there is no contest: Americans are praised as better and more faithful lovers, and, as evidenced by Mary's twins, more productive, too.

Chauvinism and patriotism color the play, applauding American motherhood and making a jab at France's declining birth rate. (While nearly half a million American Expeditionary Force "doughboys" died in the very few months America fought in World War I, that number was small compared to the horrendous decimation of France's male population between 1914 and 1918, causing births in France to drop precipitously.)

The third significant concern has to do with the character of incompetent and corrupt elected officials in Washington, a fact as relevant today as it was then. In Act II, Scene 2, in a Capitol corridor just outside the United States Senate, the discussion concerns the Constitution's ordering of succession in government leadership should President Wintergreen be impeached. It is a cunningly subversive but legal action that Senators Fulton and Gilhooley have in mind as they connive to have the easily manipulated, dimwitted Vice President Alexander Throttlebottom become the President.

The office of the presidency itself is satirized as a stepping stone to a bigger and better-paying position, such as an officer in one of the newly emerging monopolistic corporations in America. The politico knows his Washington employment is limited in time. A clever President can secure any corporate position he wants by simply supporting that industry's lobbyists, lessons that all of Washington politicos have learned well.

A serious and ironical symbol of President Hoover's indifference to the national welfare is Jenny, Paul Revere's horse who served to alert the countryside against the British invasion in 1775. The foolish, inane concern for an immediate pension for the long-deceased Jenny touches satirically on a painful reality: the contentious pension problem for World War I veterans. Congress had awarded the A.E.F. war veterans a bonus in the 1924 Adjusted Service Certificate Law, but it was not going to be paid until 1945, more than two decades later.

In the summer of 1932, the A.E.F. bonus marchers rose in anger against Washington, gathering five thousand strong, to demand that the promised bonuses be paid at once. From all parts of the nation, the marchers came with their families to the District of Columbia and made camp at Anacostia Flatts Hooverville, prepared to stay until payment was made. The Bonus Expeditionary Force of May 1932, the nadir of the Depression, saw many thousands of veterans unemployed in D.C. without enough money to feed their families.

This displeased and frightened Hoover, who had vetoed the Adjusted Service Certificate Law, declaring that government deficit spending would protract the Depression. The camp was violently attacked, the shelters burned, and the Hooverville squatters dispersed by regular U.S Army forces, fully armed with tanks and bayonets, under Army chief of staff Douglas MacArthur. President Hoover had issued the command.

Presenting a whimsical alternative to the grim reality of the day, *Of Thee I Sing* is essentially an optimistic fantasy seeking a destiny-sent hero to save the nation suffering in the throes of the Great Depression. Though the satire cuts painfully deep, the play posits faith in the democratic principles of America.

Both Your Houses (1932–1933)
by Maxwell Anderson

A Play in Three Acts. Produced by the Theater Guild, Inc. Staged by Worthington Minor. Opened on Broadway at the Royale Theater, March 6, 1933.

The Original Cast

Marjorie Gray	Aleta Freel
Bus	Mary Philips
Eddie Wister	Robert Shayne
Solomon Fitzmaurice	Walter C. Kelly
Mark	Oscar Polk
Simeon Gray	Robert Strange
Levering	Morris Carnovsky
Merton	John Butler
Dell	William Foran
Miss McMurtry	Jane Seymour

Wingblattt	J. Edward Bromberg
Peebles	Russell Collins
Farnum	John F. Morrissey
Alan McClean	Shepperd Strudwick
Ebner	Joseph Sweeney

The dramatic action of *Both Your Houses* starts with the protagonist Alan McClean's discovery of rampant corruption in the legislative Houses of Washington, D.C. The idealistic, first-term Nevada congressman contends with that dishonesty to the death of his own political career. Disillusioned by the Capitol's immoral political climate, McClean recalls Mercutio's dying curse in *Romeo and Juliet*: "A plague on both your houses," providing the cynical title to the play.

The major theme of *Both Your Houses* is that corruption destroys all human values, even unmaking a political champion-for-integrity in government. McClean, serving on the Appropriations Committee, sees the outrageous dishonesty of Washington's politicians and fights to defeat the fradulent appropriations bill, bringing about his own political demise.

In the House Office Building in Washington, D.C., Marjorie Gray, serving as secretary to her father, Simeon Gray, the chairman of the Appropriations Committee, learns that her friend Bus Nilson, a long-serving secretary in the House, has just been fired by Congressman Eddie Wister. Bus's replacement is a tall, gorgeous, and inexperienced blonde from New York who has been given the secretarial post as part of a deal the congressman has made as lobbyist for the Appalachian Steel Company.

Casually, Bus asks Marjorie how her fiance Alan McClean is doing and is baffled when Marjorie says that he's a bit out of hand and in need of some lessons in how to juggle dynamite. Alan is expected any minute for the Appropriations Committee meeting scheduled to begin shortly.

McClean won election in Nevada backed by several huge construction companies who were the responsible builders of the first portion of the Hoover Dam. But, having found that the bids for the completion of the dam are highly inflated, he has been investigating his own election. He is concerned about Chairman Gray's motivation to appoint him to the Appropriations Committee because on the upcoming appropriations bill is an item for forty million dollars earmarked for the completion of the Hoover project intended to control water flow for Nevada, Arizona, and California.

Keenly aware that the Depression, without an accountable economy, could be a mortal blow to democracy, McClean has in mind sacrificing the extra million dollar irrigation appropriation the committee has offered his state. He also wants the committee to trim the forty million dollar appropriation for the dam, so as not to play into the Nevada construction company's money-grab, knowing the U.S. Treasury has been very hard hit and thrift is the watchword against the Treasury's collapse.

McClean's idealism worries the committee members, who are beyond eager to have Chairman Gray agree to fund the items that they have requested, irrespective of their excessive cost, questionable value, or actual necessity. The projects that Gray has approved for inclusion are, among others, veteran's hospitals, river and harbor dredging, insane asylums, and post offices.

Chairman Gray has flatly rejected Congressman Wingblatt's bid for the establishment of a guard patrol of the Canadian border to rid the area of the Japanese beetle, since it is affirmed there are no beetles on the Canadian border. He has disapproved Congresswoman McMurty's request for nursing stations nationwide to dispense contraception information. He has denied the petition of Solomon Fitzmaurice, a rough, hard-drinking congressman of three decades' standing, to have the Atlantic Fleet anchored every summer at Rocky Point, Long Island, instead of at Hampton Roads, Virginia, where it has summered since 1812. This relocation would be a tremendous boon to Fitzmaurice's real estate holdings, resorts, and chain of speakeasies in the Rocky Point area.

The Bill has been porked up now to 470 million, with nearly every lobby in Washington having a section, and Simeon Gray is afraid that it's so overloaded the President will veto it.

McClean says that the entire bill should be killed: the dam work can be done for much less; pork has added two hundred million for totally useless, extravagant, and ridiculous projects; and in his close study of the bill McClean has found private graft. With this bomb-shell the conflict between Gray and McClean explodes. Angry and frustrated, Chairman Gray uses his gavel and adjourns the meeting abruptly.

Alan apologizes to Gray for disrupting the committee's proceed-ings but says he has found reason to suspect the chairman himself, since Gray owns considerable stock in a Culver bank that is in shaky condition, and the location of the proposed Culver penitentiary close by and the spending of government money would save the Culver bank from bankruptcy.

Gray protests his unawareness of the alleged Culver situation, so Alan insists that Gray eliminate the item, otherwise he threatens to fight to kill the bill.

Marjorie, who has overheard the conversation, tells her father she is not satisfied with his answer to Alan that he is not responsible for the penitentiary appropriation request, and points out that all United States banks, not his alone, are in deep trouble.

Gray admits that if the newspapers knew about the condition of the Culver bank and his relationship to it, coupled with the item on the appropriations bill, they would go after him like a pack of wolves and make him out to be a crook. Arrangements for the peniten-tiary were made when he was away, he claims, and when he learned about it, he didn't feel he could deny his own hometown people the benefit of what was offered them.

Alan understands now that he can't attack the corruption of the committee without also attacking Marjorie's father. He is more than a whistle-blower. He is going against a gang of professional grafters who have every year and for decades served in the House grabbing millions from the national treasury.

Meanwhile, even though the deadline for inclusion in the bill has passed, Eddie Wister and Sprague, the president of Appalachian Steel with whom Eddie is allied as lobbyist, have applied to Gray to be approved for twenty-five million dollars for two battleships in the Pacific to counter the growing strength of the Japanese navy. To coerce Gray, Wister has investigated the chairman and learned that he himself applied for and approved the penitentiary for Culver, showing that he is as greedy as everyone else.

Playwright Anderson's Solomon Fitzmaurice is one of the most fascinating and frightening characters in any of the Pulitzer Prize plays. He is a veteran in the tricky Washington game of "promise and don't deliver," the game all politicians play, always with an eye to how much money one can come away with, and he believes he has discovered a simple formula for determining what is right and what is wrong in politics. The one rule is that God is always on the money side and God never loses. Fitzmaurice has found in the thirty years he has been in Washington that people are completely ignorant and incompetent to see the chicanery of the money-merchants in Washington.

Given that there are far more dishonest men than honest ones, Alan McClean asks Fitzmaurice, what if the dishonest were to get control of government? Would they themselves be governed by the adage that honesty is the best policy? Fitzmaurice defends his fraudulent political life with the philosophy that the only business of government is graft, special privilege, and corruption—which is allowed because of its by-product, a seeming sense of order, without which necessary condition the IRS could not make tax collections.

Recognizing Gray as part of the brigand gang determined to steal from the people, McClean intends to overload the appropriations bill with as many items as possible, to make it impossible for any politician to vote for it. He is shocked to learn that his future father-in-law faces jail if the bill does not pass, because, as the major stock-holder of the Culver bank, he has stacked phony federal securities in the vault as collateral for the bank's Treasury cash loans.

The dramatic impact of the play lies in McClean's dilemma of how to deal with the extreme political right, represented by Gray and Fitzmaurice and the unseen, but equally dangerous extreme left, with its hidden communist cells espousing revolution.

When the Appropriations Committee meets, McClean presents a revised roster of items that reinstates every request Gray denied earlier, including also Wister's two battleships and Fitzmaurice's Atlantic Fleet relocation, these last two entered after the deadline set for inclusion. The bill now stands at 475 million, and Gray warns the committee that Alan has overloaded it on purpose.

The next day the bill, unwieldy as it is, is presented in the House and a *Washington Tribune* editorial lambastes it as a plunder-grab at the U.S. Treasury. Everyone knows the President will veto the bill, but if the House passes it with a two-thirds majority, the President's veto will be overridden.

Marjorie pleads with Alan to change his bloc of opposition, to allow the bill to pass to keep her father from going to jail. Alan refuses to be compromised, saying he's in a fight for a basic principle, something he truly believes in and has no right to give away.

In the Committee Room, a few hours later that evening, all the congresspeople are celebrating because the bill has passed with a two-thirds majority. Alan tells the celebrants angrily that they are a gang of crooks and should all get out of Washington.

Fitzmaurice disagrees with Alan, presenting his capitalist philosophy of governance: Grab all you can from everyone, rob the Treasury, plunder the natural resources. Gamble and win a fortune from the Wall Street Christmas tree. Learn the skills for graft that in the past made the robber barons of America into a rich, powerful aristocracy. In time, the capitalist trickle-down economy may lift Americans out of the depths of the Depression.

Echoing the amorality of Nietzsche's Superman, Fitzmaurice calls for the reincarnation of those Silurian giants who ruled the Earth with tyrannical force in a more magnificent age. Those Supermen stole billions and gutted whole states as they dug this country's oil wells, built the railroads, and invented a prosperity for themselves—and, knowing that there can never be an honest government, he prays to see these giants again.

Fitzmaurice conjures up the robber barons and spoilers of the nineteenth century as heroic. Alan's is the hopeful voice of the future, saying that people are better informed than this Washington gang seems to believe and will no longer tolerate politicians' greed and fraud.

Speaking as an ardent patriot, McClean says that 150 years ago, in 1779, the framers of the Constitution struggled to find the best government at the birth of this nation, but governments need constant examination and change, and sometimes even replacement, just as these congresspeople must be replaced by their constituents when their proposed legislation and their voting records are made known. The voters have to know if it is time for a change, a time to vote out the person who is *mis*representing them in government.

To his fellow congresspeople McClean is laughable. If Alan shoots his mouth off and gets some press coverage, they will answer with character assassination, but Fitzmaurice is confident there's nothing to worry about—McClean is simply confrontational, he says, and it will all blow over.

Fitzmaurice continues, pointing out with a sinister gloat that there are natural human elements—apathy, indifference, ignorance, and cowardice—working to keep a guy like him in office. With a laugh, he agrees that the committee is a gang of crooks, but he's been in the House for eighteen years now, and nobody who didn't know better would believe that an old guy like him could be a crook.

At the end of the play, Anderson's great dialogue exchange between McClean and Gray gets to the heart of the conflict. McClean asks Gray if honesty is at all possible in Washington. Gray replies that honesty is unknown in any government and impossible in the capitalist system, where every man is for himself and the nation be damned.

This spurs McClean to fight on, because he believes that the desperation of the American people in this time of Depression may move them to rise up in revolution against the government and that America might be transformed into a dictatorship as has happened in many European countries. He must fight against those lawmakers who are blind to their responsibilities—to their constituents and to the principles of democracy—though they counter with insinuations that McClean speaks treason, the words of a communist.

Anderson ends this insightful play sadly but honestly, with the brigands and robber barons on the right in control of Washington's dirty politics. They scoff that it makes no difference whether or not McClean informs the newspapers or the media about their machinations. The citizens of this nation will remain as apathetic as always. Maxwell Anderson poses the moral question: Is there any chance of finding integrity in Washington?

In the real world of the twenty-first century the Sol Fitzmaurices have survived and multiplied as corporation presidents, a new race of monstrous Silurian giants, circumventing the restriction of government regulation and law. In fact, they now have full government support as they contend with Labor, threatening the extinction of the middle class. In the marketplace of Wall Street, greed is still the moral good, and profit is the best policy . The corporate behemoths' wealth gives them incredible power, via lobbies, to create and control the making of the law in Washington and every state capital.

The dramatic power of *Both Your Houses* is Maxwell Anderson's challenge to make Americans aware of their government and the foibles of those who constitute it, not only of the legislative branch but of the executive and judiciary branches as well.

Today, after having worked for years in the Congress, making all kinds of friendships, swapping favors, and establishing long-term commitments, it has now become the custom for lawmakers to set up a lobbyist's office, even before their term in office is over. Instead of being named CEOs of thriving insurance corporations, today's politicos have made for themselves a great retirement benefit as lobbyists, private operatives, akin to private Appropriations Committees with congressional entrees and powers to harvest rewards for past and present political gifts.

Imagine Maxwell Anderson updating this play to October 2005, when the Republican Congress Appropriations Bill provided one and a half billion dollars to the House Transportation and Infrastructure Committee Chairman, Don Young, Republican from the state of Alaska, for the construction of two bridges to nowhere. As reported in the *Washintgon Post* of October 21, 2005, this appropriation was nationally recognized as pork for the Alaskan congressman, and a total waste of resources, especially since New Orleans and the Gulf Coast had been utterly devastated by the Hurricane Katrina and left to plead for monies that were not forthcoming to house and feed people who survived the disaster.

The play's major theme and message is as important today as it was in 1933. Anderson's *Both Your Houses* is deserving of close study in every American high school civics and psychology classroom. Despite the fact that on the surface the play decries politics as a viable career for any idealistic, ethical American youth, portraying Washington as the wrong place and elected politicos as the wrong people to associate with, Anderson's play asserts that Washington is exactly where idealistic and ethical young people must go to protect American democracy and run crooks out of government.

Anderson's play disturbs one's equanimity as it incites citizens to consider what they can do to insure that corrections are made in the selection process of candidates and that there be close, follow-up evaluation of each politician's activities, liaisons, and voting records.

Both Your Houses is a very angry play about the nature of the people in Washington in whom Americans have put their trust, and with blind faith continue trusting even when they are not worthy, having proved themselves immoral, making a mockery of the law and order of government.

State of the Union (1945–1946)
by Russel Crouse and Howard Lindsay

A Play in Three Acts. Produced by Leland Hayward. Staged by Bretaigne Windust. Opened on Broadway at the Hudson Theater, November 14, 1945.

The Original Cast

James Conover	Minor Watson
Spike McManus	Myron McCormick
Kay Thorndyke	Kay Johnson
Grant Matthews	Ralph Bellamy
Norah	Helen Ray
Mary Matthews	Ruth Hussey
Stevens	John Rowe
Bellboy	Howard Graham

Waiter	Robert Toms
Sam Parrish	Herbert Heyes
Swenson	Fred Ayres Cotton
Judge Jefferson Davis Alexander	G. Albert Smith
Mrs. Alexander	Maidel Turner
Jennie	Madeline King
Mrs. Draper	Aline McDermott
William Hardy	Victor Sutherland
Senator Lauterback	George Lessey

In his home study in Washington, D.C., James Conover, a high-ranking Republican politico, is a member of the party's search committee looking for the right candidate to be nominated at the 1948 Republican National Convention, hopefully to go forward to win the national election.

Franklin Delano Roosevelt has occupied the White House since 1933, winning over the incumbent, one-term President Herbert Hoover, and then defeating the Republican contenders Alfred Landon in 1936 and Wendell Willkie in 1940. In the election of 1944, Roosevelt ran for an unprecedented and controversial fourth term and won against the Republican Thomas E. Dewey.

Roosevelt's innovative New Deal saved the nation from a societal revolution. Then he mobilized America's war effort to fight and defeat the Axis powers in 1945. Now, with the war over, America has to resolve many national problems. Among the most critical, just as today, is the status of unions and the relationship between labor and management.

The major symbol of *State of the Union* is Washington, D.C., itself, a hotbed of political intrigue, fraud, and deceit. Grant Matthews is a home-front hero who uncomfortably finds himself in that hostile environment.

In the meeting taking place in Conover's Washington, D.C., study are Mrs. Kay Thorndyke, the owner-publisher of several major city newspapers; Spike MacManus, a newspaperman reputed to be the best informed PR man and political organizer in Washington, D.C.; and Grant Matthews, CEO of one of America's largest airplane manufacturing groups, who has reluctantly allowed Mrs. Thorndyke to entice him to Conover's home.

As a productive and patriotic CEO of an unnamed aircraft factory system that could be likened to Ford's Willow Run factory, hailed as one of the seven wonders of the world, Grant Matthews is a youthful American industrialist, endowed with a pragmatic sense of reasonableness in his relationship with labor and management. However, being human, Matthews has failings and has made inappropriate choices in his personal life, namely an extramarital sexual liaison that will be terminated and fully forgiven by the time the final curtain falls.

Recently Matthews has made front page headlines addressing the Senate Investigating Committee about his concern that the nation is in danger of an economic civil war, its unity shaken by devastating inflation. In a speech given in Cleveland, Matthews distinguished himself as he exhorted management and labor, big business and unions to work together with the same united effort that brought the Allied victory in World War II.

Conover believes Matthews to be the strongest candidate the committee has considered to go up against Roosevelt. In order to test Matthews' persuasive power, stamina, and charisma as a possible candidate for the presidency, the political boss proposes that Matthews tour the country and speak informally on national issues. Conover is aware that Matthews' extramarital affair with Kay Thorndyke has been going on for more than a year, and to dispel any possible rumors that would be injurious, he asks that Matthews' estranged wife Mary accompany him on the tour.

Skeptical at first, Mary finally agrees to go, aware that she is contesting with the duplicitous Kay Thorndyke to influence the shaping of Matthews' political character.

As Mary gives Grant courage to realize and declare his own personal political philosophy, she wins back his love. Matthews stands up to champion democratic principles in fearless opposition to the fascistic political positions commanded by Conover and the powerful politicos.

In this sophisticated, political comedy, playwrights Lindsay and Crouse present a portrait of the mid-century, profit-oriented businessman as idealistic, a change from the common image of the self-centered businessman inspired only by the profit motive. Matthews' foil and dramatic antagonist is Jim Conover, the professional Republican politician who rides roughshod over principles and people in his unrelenting quest for power and profit.

As drawn by the playwrights, Jim Conover and Kay Thorndyke are a power-hungry pair as cunning as they are charming. To ensnare and control Matthews, Kay Thorndyke, a recent widow, is conducting an immoral sexual liaison. Both she and her confidant Conover are scheming to win the nomination for Matthews and then control mass media to promote "silent money" contributions to the campaign from special interest groups who have been promised gain via political favors if Matthews wins.

As a result of head-on collision with Conover's super-conservative and anti-liberal principles, Matthews comes to realize that the conflicts in leadership in government are far different from those he knew in airplane manufacture. In many ways American politics is governed by those same ruthless principles that govern the corporate world's warfare associated with takeovers and the control of markets. Matthews will not follow the party line, which calls for legislation that will result in inflation, making the rich richer, indifferent to the welfare of the middle and lower classes.

The play is a dramatic admonition to anyone interested in government service to be prepared for the subtle and controlling ferocity of Washington's jackals. Like Charles Dickens, the playwrights have utilized telling names for the two antagonists: Conover, the politico-con-artist, and the dangerous Kay Thorndyke, a rugged player in politics and big business, a power-woman for the twentieth century.

Thorndyke is determined to control the aspiring presidential nominee via her wealth, her sex, and the power of the Fourth Estate, her newspaper presses. The inspiration for this unique character is probably the powerhouse Katherine Graham, who inherited ownership of the *Washington Post*, the most influential publication in Washington, and whose strong will to control is evident in this excerpt from a 1988 interview:

> We live in a dirty and dangerous world. There are some things the general public does not need to know and shouldn't. I believe democracy flourishes when the government can take legitimate steps to keep its secrets and when the press can decide whether to print what it knows.[3]

How different is this censorship from the concept of the controlled presses of the German Nazis or those of the Russian Communists or today's Chinese Communist media? Mrs. Graham's philosophy of privileged, secret, restricted and controlled information is fundamentally undemocratic as it ironically demeans the public mind. The easy defense is that national security disallows informing this country's enemies of privileged information that would be useful to them.

When Matthew indicates he is withdrawing from the political fray at the play's end, we, the American audience, are disappointed because we had hoped for a courageous champion, a political Superman-to-the-rescue. It is painful to realize that democracy can so easily be defeated by the powerful greed and cunning of insatiable politicians. We hope that Mary will encourage Matthew not to surrender, but to come forward to support America in time of crisis, to champion democratic principles and set the state of the Union straight.

State of the Union ends on a compassionate and prophetic note: the character of the hero is known by his works. Grant Matthews cares about the American people and proposes that the nation that came together so strongly in wartime can come together in peacetime to win the fight against poverty and ignorance and greed.

PART FOUR

Morality and Survival in a Materialist Society

CHAPTER THIRTEEN

The Agrarian Hero

From the first English settlement in the seventeenth century to 1850, America was essentially an agricultural country, its economy bolstered by farmers selling grain and dairy products in excess of their own families' needs to regional and European markets. Farming was a family business. The individual farmer was solely responsible for its operation and he could hire workers or enlist his own childen to bolster his labor force.

Throughout the eighteenth and nineteenth centuries the gross national product of the United States was based on its agricultural production. During the First World War American farmers reaped a bonanza supplying France and Britain with meat and grain But after the 1918 Armistice,when France and Britain were able to operate their farms, the market became glutted, prices fell, and many American farmers went bankrupt.

Meanwhile, with the advent of the Industrial Revolution, city life had become a magnet for trade and entertainment. European immigrants were pouring into American cities to work in sweatshops, factories and mills, and the culture they brought with them from their native lands made the cities interesting and attractive to young people growing up on the farms.

Some of those young people had already become acquainted first-hand with the excitement of urbane European culture when serving in the AEF during World War I. Attesting to the significance of this Americans-abroad experience is this popular song of the period, the 1919 ballad by Sam M. Lewis and Joe Young, "How Ya Gonna Keep 'Em Down on the Farm (After They've Seen Paree)?"

The chorus asks the question about the doughboys who will be coming home after the war:

> How ya gonna keep 'em down on the farm,
> After they've seen Paree?
> How ya gonna keep em away from Broadway,
> Jazzin' around, and paintin' the town?
> How ya gonna keep 'em away from harm?
> That's a mystery.
> They'll never want to see a rake or plow,
> And who the deuce can parley vous a cow?
> How ya gonna keep 'em down on the farm,
> After they've seen Paree?

In 1908, the Country Life Commission was established by President Theodore Roosevelt to help improve farm living conditions and to explore the attitudes and problems that beset farm wives, ultimately aiming to keep farmers' children on farms to share in their ownership and management rather than have them move to the cities. While the wages in industry were kept very low, even as most industries showed ever-increasing profits, they were still many times higher than the earnings of hardworking farm laborers.

Life on the farm was a rugged, sunup-to-sundown endless effort in cultivating, harvesting, and caring for livestock. Very few farms had electricity or hookups for running water and sanitation. The kerosene lamp, home-dug wells, and outhouse did not enhance the farmer's strenuous existence. In addition to the downturn in the economy that sent hundreds of thousands of farmers into bankruptcy in the 1920s, the hazards of farm life were beyond human control; storms, droughts, flooding, or insect infestation could turn a growing season into a total economic disaster.

The protagonists of these two Pulitzer Prize plays of the early 1920s, *Beyond the Horizon* and *Icebound*, confront the substantial trials of farming the soil, struggling with their families, their land, and their own longing for the excitement of the world beyond the farm. In tandem with their empathy for the reluctant farmer, these plays present the essential morality and unique nature of the farmer as a hero, a stalwart individualist who enjoys the muscular challenge of working with the earth and the peace that living close to nature brings—to those who were born to feel it.

Beyond the Horizon (1919–1920)
by Eugene O'Neill

A Play in Three Acts. Produced by John D. Williams. Staged by John D. Williams, Eugene O'Neill, and Homer Saint-Gaudens. Opened on Broadway at a Special Matinee at the Morosco Theater, February 3, 1920.

The Original Cast

Robert Mayo	Richard Bennett
Andrew Mayo	Edward Arnold
Ruth Atkins	Helen MacKeller
Captain Dick Scott	Max Mitzel
Mrs. Kate Mayo	Mary Jeffery
James Mayo	Erville Alderson
Mrs. Atkins	Louise Closser Hale
Mary	Elfin Finn
Ben	George Hadden
Doctor Fawcett	George Riddell

Beyond the Horizon (1920) is a dramatic precursor to *Long Day's Journey into Night* (1957), O'Neill's masterpiece. Together both plays flesh out a view of the people and problems that shaped the greatest American playwright.

The major symbol of Eugene O'Neill's *Beyond the Horizon* is the Road, the central dynamic that beckons the tormented Robert Mayo throughout the play. The Road that destiny promised him is there to lead him beyond the horizon, but the Road is *not* taken.

Robert's failure to leave the farm creates tensions and a depressing state of mind that grievously aggravate his tuberculosis.

It is Robert's own free but ill-fated choice to stay on the farm, rather than ship out to explore the mysteries of the world, his life's dream. Ruth's declaration of love for him, for his poetic nature, for his love of learning, move him to stay. Ironically, just a few years later, there is an awful reversal as Ruth expresses her utter contempt for him, having come to see his reading and contemplation as an atttempt to escape from responsibility. As Ruth torments him for his incompetence in practical farm management, Robert realizes he has been untrue to his deepest nature, his aesthetic self.

One of the greatest dramatic moments in the play is Ruth and Robert's cruel confrontation over their failed marriage. Ruth asks her husband what he thinks about a woman forced to live with a man she can't love or respect, who considers her ignorant and makes her feel inferior. Viciously, she declares that if she had known then what she knows now—that he is weak and spineless—she would have killed herself rather than marry him. But instead she allowed herself to be wooed away from his brother Andrew by his Romantic notions, knowing within a month that she had made a grave mistake.

Throughout the play, hopeless of ever realizing his dream of an adventurous life in search of the beauty of nature, Robert has been slowly dying of tuberculosis. In the last scene, knowing his death is at hand, he rushes out to the Road to see the sun rise over the horizon. For Ruth and the brokenhearted Andrew there is no triumph in Robert's defeat.

O'Neill's life was filled with physical and emotional suffering that fostered his psychic introspection; he discovered within himself themes that he believed mattered and gave them undying life in the vision of his plays. The major theme of *Beyond the Horizon* is the wisdom of Socrates voiced by Polonius in Shakespeare's *Hamlet*: "To thine own self be true." Neither of the two protagonists of the play, Andrew Mayo or Robert Mayo, is true to his nature, and both live out joyless, loveless lives.

Their authoritarian father, Edgar Mayo, knows full well the nature of his sons: that Andrew has herding and farming in his blood and has committed himself to assume the responsibilities of farm management; and that the younger Robert, emotionally and physically damaged by tuberculosis, looks on the farm as a prison and wants to sail out in search of the aesthete's Truth, Beauty. The old man is angered when Andrew and Robert swap life-directions, Andrew going out to sea and Robert attempting to manage a farm, both destined for a failed life. James's negative and ungiving nature is destructive of both his sons, first damaging Robert by not paying for his college tuition and failing to provide proper medical support for the youth's ill health, then cursing Andrew for turning his back on the land they had farmed together and the future they had planned.

Nothing that Andrew experienced as a sailor is of any value to him emotionally or intellectually. To him, the mysterious East Robert pined to explore is only the filthiest place he has ever seen, with dirty, ragged crowds and narrrow streets littered with all kinds of garbage rotting under the hot sun. His appreciation for Buenos Aires or the Congo is typically pragmatic, noting that one could make a fortune in the grain business in Argentina or in mining diamonds in the heart of Africa.

Unlike the negative and competitive relationship of the Biblical Cain and Abel, Andrew and Robert are loving and supportive brothers. When, in the beginning of the play, Robert asks Ruth to marry him, the shattered Andrew does not declare his own love for Ruth, but opts to leave the Mayo farm and try the seafarer's life, volunteering to ship out with his Uncle Dick in Robert's place. In his sorrow and frustration, he repudiates the farm and all it has meant to him, infuriating his father.

Deeply depressed because he believes he is guilty of creating the irremediable schism in the Mayo family, Robert begs Andrew's forgiveness and swears that if he could have foreseen what was going to take place, he never would have said a word to Ruth about love and marriage and he would have gone with Uncle Dick himself.

There is no turning back, Andrew says, hoping his father will come to understand him without acrimony. In his heart he knows he has to get far away from the farm, that his going clears the air of what could have been a psychologically fierce hostility between the brothers.

In *Beyond the Horizon* and several other of his plays, O'Neill uses the idea of a mysterious Fate motif that drives his characters to a tragic end. No one character is to blame for the fate of all; rather O'Neill suggests that if his players could summon the strength of will, they might find the courage to change their lives. But they lack the maturity for true self-knowledge, which only comes too late.

Why are O'Neill's plays so lauded? What are the qualities that make his plays worthy of the most illustrious prizes?

The poetic power of O'Neill's scenes and characters is unforgettable, impressing us with the power of the playwright's deepest emotions. When Robert is dying, he is convulsed with an unnatural, joyous excitement, declaring that Ruth and he are going to sell the farm and make a new start—that life owes them some happiness after all they've endured; otherwise their suffering is meaningless. There is such passion in Robert's hopeless hope when he says that he believes that all their suffering has been a test by which they might prove themselves worthy of a finer realization, and their dream is going to come true.

In each of his superb plays O'Neill fashions complex characters, drawn out of his own psyche. He writes copious playing notes as if he were director as well as playwright, specifying inflections and smiles and what the players must do with their hands to interpret and convey the passion of the characters. He wishes his actors to slip in under the skin of the characters, with full psychological awareness of their thoughts and feelings. His colloquial, real-speech dialogue has the cadence and power of poetry, as each character reveals flesh-and-blood feelings of hope, fear and love.

Great plays are not specific to one place, one time or one culture. Like the great classics of Aeschylus, Sophocles, Euripides, and Shakespeare, the dramatic voice of the genius speaks with a universality that informs audiences of all cultures and of all eras what it means to be human, to have failings, to strive for goals and win and fail, and to lose both love and life. O'Neill's plays create timeless theater-human-beings who merge into our hearts and minds and teach us the dimension of our own humanity. They teach us humanity's capability to love, to hate, to curse, to bless, to kill, to nurture, to envy, to applaud, to command, to submit, to cry, to laugh, to live, and to die.

Icebound (1922–1923)
by Owen Davis

A Play in Three Acts. Produced by Sam H. Harris. Staged by Sam Forrest. Opened at the Sam H. Harris Theater, February 10, 1923.

The Original Cast

Emma Jordan	Lotta Linthicum
Henry Jordan	John Westley
Nettie Jordan	Boots Wooster
Ella Jordan	Frances Neilson
Sadie Fellows	Eva Condon
Orin Fellows	Andrew J. Lawlor, Jr.
Doctor Curtis	Lawrence Eddinger
Jane Crosby	Phyllis Povah
Judge Bradford	Willard Robertson
Ben Jordan	Robert Ames
Hannah	Edna May Oliver
Jim Jay	Charles Henderson

Icebound, set in the town of Veazie in the farmlands of Penobscot County, Maine, is a portrait of American agrarian society in the 1920s, depicting the transformation of the renegade, shiftless Ben Jordan into a successful farmer and respect-worthy citizen.

The major theme of reformation by love and hard work on the farm supports the foundations of agrarian capitalism, which in 1922 still constituted fifty percent of America's wealth and gross national product. In the early 1900s Maine was largely an agricultural

economy, with urban growth in the state spurred mainly by immigration from French Canada, supplying the labor force for newly
established factories.

The dramatic conflict of *Icebound* revolves around the ownership
and administration of the hugely successful farm managed by the
dying matriarch Mother Jordan, who always favored her last-born
child, Ben. He is accounted a ne'er-do-well, and in the beginning of
the play he is a fugitive from justice, accused of arson.

Mother Jordan's inability to express maternal warmth to her
children seems to have produced a brood of icy-hearted and mean-
spirited offspring, who are ruthlessly greedy in their intra-family
dealings. The title of the play is a metaphor that describes the icy
restrictions of Maine winters and the icy hearts of the Jordan clan.

Over the years, none of Mother Jordan's children has shown any
interest in taking part in the farming business, which has sustained
the Jordan family for generations. Jane Crosby, a distant relative,
has for eight years been Mother Jordan's right-hand administrator,
supervising the farm's dairy, poultry, and agricultural production.
So it is with a modicum of guilt and guarded expectations that the
Jordan heirs gather in Mother Jordan's parlor anticipating her imminent death, waiting to hear the reading of her will.

Henry Jordan, a stout man of fifty, worn down by store-keeping
on Main Street, is the oldest Jordan and is married to Emma, a
heavyset and formidable woman of forty who dotes on the shallow
Nettie, her daughter from a former marriage.

Impatiently waiting for news are Henry's two younger sisters, Ella
Jordan, a jittery, thirty-six-year-old maiden lady, and the widowed,
fortyish Sadie Jordan Fellows with her pasty-faced ten-year-old son
Orin. They are all uncomfortably aware that their mother is dying
upstairs in her bedroom, attended by Dr. Curtis, Jane Cosby, and a
house servant Hannah, while they, her children, have been banned
from her bedside.

Ben, the youngest Jordan and the black sheep of the family, is
absent and unheard from.

As the scene unfolds, the Jordans express their open dislike and
envy of their step-cousin Jane, who has secured the trust of the

dying matriarch and is characterized by Dr. Curtis as one of the most dependable girls he has ever known. Bickering and maligning each other as they sit in the farm parlor, they reveal their petty, malicious natures.

Never able to get along with her mother, Ella shunned the farm and lived in town. She complains that Jane took *her* rightful place and lived free while she had to slave to make hats to pay for her room and board in town.

Henry's wife Emma demands that Henry dismiss Jane from the premises immediately on the old lady's death.

The most virulent criticism is directed against their young brother Ben, who was born very late in their parents' life, when the others were already grown. He is especially scorned because he has always been catered to by his mother. Recently he was indicted by a grand jury on a charge of arson, but he hid away in Bangor and the sheriff couldn't track him down to put him in jail. They name him a good-for-nothing and would like to see him caught and locked up in the state penitentiary in Thomaston.

Suddenly Jane enters with Judge John Bradford, who has served as confidant and advisor to Mrs. Jordan, and in whose office the matriarch's will has been deposited for safekeeping. The Jordan children tell the Judge they hope the money from the estate will be divided into three parts, to exclude Ben, who dramatically appears at that moment, explaining that Jane sent word to him in Bangor of Mother Jordan's grave illness, enclosing money for the trip home to Veazie.

Henry warns Ben that the authorities will be here to get him and that he had better run away again. The brothers come to blows, and Ben throws Henry back against a table.

Dr. Curtis appears on the stairs to tell the Jordans that their mother is upset to hear the fracas below. Just then, however, Hannah comes out of the bedroom calling sharply to the doctor to come into the bedroom right away—that Mother Jordan is expiring.

Emma insists that Henry rule the roost and order Jane off the premises, but Henry says that Jane need not leave until after the funeral, which she readily agrees to do.

But the Judge explains that Mrs. Jordan, who saw her children as vultures waiting for an ailing cow to die in the pasture, decided to leave everything to Jane because she was the only levelheaded, unselfish person whom she could entrust to handle the estate. The Judge, who drew up the will according to Mrs. Jordan's dictation, informs them that Mother Jordan bequeathed to each of her children the sum of one hundred dollars. He adds that in his office he has a sealed letter that Mrs. Jordan wrote to Jane, possibly about the disposition of the property.

Suddenly Jim Jay, a policeman, rings and enters with a warrant for Ben's arrest, having been informed of his presence by his brother Henry. When Jane hears Ben say that he would like to go to his mother's funeral before he goes to prison on the felony charge, she makes a deal with Ben: she will keep him out of prison if he will stay on the farm and work until his trial comes up in the spring. He agrees to work on the farm.

It becomes more and more evident that young Ben has not hardened to the same extent as his brother and sisters. One afternoon he tells Jane that after he served with the American Expeditionary Force in World War I, he stayed on for a while in France after the Armistice. He liked the French people and thought to take up farming there, where farms were small compared with those in America and winters weren't as severe as Maine winters.

He points outside through the window at the huge banks of drifted snow and says that six months of the year, it's like that, "froze up," just like the small, mean-spirited Jordans, half-frozen even before they were born, ice-bound people coming into the world mean and hard so they could live mean and hard lives.

In France people laughed and sang, even though they didn't have much to sing about. He recalls the house where he was billeted, belonging to a French lady whose six merry children were so different from the sour-faced, complaining family he remembered at the dining-room table back home.

Romance begins when Jane buys a sky-blue gown like the one Ben admired worn by the lady who hosted him in France. Asked to come to the homestead by Jane, Judge Bradford spies the light-blue dress popping out of the box beneath the sofa and is delighted to learn that Jane has given herself a lovely birthday gift, and that tonight she'll wear it. The Judge's proposal of marriage comes as a surprise to Jane and to the audience, since the playwright has given us no prior hint of his interest. Her swift rejection brings the focus of the play back to Ben.

Jane wants the Judge to offer Mr. Kimball a new barn to replace the one that burned and to have the indictment against Ben withdrawn, since even the grand jury has not concluded a crime was committed, finding that the fire could have been accidental.

The melodrama ends with Ben exonerated and his most unbelievable character change from wastrel to wonderful. Lastly, Jane follows Mother Jordan's letter-request to transfer ownership of the estate to Ben after his reformation. It is then that Ben realizes for the first time how much he owes Jane, and how much he loves her.

The swift and happy resolution to all the problems in the play is sketchily drawn, as are the characters, resulting in cartoon-like portraits. This is especially true of the hero-protagonist Ben Jordan, whose character provokes so many unanswered questions. How did Mother Jordan show favoritism to Ben? Why did Ben enlist in the A.E.F.? What were his war experiences beyond his being billeted in a French home? What were his army friendships? Who were the other women in his Lothario life?

How did Mother Jordan know that Jane loved Ben? Did he ever know his father? What inspired Jane to love a seemingly angry and unloveable person like Ben? What was his education? His ambition? His work experience? Was he a loner, dismissed by is immediate family? What influence did his peers, such as the Kimball boys, have on his development? Why did he have trouble and fight with his friends? When Ben came back from the war, why didn't Jane go to meet him as he wanted? Did he correspond with his mother? With Jane?

How often did Ben get into fights, in and outside of bars? Was he a notorious character? Was he respected as a veteran of the war? After the grand jury hearing, why couldn't the authorities locate Ben? How did Jane manage to send him the money to come to Veazie? Why did he run away in the first place, hiding out as an outlaw, if he was innocent?

Why did Mother Jordan believe that Jane could change him? What was the earlier relationship between Ben and Jane?

Despite all the lacunae in its structure, *Icebound* is fascinating theater and has great appeal as a regionalist melodrama reflecting the local color of Veazie, Maine, a real rural community. Its major theme is an affirmation of the health of the outdoor, agrarian life which creates upright, rugged, American individualism.

Icebound's symbolism is easily translated: love thaws the icy heart; love disciplines the irresponsible spirit.

CHAPTER FOURTEEN

The Capitalist Hero

Almost two hundred years ago, in 1831, Gustave de Beaumont, a friend and traveling companion of Alexis De Tocqueville, the French social historian and author of *Democracy in America*, came to America to study the young country's social and political system. De Beaumont wrote in his *Journal*:

> The American male from his earliest youth is devoted to business; hardly has he learned to read and write when he becomes a merchant. The first sound in his ears is the clink of money; the first voice he hears is that of self-interest; he breathes at birth the air of industry and all his early impressions persuade him that a business career is the only one becoming a man.[1]

Probably the most popular books of the entire twentieth century on this same subject are Eric Fromm's *Man for Himself* and Dale Carnegie's *How to Win Friends and Influence People.* Arthur Miller's Willy Loman, a failure, and Shepherd Mead's J. Pierpont Finch, a success, are dramatic realizations of both Fromm and Carnegie, diametrically opposite portraits of the American male "devoted to business," the salesman-middleman and corporate man in the twentieth century.

Willy Loman is a model of the marketing orientation personality, selling himself even before he attempts to sell his product. Finch follows the corporation marketing orientation, with no personal contact with customers but absolute concern for in-house status.

Both Loman and Finch are faithful to the commandments of the American businessman's ethics, that persistence and loyalty pay off—in some way mirroring the Calvinist ethic that asserts that God preordains election and gives prosperity to His faithful. However, in neither play is Divinity ever summoned.

How to Succeed in Business Without Really Trying and *Death of a Salesman* both dramatize the amorality or immorality of capitalism. The hero is in conflict within the system, under constant pressure to produce in a ruthless competition, with tenuous security.

Like a Marxist script, *Death of a Salesman* raises questions about an economic system that does not provide job security, health benefits, or provisions for retirement to a worker after thirty years of faithful service to an indifferent, self-centered, self-indulgent management.

In historical time Miller's play looks backward and forward, from before the stock market crash of 1929 throughout the Depression years, dramatizing Willy's failure as a father, as a husband, and finally as a salesman.

After the onslaught of the Depression, the Roosevelt New Deal program saw the middle class and the small businessman as the strength of the American economy. Unemployment, bread lines, vagrancy, and poverty were causing a dangerous panic. People had to struggle to make a living in an unstable economy without job security.

But Willy Loman values what he believes is his job security, working with dedication for the small, Wagner family–controlled business. The distribution of the manufactured product has been dependent on a team of salesmen assigned to prescribed territories, working on commission and writing orders directly with the purchasing agents of department stores. With his sample cases full, Willy travels the New England territory, far from his Brooklyn home, driving alone in his prized Chevy.

More than two decades later in the 1960s, *How to Succeed in Business Without Really Trying* reflects a new brand of marketing that extends worldwide by means of electronic communications and air transportation. World Wide Wicket's home base may be in New

York City, but satellite offices exist around the world. With every imaginable subterfuge, Finch charts his route of advancement beginning in the lowly mailroom, where orders are first processed, to the Madison Avenue penthouse suite of the chairman of the board.

Each play offers dramatic evidence of the ruthlessness of the American business world—a world that is beyond human, as full of feeling as an adding machine.

Death of a Salesman (1948–1949)
by Arthur Miller

A Play in Two Acts. Produced by Kermit Bloomgarden and Walter Fried. Staged by Elia Kazan. Opened on Broadway at the Morosco Theater, February 10, 1949.

The Original Cast

Willy Loman	Lee J. Cobb
Linda	Mildred Dunnock
Biff	Arthur Kennedy
Happy	Cameron Mitchell
Bernard	Don Keefer
The Woman	Winifred Cushing
Charley	Howard Smith
Uncle Ben	Thomas Chalmers
Howard Wagner	Alan Hewitt
Jenny	Ann Driscoll
Stanley	Tom Pedi
Miss Forsythe	Constance Ford
Letta	Hope Cameron

In *Death of a Salesman* Arthur Miller aims to portray Willy Loman as a typical American "Everyman" breadwinner during America's Depression years, any time between 1929 and 1941.

The stage set allows movement throughout the two-story frame house whose fourth wall is gone, revealing the various rooms of the interior, while downstage, outside the house, there is an area that presents a variety of imagined settings for simultaneous and continuous action, representing disparate times and places, past and present. The sound of a lonely flute, the musical instrument that Willy's father played, signals an interweaving of the realism of the present moment with visions recalled from the past or imagined beyond the realm of normal experience.

The playwright does not indicate how Willy and Linda met and married. We meet them in the house they bought as a young couple, where they raised their two sons. Now, in late middle age, with his energy and confidence waning, Willy must still work hard to make the monthly mortgage payments and to maintain his home and his car, a salesman's major expense. His children have grown up and left, and he and Linda are alone. This is the simple, skeletal narrative of *Death of a Salesman*, it may be the bare-bones scenario of all family life, which may account for this play's singular popularity around the world.

In the very first scene of the play, Willy is identified as mentally ill, his neurosis evidenced by his anxiety-ridden behavior, obsessive thoughts, and feelings of guilt. As the first act progresses, Linda reveals that she has discovered a gas pipe extension in the cellar and realized Willy's intention to commit suicide. She tells her sons, but neither of them considers consulting a psychiatrist—probably because Willy has no health coverage with his firm, the Wagner Company. The cost of private psychiatric treatment is prohibitive to the Lomans, as is the embarrassment of facing the dire truth of mental illness.

In the first scene, Willy has just turned his car around and come home, unable to focus on the road. He is veering irresistibly toward self-destruction. For seventeen long years, he has been living with terrible feelings of guilt at having been found in a sexual encounter with a Miss Francis, a secretary to a department store buyer, in a Boston hotel room by his son Biff.

When Biff happened upon his father's extramarital liaison, he was nineteen and about to graduate from high school. Since then, Biff, now thirty-six, has been away from home, bumming around the country, and has never disclosed his father's secret to anyone.

But all the time, in Willy's disturbed mind Biff looms like Banquo, the specter pointing a finger at him, unrelentingly, unforgivingly.

Perhaps even more painfully, Biff has had his revenge by failing to make something of himself as Willy always trusted he would. Sabotaging every opportunity, he is determined to prove to his father that Willy's great faith in him—just like his own faith in his father before he surprised him at the hotel—was misplaced. "I'm a dime a dozen," he pleads with his father, "and so are you!"[2]

While Willy's scenes with Biff are either memories or real-time confrontations, we see him conversing with another ghostly figure, his brother Ben, who seems to speak to Willy from beyond the grave. When Willy receives news of Ben's death, Ben's doppelganger appears onstage and checks his watch, saying he has to catch a train to Alaska. He asks why Willy's not up there already, where the opportunities for making a fortune are terrific. But Willy has no courage to venture into unknown territories.

Later Miller repeats his remarkable use of the real/surreal in the gripping scene between the brothers reflecting their early family life. Their father left when Willy was only three, and Ben, who was much older, soon followed him. Ben identifies with their father and has definite memories of him, while Willy has always felt denied father-love and has hungered throughout his life to be well liked by everyone he encounters.

Ben's cruel assessment is that Willy wouldn't have merited love or praise from their wonderfully creative father because he lacked inventiveness and talent, so unlike the father who made more in a week than Willy could make in a lifetime. Ben presents the materialist definition of a creditable man, measuring his worth is his earning power in America's capitalist society.

Willy wants his sons to emulate Ben's model, to have the courage to walk into the jungle and come out millionaires—and on his single brotherly visit while Biff and Happy are growing up, Ben tells Willy he is doing a first-rate job with his sons. It is a baseless comment; without his father or his brother in his life, Willy is floundering, uncertain how to teach his sons to succeed in the world, and during

Ben's visit they are caught stealing lumber from a construction site with Willy's approval. But Willy believes they can be forgiven anything and are bound to succeed, so long as—like the best salesmen—they are well liked.

Ironically, at Willy's gravesite, where evaluations of his life are voiced, Biff discounts everything Willy achieved as a salesman, saying that he taught his sons the wrong values, and that there is more of his spirit in the front stoop that he built than in all the sales he ever made.

Charley agrees that Willy was a happy man if he had a batch of cement, lumber, something tangible to build with, that the intangibility of sales gave him no reassuring foundation on which to build his life. Peddling what he believed was the best product he could get hold of, Willy had the salesman's veneer, a smile, a joke, a handshake, and a shoeshine.

Only Linda, his wife for thirty-five years, questions the morality of his suicide, rationalizing that no one has come to the funeral because they blame him, instead of having pity on him.

This raises the question: Is Willy a tragic figure to be pitied?

On the first anniversary of the Broadway opening, playwright Miller wrote in the *New York Times* that "the tragedy of Willy Loman is that he gave his life, or sold it, in order to justify the waste of it." Miller identifies the play as a tragedy and Willy Loman as a tragic hero.

Yet *Death of a Salesman* is not a tragedy in Aristotelian terms. In his *Poetics*, Aristotle wrote that the character of the hero must be one whom the audience can admire, even though as a human being he is flawed. The Fates have given the hero a tragic flaw, though he has no knowledge of it until it comes to the fore when the hero is caught in overwhelming circumstances. He struggles valiantly but in vain to choose the right path, to extricate himself from the encircling web of damning circumstances that serve to bring about his downfall or death.

Is Willy Loman's having extramarital sex for a business purpose (access to buyers) a tragic flaw? Is his intent to commit suicide to benefit his family—believing his life insurance policy made him worth more dead than alive—heroic?

Willy is a complex character, an adulterer, a compulsive liar, a braggart, a user, a phony, a brand-name materialist, a man whose smile must be decoded, whose deep-rooted envy breeds self-hate. So, the question must be asked: Does Willy Loman have any qualities that one can admire?

A true hero, Aristotelian or otherwise, is to be admired despite his tragic flaw; he can be forgiven his wrongdoing since he pays the price for that failing. Willy has too many flaws and too few redeeming features. His greatest flaw and sin is having inculcated his sons with the wrong set of values, encouraging their immorality.

However, Willy *can* be pitied for his lack of courage to battle the economic hardships that nearly all Americans had to suffer to survive in the Depression during the thirties, when Marxist communism was popular among the young intellectuals and liberals. *Death of a Salesman*'s strong popular appeal comes from the playwright's denunciation of the insensitive immorality of the American capitalist system that cares so little for the plight of the ordinary worker. Though he never articulates it specifically in this play, Miller is implying, as a one-time fervent political leftist, that changes are needed in the current capitalist system.

For Willy, there is little meaning to life except his vanity as a salesman. His dream is to become a sales celebrity, like his model and the major symbol of the play, David Singleman, the best-liked salesman of all time, greeted with respect by all the city mayors in New England.

Again and again Willy tries to make himself and his family believe he has been establishing a respectful personal relationship with all the major stores' merchandise buyers with his cultivated smile and a kind of thought-power that encourages them to smile back at him, friend to friend.

Willy's bitter failure takes solid form in the poignant scene between employee and employer, Willy Loman versus Howard Wagner, the firm's new director, probably the greatest scene of the play.

It is with intensely submerged and conflicting emotions that Willy has come to plead with Howard Wagner, his own godson whom he named at birth. Now the godfather is begging the godson to give his old New England territory back to him, painfully aware that his economic survival depends on it. It is ironic that Howard Wagner addresses Willy, his senior by forty years, demeaningly as "kid."

There is no trace of compassion in Howard Wagner for Willy's plight. Willy's helplessness moves audiences most deeply, because they too have lived through times when the cry for survival was like a raw wound.

The cruelty of management is compounded beyond indifference when Howard proudly tells Willy to listen to his five-year-old child recite, on a tape deck, an alphabetical listing of all the state capitals. The playwright makes the moment both ironical and poetical as state after state is named by the child in a Whitmanesque vista of America's boundless business territories, infinite possibilities for salesmen to come, but not for Willy. Still, though we pity him, Willy is not heroic.

Linda is the hero of *Death of a Salesman* and its most compelling force, but also the person whom we know least about. We know more about Miss Francis, the Woman in Boston, about her work, her sisters, and her daily life. We know more about the prostitute Miss Forsythe's background than Linda's. We wonder about Linda—where she grew up, in what kind of family, with what kind of education. And, above all, why did she marry Willy?

As a hero Linda is long-suffering, totally devoted, and in the end betrayed, bereft, and uncared for. The moral voice of the play, she understands that the Loman men are less than they believe themselves to be, but she encourages them constantly to do the right thing, to be honest, and, by her example, to build within themselves a solid foundation of self, based on integrity and responsible performance, not vague, false, superman dreams. Ever faithful, Linda stands behind Willy, a positive supportive force, never adding the destructive burden of negative criticism. She is the sole person of the play who is selflessly other-concerned, motivated by love, accepting each hardship as it comes with dignity and courage.

The lone flute that played at the beginning of the drama starts to play Willy's theme as Linda muses at her husband's gravesite that she doesn't understand why he did it, why he left her alone. She wants to feel he's just away on another trip, but she knows that he will never come back. And the house he loved so much is empty with no one but her to live in it now.

The flute plays its sad obbligato as the lights begin to fade over the Loman house and the towers of the apartments come into sharp focus.

How to Succeed in Business Without Really Trying (1961–1962)
by Abe Burrows, Jack Weinstock, and Willy Gilbert

A Play in Two Acts. Based on the novel by Shepherd Mead. Music and Lyrics by Frank Loesser. Produced by Cy Feuer and Ernest Martin in Association with Frank Productions, Inc. Staged by Abe Burrows. Opened on Broadway at the 46th St. Theater, October 14, 1961

The Original Cast

Finch	Robert Morse
Gatch	Ray Mason
Jenkins	Robert Kaliban
Tackaberry	David Collyer
Peterson	Casper Roos
J. B. Bigley	Rudy Vallee
Rosemary	Bonnie Scott
Bratt	Paul Reed
Smitty	Claudette Southerland
Frump	Charles Nelson Reilly
Miss Jones	Ruth Kobart
Mr. Twimble	Sammy Smith
Hedy	Virginia Martin
Scrubwomen	Mara Landri and Silver Saundors
Miss Krumholtz	Mara Landri
Toynbee	Ray Masom
Ovington	Lanier Davis
Policeman	Bob Murdock
Womper	Sammy Smith

A manned window-washing platform descends on the exterior of the World Wide Wicket Company building. One of the window washers is J. Pierpont Finch, who holds a squeegee in one hand and the paper-bound *How to Succeed in Business Without Really Trying* in the other.

As Finch scans the first page, the Book Voice speaks, saying that this little book will tell everything one needs to know to rise to the top of the business world, even without education, intelligence, or ability, as thousands have done before. One must only have courage and memorize the simple rules offered here to make it to the top.

Putting the squeegee into a pail, Finch sings the Book's schematic outline, the all-significant "How To's": how to get a job, how to make significant contacts by observing who to have lunch with, and how to advance to an executive position from the lowly mailroom.

Finch enters through an open window and slips out of his window washer's overalls, adjusting his jacket and tie.

As Finch is in search of the Office of Personnel, J. B. Biggley, the president of the the company, strides along with four of his henchmen, blindly bumping into Finch and knocking him to the floor. The henchmen pick up the abjectly humble, apologetic Finch. Biggley announces proudly who he is and Finch says that he wants to apply for a job. Biggley tells him to go to the personnel office.

Rosemary Pilkington, a secretary in the advertising office, sees Finch and is enamored at once of this helpless-looking young man. Trying to be helpful, she tells him that Smitty, the secretary to Mr. Bratt, head of Personnel, is a good friend of hers and will help him get in to talk with her boss.

Just at that moment, Bratt comes out of his office and is confronted in his private doorway by Finch, who tells him he's here to apply for a job. Bratt says he's not hiring anyone today. Unthwarted, Finch says that he was just talking with Mr. Biggley, who told him to see Mr. Bratt in Personnel. Flattered and flustered at the coupling of his and the president's name, Bratt asks if Biggley is a personal friend.

Cleverly, Finch replies that he would never use a friendship to get a job. Duly impressed with the good looks, candid manner, and keen intelligence of someone he believes is close to the President and therefore deserving of special attention, Bratt invites Finch into his office, suggesting that a name like Pierpont Finch deserves to have the elegance and power of the initial J. in front of it. And as a matter of fact, John Pierpont Finch says as they exit into Bratt's office, he very conveniently has one. As a new Horatio Alger, from lowly window washer to mail room clerk to corporate chief in the executive suite, Finch has the requisite self-assuredness and cunning aggressiveness to master the power to manipulate people and create reverence for his corporate leadership. *How to Succeed in Business Without Really Trying* ends on a note of personal triumph—a marriage and a prophetic prescription that the president of the United States has to be a man cut out of the same cloth as Finch—a compulsively driven Economic Man intent on consummate leadership, selling the "Brotherhood of Man."

How to Succeed in Business Without Really Trying predicts the exuberance of American corporations moving into booming production by outsourcing, establishing factories in poorer countries where cheap labor helps to produce wealth that will enhance the corporation's bottom line and avoid a host of taxes at the same time. It rejoices in the opening of new markets all around the world, and with moneyed Washington lobbies taking power over legislation, it looks to buy congressional influence, moved forward by politicians' insatiable greed.

In its corporate orientation, World Wide Wickets is a depersonalized, well-advertised entity whose leadership is entrusted to a man of breadth, vision, and daring, open to new ideas to gain power and markets. The W.W.W. TV show is a farce that informs the banality of Madison Avenue's advertising mentality.

Flatteringly, Finch convinces Biggley of his idea-ability, saying that even if you know an idea in itself is nothing, it's the development, production, and promotion that count. For example, he continues, Leonardo da Vinci drew some sketches for a flying machine in the 1500s, but it was American know-how that developed them into the Boeing 707. And there was a man named Gatling who invented a gun that could keep firing automatically, but it took a great brain to develop this into the machine gun—and another to develop it further into a TV program like *The Untouchables*, a violent television show of the period.

The play reflects capitalist America's emphasis on material values and the compulsion to win, with the absolute assertion that the end justifies any means. Success is success, to be honored no matter by what immorality, ploy, or crime one may have accumulated one's wealth, so long as one has been smart enough to cover one's tracks to avoid grand jury indictment.

In the years following World War II, the American economy rose sharply out of the stranglehold of the Depression. *How to Succeed in Business Without Really Trying* epitomizes the determined attitude of post–World War II America, satirizing the anything goes techniques and strategies that bullish young Americans yuppies might emulate to climb to the top rung of the American financial ladder.

It may be that there is an unconscious fear in the brilliant but ironically symbolic song that proclaims the "Brotherhood of Man." In this rousing song, Finch forgives himself and everyone else who has played rotten, dirty tricks in business. Finch smiles as he explains, with an expression of Rotarian fraternality, that there is a noble tie that binds all human hearts and minds. And he winks, "I'm kidding," at the audience as he sings. The fact is that one must be on guard. The message of capitalism is clear: there is no security in today's business world. Don't expect to find security, no matter how many songs may proclaim its existence.

Given that the "Brotherhood of Man" song from *How to Succeed* is an absolute lie—a deceitful, Machiavellian capitalist pronouncement—it is nevertheless a heartwarming song to sing as one goes on the offensive-to-the-death for the next guy's higher and better perked position, or possibly the next corporate takeover.

As the American economy surged following World War II, there were countless corporate executives ruthlessly discharged as the super-competitive J. Pierpont Finches replaced them, soaring high onto executive, multimillion-dollar salaried perches with amazing perks. In the brilliant Executive Washroom scene the male employees of World Wide Wickets sing about how threatened they feel by

Finch's spectacularly rapid rise from window washer to mail room clerk to junior executive officer, now the proud possessor of his own office. Fearing his machinations to oust and replace them, each vows to take action to get rid of him.

To his reflection in the bathroom mirror, Finch sings the show-stopping song "I Believe in You." The lyrics narcissistically reconfirm the calculated design for ascent to higher and higher levels of executive power, with the single objective that one day Finch himself will formulate company policy standing on top of the pyramidal corporate structure.

Finch's personality shares aspects of Eric Fromm's characterization of the marketing orientation personality. Finch's concern is not the selling of a commodity; it is essentially the selling of one's own self, whose market strength is measured by the strength of one's ego, one's cunning understanding of human nature, and one's assessment of oneself as a committed person.

The house that Finch will buy for Rosemary Pilkington, when they marry, is to be a gorgeous mansion with acres of green, rolling lawns and flower gardens in suburban New Rochelle, one of the the bedroom towns for corporation executives and bankers, far from the tumultuous financial markets of Manhattan.

Not a budget-conscious housewife-homemaker but a resourceful secretary, Rosemary Pilkington serves as a romantic inspiration, Finch's confidence builder, and a savior in complicated intrigues within the corporate structure.

She is the American Chief Executive Officer's wife to whom the upscale advertising in all the slick magazines is directed. Shopping for the latest Paris fashions will be one of her major occupations, cleverly satirized in the "imported French creation" scene of Act I. The play spoofs the fantasy of the would-be-Cinderella secretary dreaming about marrying the boss, which is exactly what must happen in a fantasy musical.

The cautionary song "A Secretary Is Not a Toy" aims to show the serious repercussions that arise when imprudent boys fool around sexually. Hedy LaRue is the Treasure Hunt Girl, that is to say, the major symbol of the Gold Digger whose insatiable man-hunger, inane giggle and buttocks-wiggle entice all the boys with high levels of testesterone.

Gratefully relieved of his girl toy, Hedy, J. B. Biggley can now face his jealous, carping wife Gertrude without feelings of guilt because of his adulterous relationship. He enthusiastically surrenders Hedy to Womper, the chairman of the board, who marries her.

Womper is destined to pay the cuckold's price, as Hedy is truly the untamed shrew who promises to torment the chairman with extramarital affairs and a subsequent divorce with an obscene financial settlement.

Throughout *How to Succeed in Business Without Really Trying*, we recognize that Rosemary is the perfect woman for Finch. She is reasonable, practical, and intelligent, unlike ditzy Hedy or complaining Gertrude. Rosemary suggests she is a direct descendant of Mother Eve, promising children to fill the mansion in the suburbs. She avows her love with an adoration that would flatter any man, saying that she doesn't care if her darling husband Finch works in the mailroom or becomes the chairman of the board or even the president of the United States, that she loves him for just what he is.

In the film version, the last scene of the musical shows J. Pierpont Finch washing the windows of the Oval Office. A lookalike President Johnson is intrigued by the cocky young man, who enters through the window, with the smile of a hungering crocodile intent upon success, to sit at the desk in front of the great Seal.

The Teahouse of the August Moon (1953–1954)
by John Patrick

A Play in Three Acts. Adapted from the novel by Vern Sneider. Produced by Maurice Evans. Staged by Robert Lewis. Opened on Broadway at the Martin Beck Theater, October 15, 1953.

The Original Cast

Sakini	David Wayne
Sergeant Gregovich	Harry Jackson

Col. Wainwright Purdy III	Paul Ford
Captain Fisby	John Forsythe
Old Woman	Naoe Kondo
Old Woman's Daughter	Mara Kim
The Daughter's Children	Joyce Chen,
	Kenneth Wong
	and Moy Moy Thom
Lady Astor	Saki
Ancient Man	Kame Ishikawa
Mr. Hokaida	huck Morgan
Mr. Omura	Kuraji Seida
Mr. Sumata	Kaie Deei
Mr. Sumata's Father	Kikuo Hiromura
Mr. Seiko	Haim Winant
Mr. Oshira	William Hansen
Villagers	Frank Ogawa, Norman Chi,
	Richard Akagi, Lawrence Kim,
	and Jerry Fujikawa
Ladies' League for	
Democratic Action	Vivian Thom,
	Mary Ann Reeve, Naoe Kondo,
	and Mara Kim
Lotus Blossom	Mariko Niki
Captain McClean	Larry Gates

In front of a trio of bamboo curtains the protagonist-interlocutor Sakini, dressed in shabby shorts and a native shirt, comes forward to bow to the audience in greeting, as offstage the sound of a plucked string instrument creates the atmosphere of peacefulness that now pervades Okinawa.

Before Sakini begins to speak, he takes a wad of chewing gum out of his mouth, and in clipped and musically nasal Sino-English speech informs us that the flavor is tutti-frutti, a gift from an American sergeant. He introduces himself as Sakini, an interpreter and educator and native of Okinawa. He swiftly reviews Okinawa's history as an endless series of conquerors, with invasions starting in the fourteenth century by Taiwanese and Chinese pirates, extending to the eighteenth cenury when Japanese warlords took possession of the country, until 1945 when American Marines invaded and eliminated the Japanese.

Sakini's theme is the resilience and courageous survival of the Okinawans in the face of all the invasions and disasters: typhoons, locusts, cockroaches, and even the sweet potato moth. Okinawa will survive and not sink into the ocean.

Through the centuries Okinawans have been eager to eliminate the pain of social friction with the conquerors. Though learning is sometimes painful, Sakini admits, pain makes people think, and thinking makes them wise—and wisdom makes life bearable.

Interlocutor Sakini sets the action of the play in motion to tell the story of post–World War II America's Occupation Army's intention to bring democracy to Okinawa. Colonel Wainwright Purdy III is in charge of installing this educational process as spelled out in Plan B by Washington's think tank at the Pentagon with the building of a prototype, pentagon-shaped schoolhouse in the small village of Tobiki, Sakini's birthplace thirty or so years ago.

We are then introduced to the playwright's American hero-protagonist, Captain Fisby, forty years old, who describes himself as an ineffective propaganda creator and disseminator in Psychological Warfare and a former Humanities professor at Muncie College, and who has just now been assigned to Colonel Purdy's team to implement the Tobiki project.

The objectives of an army of occupation vary with the occupier. The Japanese, who annexed the island as a prefect-county, legislating the laws and levying taxes, were ruthless in their subjugation of what they deemed an inferior people. The American occupiers were intent on establishing American air bases for the military in Okinawa because nearby China and Korea were both allied with Communist Russia as the Cold War moved into deep freeze.

The American military realized the heavy toll taken by the Okinawan civilians in the war to win the island and must now strive to eliminate all the negative feelings engendered in that aggression. It must evaluate how the new peace could best serve and make amends to the Okinawans by introducing new ideas in language, government, morality, technology, and life styles.

Colonel Wainwright Purdy, III, Fisby's commander, is a humourous and clownish character who relies completely on the Pentagon's military strategy, Plan B, to solve every problem that may be encountered. He wants daily reports from Fisby about the progress he is making in constructing the schoolhouse and teaching the principles of democracy. He cites Major McEvoy as a model achiever in another village, as the major's fourth graders know the English alphabet by rote through "m"—and whose whole village can sing "God Bless America" in English.

The success of Captain Fisby's particular Okinawan capitalist-industry-venture provides the play with its humor as well as its major theme: American capitalism can be shipped abroad, but a democratic government cannot be imposed upon a foreign culture whose societal mores are deeply rooted in its history.

The Okinawans of Tobiki let their opinions be known. No, they are not interested in having America give them a schoolhouse. They already have schoolhouses where children go to learn. But they have never been wealthy enough to build and maintain a teahouse, which represents the proudest achievement of a community. Only large cities offer their citizens this meaningful sanctuary for peaceful relaxation and social interaction.

The ultimate beauty in life for Okinawans is symbolized by the teahouse, the *chaya*, a communal house of entertainment, colored lights, tinkling sounds, and sweet perfumes, where peace and friendship reign, a public palace-temple of leisure where companionship is shared in the gentle, relaxed atmosphere. Its closest equivalent in the West is an entertainment venue like the cabaret at the fashionable Hotel Carlyle. In the teahouse a geisha may sing, dance, or play her lute, or a sporting event like a wrestling match may take place as teas or liquors are imbibed.

Since Okinawan culture has been based on a noncompetitive, nonmaterialistic socialism, the communal teahouse assumes a dream-character, where a poor man can feel that he is rich, a rich man can dream that he is wise, and a sad man can laugh and feel happy. It becomes the Americans' role to help the Okinawans create the means of realizing this dream.

When Frisby first arrives in Tobiki, he is given presents from the welcoming but poor Tobiki inhabitants, a sampling of the handicrafts that they make to market in a neighboring city. Frisby is fascinated with the intricacy and beauty of the empty cricket cage presented to him. The caged cricket is a symbol of the constrained life, but also an icon of hope and good luck. The message of the empty cage is clear: one must find one's own cricket, one's own good fortune.

In the play Captain Fisby discovers his cricket the moment he hears that Tobiki brandy can be made of sweet potatoes in the space of a week, and the cricket is securely in its cage the moment he tastes the one-week-old liquor, which is almost ninety proof and as smooth as any one-year-old brandy in the West. Immediately Frisby begins a campaign to market the three-star brandy to officers' clubs around the island, and the distillery village of Tobiki begins to realize amazing profits.

Capitalist know-how has put a cricket in every Tobiki villager's cage and real hard currency deposited in each villager's name in a Seattle bank's savings account. The play proves that underdeveloped nations can pull themselves up by their own version of capitalist bootstraps if they explore their resources and use their imaginations to find a profit-producing, saleable product with wide-ranging appeal.

The economist W. W. Rostow observes that the social structure of most under-developed nations is not ready to accept the infrastructure of modern capitalism:

> Most of the presently under-developed nations, in the stage of pre-conditions or early take-off, must allocate much of their resources to building up and modernizing the three non-industrial sectors required as the matrix for industrial growth: social overhead capital; agriculture; and foreign-exchange-earning sectors, rooted in the improved exploitation of natural resources.[3]

Rostow's pre-conditions for launching a third- world country's development are instituted by Fisby when he establishes the Cooperative Brewing Company of Tobiki, organizing the village stills into coordinated production.

Captain Fisby successfully teaches the concepts of production and marketing to the citizens of Tobiki, sparking capitalist growth, and in the newly constructed houses of Act II the citizens of Tobiki have remarkably upgraded their lifestyles. The white suits worn by the men and the beautiful silk costumes worn by the women reflect a high degree of self-consciousness in fashion and self-image and an improved standard of living.

The Okinawans, who earlier in the play had expressed shame over their tattered clothes, have need to be proud of all the things they are. Humility was forced upon them by the conquerors, but they are intensely concerned with never being ashamed of themselves, maintaining the image of contented self-respect with a smile, and the show of respect to others with a bow.

There are significant face-saving moments in the play. The wrestling match in the teahouse represents the model of this societal principle. The loser by one standard may be accounted the winner by another. It is unconscionable for an Okinawan to shame anyone by outwitting him or her in any kind of contest or transaction. The belief in saving face offers a basic contradiction to the capitalist way. The American capitalist philosophy dictates winner-take-all in every competitive endeavor in American society, with no concern for saving anybody else's face or even caring for anybody else, including widows and orphans.

The Teahouse of the August Moon strives to teach its American audiences the need to respect and appreciate the culture of poorer nations, no matter how different their values. Okinawan culture is peace-loving and deeply-rooted within a proud people who have suffered much in their history, and the equality of the sexes in this culture is indicative of its basic democratic rightness.

The most powerful impact of the play arises out of the interracial love affair between Fisby and the geisha Lotus Blossom. Here lurk the shadows of Madame Butterfly and Lieutenant Pinkerton, and Lieutenant Joseph Cable and Liat of *South Pacific*. Captain Fisby is a carbon copy of those American military men whose inherent but unconfessed racial prejudice is threaded to tragedy or disappointment in love.

In Act I, Scene 3, Mr. Sumata comes toward Fisby's office carrying a couple of pieces of battered luggage. He is followed closely by a lovely young woman, a geisha, Lotus Blossom, in traditional dress with full hairdo and make up. Almost immediately behind them Mr. Seiko comes running, calling to Lotus Blossom. In their native tongue Mr. Sumata tells Sakini that Lotus Blossom has rejected her wealthy suitor Mr. Seiko and is very happy to be considered as a gift to the handsome Captain Fisby.

Fisby says he can't accept a human gift and tells Sakini to return Lotus Blossom at once to Mr. Sumata. But Sakini reports that the generous donor has gone away into the mountains and Lotus Blossom has no place to stay and no place to go.

Lotus Blossom, a geisha, represents the highest professional platform a woman can reach in Okinawan culture. She is a celebrity, schooled and skilled in the disciplined Japanese arts of dance, singing, playing the three-stringed *shamisen*; a perfect ritualist in *sadoh*, the tea ceremony; an esthete, trained in the art of flower arrangement; expert in *shodoh*, the art of calligraphy; and a practitioner of *kimono*, the epitome of Japanese/Okinawan etiquette, social graces, conversation, and charming presence.

Fisby is enchanted with the lovely and accomplished Lotus Blossom, but refuses to believe she could thrive in the America he knows. As he prepares to leave Okinawa, Fisby chooses not to fight the battle against prejudice in his American home town, even though Lotus Blossom, who worships him, pleads to go back with him and become an American citizen.

Verne Sneider's serious yet farcical novel *Teahouse of the August Moon*, published in 1951, becomes John Patrick's play in 1953 eight years after V-J Day. On the morning of August 6, 1945, the Enola Gay bomber dropped the first atomic bomb on Hiroshima and subsequently another on Nagasaki, killing hundreds of thousands of Japanese civilians.

The Teahouse of the August Moon is a uniquely gentle play with slight political implications. It avoids any negative element of confrontation and aims to prove that America is a kind conqueror, who does not punish the already downtrodden Okinawans by stripping them of their valuables or taking advantage of their naivete. Rather, America is shown earnestly intent on teaching the principles of democracy along with the capitalist economic system to improve the Okinawans' living standards.

The destruction of the teahouse by the colonel's order is a dramatic reversal, eradicating the joy that thrilled the audience in the scene of the teahouse in full operation. Pentagon Plan B appears to have triumphed over the wishes of the people of Tobiki, until the right of the Okinawans to choose their own destiny is allowed and the teahouse reappears in all its beauty.

Sakini explains that over the centuries Okinawans have learned the technique of hiding what they do not want the conquerors to see and steal or destroy, that under no circumstance were they themselves going to destroy their teahouse, that Tobiki's precious landmark is to be preserved at all costs.

Lotus Blossom enters with flowers and arranges them in vases. Sakini snaps his fingers and magically an August moon lights up in the sky. Captain Fisby orders a snifter of Twenty Star brandy for the Colonel.

The bamboo curtains begin to lower on this joyous, feel-good scene as Sakini steps forward to wish everyone happiness and gentle sleep, the blessings of the August Moon.

The bloody war of the South Pacific has been transmuted in *Teahouse of the August Moon* to provide the meaningful realization that the enslaved people of Okinawa have been given freedom from tyranny and the gift of American capitalism to take off effectively into the twentieth century.

PART FIVE

The Spiritual Condition of Humankind

CHAPTER FIFTEEN

Inferno and Purgatory

Hell-Bent fer Heaven and *A Streetcar Named Desire* are different in literary and dramatic values, and unequal in quality, but share a similar moral major theme. Carnal sinners who have damaged or destroyed the lives of others will be punished severely by Divinity.

In his *Divine Comedy*, Dante assigns each human soul to one of the nine circles that exist in each sphere: the Inferno, Purgatory, and Heaven. In this medieval Catholic vision of morality, saints find and fill choral vacancies in heavenly choirs; small sinners atone in the rehabilitation circles of Purgatory. Those who are guilty of great offenses against the Church and State (in Dante's time, government was considered to be divinely sanctioned) are punished in the circles of Hell.

Wearing masks of innocence, Rufe Pryor of *Hell-Bent fer Heaven* and Blanche DuBois of *A Streetcar Named Desire* are guilty of deceit, sexual incontinence, and deliberate harm to others. The resolutions to the dramatic conflicts of these two plays provide pseudo-Dantesque retributions: eternal damnation in the Inferno for the God-cursing Rufe Pryor, but a possible redemption through Purgatory for the manic-depressive, sexually conflicted Blanche DuBois. Both Pulitzer Prize plays delineate a moralistic disorder that persists in contemporary America.

Hell-Bent fer Heaven (1923–1924)
by Hatcher Hughes

A Play in Three Acts. Produced by Marc Klaw, Inc. at the Klaw Theater, January 4, 1924. Staged by Augustin Duncan.

The Original Cast

David Hunt	Augustin Duncan
Meg Hunt	Clara Blandick
Sid Hunt	George Abbott
Rufe Pryor	John F. Hamilton
Matt Hunt	Burke Clarke
Andy Lowry	Glenn Anders
Jude Lowry	Margaret Borough

The eighty-year-old David Hunt and his daughter Meg are awaiting the homecoming of Sid, Meg's twenty-three-year-old son, who has earned a distinguished mark of heroism in World War I's European trench warfare. The fictional protagonist Sid Hunt is fashioned after the real Sergeant Alvin York, the superb marksman who with a standard-issue Springfield rifle killed twenty-five German soldiers and captured an entire battalion, for which he was awarded the American Medal of Honor.

When Meg asks her son where his medal is, he says he's using it to hold up his underdrawers, because the button fell off. Sid Hunt is a hillbilly type like the ruggedly handsome cartoon character Li'l Abner. Asked to tell how he came to win the medal, he modestly recounts his derring-do, which he doesn't think worthy of any honor.

Suddenly Rufe Pryor, an unattractive, swarthy thirty-year-old, appears at the top of the stairs leading from the bedrooms. When Sid went off to serve in the A.E.F., Rufe came to live with the Hunts, helping David as a clerk in his general store.

Rufe's personality has changed for the worse, the Hunts all agree, ever since he became a fervent participant in the local fundamentalist Presbyterian camp meetings.

In the early nineteenth century this outdoor religious communion flourished in Kentucky and Tennessee, attracting Appalachian

woodsmen, farmers, pioneers, and their families. The revivalist
meetings took place in a large tent over several days with sinners
acting out dramatically in their confessionals, often inflicting great
bodily self-injury. In a mad rapture, the inspired cried out their visions of Heaven, Hell, and Divinity.

Rufe's religious belief is the universal fundamentalist's demand
that everyone follow the same path to salvation—or else they are
doomed to burn in Hell.

When Andy, Jude's younger brother, says that Sid was always very
good in shooting matches and that experience probably saved his
life in the war, Rufe attributes Sid's survival to God's will and warns
that, according to the Lord, shooting matches are a source of evil.
He reminds Sid that it was a shooting match between their grand-
daddies Lowry and Hunt that caused the families' feud in the last
generation with many deaths on both sides—an unequal outcome,
with three more Lowrys than Hunts shot dead.

Intent on stirring up Andy Lowry's hostilities against Sid, Rufe
invites both men upstairs to his room, where he offers some potent
twenty-year-old moonshine. They are about to go when the beautiful Jude Lowry comes into the store, and begging off Rufe's invitation, Sid goes to help her.

Upstairs, Rufe manufactures lies to incite Andy's drunken hostility against Sid, hoping that Sid will be killed and Jude, for whom
he has been secretly lusting, will be his. In an ensuing scene, Rufe
tries to woo Jude, to convince her of his devotion to her, of their
shared Christian values, and of his personal religious experiences in
camp meetings where he has been inspired by the Lord to love her
spiritually. A villainous sensualist, he hides his dark desires behind
a religionist's mask.

Devilishly, Rufe tells Andy that the whole Hunt family is privy to
a plan to have Sid shoot Andy dead when they are riding together
alone in the woods and claim self-defense. Just as Iago warns Othello to be on guard against everyone else's duplicity, Rufe plays a malevolent game with Andy, saying that Sid's friendship is feigned, and
he must not wait for Sid to get the drop on him.

Sid decides he will accompany Andy on his way home so he can
speak with Mr. Lowry about marrying Jude, and the two set out on

horseback, leaving Grandpappy David, Meg, Rufe, and Pappy Matt gathered in the living room. Suddenly a gunshot is heard in the distance. And then a second. Bewilderment and fear are in the faces of all in the room—except for Rufe.

Then there is the sound of a galloping horse coming toward the house. In a panic, Meg rushes out onto the porch and nearly faints when she sees Sid's horse is riderless as he goes through the gate to his stall. She cries out that Andy has shot and killed Sid.

Both Grandpappy David and Pappy Matt take their rifles against Meg's protestations that another killing won't bring Sid back to life. The men leave the house, bent on vengeance. In this lawless region of early twentieth-century America, deadly feuds rage and a spur-of-the-moment armed posse acts as avenger without a trial by peers.

Where is God? Meg cries out melodramatically. Why doesn't He stop terrible things like this from happening?

God's judgments are righteous, Rufe declares, and require no justification to humankind. Besides, Scripture dictates that wicked heathens are destined to destroy each other, according to God's plan.

When suddenly Sid comes in through the kitchen door, Rufe screams in terror, believing he sees Sid's ghost. But Sid, in the flesh, explains that as he was riding alongside Andy, his saddle became loose and he got off his horse to fix it. When he reached in his back pocket for his knife, Andy whipped out his pistol and shot a bullet through his hat. Realizing at that moment that Andy intended to kill him, Sid darted into the woods and let his horse run loose.

Sid is alarmed when he sees the rifles are missing from the wall rack. Rufe says that David and Matt took them and must have taken the shortcut over the mountain to meet and settle the score with Andy.

During the early 1920s, the problem of frequent flooding due to deforestation in the Tennessee Valley required the U.S. government to build a series of dams on the Appalachian rivers. So far, only one wing of the huge proposed dam in this area has been finished, but it is solid enough to withstand any amount of water buildup. According to Rufe, only a boxful of dynamite could ever make a dent in it.

The local farm and mountain community, resentful of the intrusion of the government, has in fact threatened to dynamite the dam. Rufe knows a couple of very angry farmers who have a heap of dynamite on hand to dig out wells.

There is a telephone in the tool house on a ledge right under the dam that connects to the workers' settlement that Andy must pass. Sid wants to phone ahead from the tool house to the settlement office to stop David and Matt from pursuing Andy. But Rufe contends that if Andy were stopped, he'd simply blame Rufe, saying Rufe egged him on—all lies, of course, he assures the incredulous Sid. Hearing this as Rufe's confession, Sid hurls the cowering Iago into a far corner of the room and rushes out to the dam to see if he can prevent bloodshed.

In a dramatic monologue addressed to God at the end of Act II, Rufe asks God why He allows the wicked to prosper, to get the best of everything in today's world. As an avenger, God should strike down sinners with a lightning bolt and bring the fear of God back to these mountains. But if God so wishes, Rufe will act as His avenger, punishing transgressors and blasphemers, even if he is to be hanged for it, because when he was a sinner and God came knocking at his door, he knew he belonged to God.

Still raving, Rufe runs into the storm with a whole box of dynamite and a time-fuse long enough to light and get away before the whole dam explodes. He is setting it to go off when Sid is under the dam making the phone call. (His many contrivances and conspiracies to eliminate Sid begin to approach the ludicrous unreality of a *Tom and Jerry* cartoon or the serial near-death escapades of Hairbreadth Harry.)

Act III begins with the Hunts' entrance commanding Andy at gunpoint. When they tie him to a chair and question him, he confesses to having shot at Sid, but doesn't know whether he hit or missed, blaming his own unsteady hand and poor marksmanship on the liquor he drank.

Suddenly, from the dam, Rufe enters cold and drenched. A moment later there is an explosion, a boom that echoes and re-echoes through the valley as if a giant still has been exploded by the

Revenuers. Immediately, the sound of the river torrent thunders as the flood rolls into the valley.

The Hunts run out onto the porch, shocked to see the flood waters.

Inside, Rufe behaves as a man possessed, spouting damnation prophecies and threats to keep Andy from revealing his plot. But Andy is still drunk, and when Rufe sings a snatch of a revivalist hymn, Andy starts to sing in response, much to the annoyance of the distraught Hunts, who are concerned about the livestock in the barn and poultry house as the waters rise to the front porch level. To silence Andy, who is singing wildly, Rufe suggests to the Hunts that he be moved down into the cellar, and they comply, tying Andy to a chair and locking the cellar door to prevent his escape should he free himself.

Andy's sister Jude is extremely perturbed by her brother's behavior, but doesn't know what to do as the flood rises to the back porch level and begins to flow into the cellar. Meg asks Jude to help her in the poultry house to save the turkeys, as David and Matt go out back into the barn to save the cattle, to move them all to high ground.

Suddenly, like an apparition, Sid appears in the front door, his clothes torn and his face and arms bruised and dirty. He has overheard Rufe's manic address to God, and in a deep and haunted voice croaks, "Mene, Mene, Tekel, Upharsim"—the words of warning that God mysteriously wrote on a wall with a moving dismembered hand at Belshazzar's feast.

Fearfully, Rufe asks aloud if that is God Himself speaking. Sid answers that he is the ghost of Sid Hunt and has come to identify his murderer to bring him to the bar for God's Judgment.

Then, like a weird happening in a revivalist meeting, from below in the cellar comes Andy's voice shouting the command for the brethren to pray, as he begins to sing the hymn "Roll, Jordan, Roll," as the rising river waters flow into the cellar.

Coming from the barn, Meg, Jude, and David see that the river water has risen up to the kitchen doorstep. Rufe tells them he's talked with Sid's ghost and it has just gone down into the cellar. So far as David is concerned, Rufe has lost whatever little rational mind he once had, but suddenly the cellar door opens and Andy emerges with Sid, who humorously discounts the attempted murder in the woods, faulting Andy only for his poor aim.

Rufe disowns any responsibility for the dam explosion, saying that God appeared in the flesh and did it.

Matt looks out and says there's six feet of water around the house, and Meg cries out that she can't swim.

How will this flood disaster end?

Mirabile dictu, Sid says he has a boat! As he was coming down the river in the swollen turmoil of the broken dam, he saw a loose boat and hooked onto it, and has hitched it up alongside the outside porch. He orders everyone to get out and into the boat before any more dynamited sections of the dam fall apart and send new surges down the river.

Rufe asks if they are going to take him with them. Andy tells him that God will come to save him if he's really done as much service to Him as he says. They all clamber into the boat.

Alone in the living room, Rufe begins his prayer to God to prove His existence and save him. Water is beginning to flow into the living room, and Rufe fears he has been abandoned after all. Now, in a fit of anger, he cries out curses against God. There is no God, he despairs, and if there is, that God has no concern for him, but only for folks who are on top. Terrified by his own blasphemy, an unpardonable sin, Rufe screams hysterically for help—where there is none, as the flood overwhelms the living room.

Rufe might well have escaped the flood by going upstairs or onto the roof, but his terror and blasphemy are dramatically necessary. The playwright has stacked the deck against Rufe. He is the essence of evil and deserves to be destroyed.

Rufe's unmitigated villainy is just one of the aspects of *Hell-Bent fer Heaven* that suggests a strong Shakespearean sensibility in playwright Hughes, who taught English and drama at Columbia University. Echoes of Othello are most prevalent, with Sid Hunt like the returning hero-soldier Othello, and Rufe Pryor the shadow of an envious and murderous Iago.

When Rufe woos the beautiful Jude Lowry, Sid's inamorata, with erotic cunning, there is the specter of malformed Richard III seducing the Lady Anne.

The moment Rufe sees Sid, and in his terror calls him the ghost of the man he believes he has just murdered, Banquo and King Hamlet glide past.

When Andy is chained in the cellar and only his booming voice is heard, do we hear the shade of Caliban imprisoned by Prospero, calling out in irrational fear?

The generational feud between the Montagues and the Capulets is refigured in the feud between the Lowrys and the Hunts, paralleling the real hillbilly feud between the Hatfields and the McCoys.

Yet Hatcher Hughes' university teaching, in addition to informing his writing with classic dramatic scenarios and effects, also raised problems in the consideration of his play for a Pulitzer Prize. The playwright's close professional relationship with Dr. Brander Matthews, head of Columbia's drama department, set off an uproar among the jurors, who felt undue pressure to honor Hughes' play. They were reluctant to award the professor the prize, noting the work's improbable story line, melodramatic excesses, and failure to show character development.

Despite these legitimate criticisms, the play does have the value of raising significant questions for the audience, calling out for after-curtain discussion: Is prayer just lip service, a vain personal petition for God's favor? Does He hear? Or are we at the mercy of fate or accident, fortune or luck? Was it serendipity, fate, or his own skill that guided Sid to subdue a German battalion, escape being killed by a bullet that went through his hat, survive a blast of dynamite that destroyed a dam, and find a boat in a raging flood to save everyone he chooses to save? Or is the playwright implying that there is a God, who is offended by self-satisfaction and hatred, and shows His favor to those of humbler faith?

Late in the play, Sid recognizes Rufe's religious madness and declares that God, if He does exist, must be tired of being used as the scapegoat by so many mean, narrow-minded and psychologically disturbed people who set themselves up as models of morality and righteousness and call their distorted beliefs religion. Does Hughes' profound major theme present evidence of the playwright's belief?

Hatcher Hughes, born in Polksville, North Carolina in 1881, boldly reflects the Appalachian regionalism he knew first hand in his depiction of the folkways of these mountain people, their daily lives, diction, and cultural values. Beginning with the first quarter of the twentieth century, the fundamental-revivalists in the South dissented vehemently with the liberal philosophies in the social sciences and Darwinian theory that moved the human race away from the center of creation as physics and astrophysics contemplated an ever-expanding universe.

In the Scopes trial in July 1925, fundamentalism failed in its attempts to prevent scientific inquiry in America, but it did not halt the fundamentalists. Today fundamentalism, in the radical right, persists in using its political power to legislate the teaching of religious doctrine in the classroom alongside the natural sciences. The fundamentalists' prejudice and ignorance takes away the freedom of thought and experimentation that is basic to democracy, and is as stultifyingly gross in its brainwashing as are Communism, Fascism, or Islamism.

The major theme of *Hell-Bent fer Heaven* is contained in the boomerang-title. Fundamentalism, though it promises a relationship with God in Heaven, creates so much evil on Earth that the fundamentalist Rufe is himself doomed to go to Hell.

Though Hughes' play is a bitter, realistic appraisal of religion and its adherents, its characterization of Rufe becomes a melodramatic, villainous caricature of a man. One cannot question the prize-worthiness of such a serious and mature theme, but the play fails the litmus test of *best*.

A Streetcar Named Desire (1947–1948)
by Tennessee Williams

A Play in Three Acts. Produced by Irene M. Selznick. Staged by Elia Kazan. Opened at the Ethel Barrymore Theater, December 3, 1947.

The Original Cast

Negro Woman	Gee Gee James
Eunice Hubbel	Peg Hillias
Stanley Kowalski	Marlon Brando
Stella Kowalski	Kim Hunter
Steve Hubbel	Rudy Bond
Harold Mitchell (Mitch)	Karl Malden
Mexican Woman	Edna Thomas
Blanche DuBois	Jessica Tandy
Pablo Gonzales	Nick Dennis
A Young Collector	Vito Christi
A Strange Woman	Ann Dere
A Strange Man	Richard Garrick

A God of mercy and compassion sends His messenger in the concluding moments of *A Streetcar Named Desire*, Tennessee Williams' masterpiece morality play of carnal sin and expiation. The playwright dramatizes Blanche DuBois' life-experience using a multiplicity of Christian, pagan, and Freudian symbols to show the progress of one Southern woman's spiritual, moral, and psychological disintegration.

Blanche arrives in New Orleans to visit her younger sister Stella, and Stella's husband, Stanley Kowalski. The atmosphere of New Orleans is sensual and frightening, rumbling with symbols of carnality and death like the streetcars named Desire and Cemetery that take Blanche to Elysian Fields, where the Kowalskis live. We first see Stanley bellowing his wife's name in front of the weathered frame house where they rent a two-room apartment, and tossing her a package of meat. The neighbors laugh heartily at the sexual innuendo of Stanley throwing the meat to Stella. Sexuality underlies every action of every character in this Freudian-Christian play.

Next Blanche DuBois comes around the corner with her valise, looking for her younger sister's apartment. In Greek mythology, Elysium is the Land of the Blessed Spirits, with its counterpart, Hell, for the damned, governed by Hades. Elysium seems an ironic misnomer for this part of the carnal city of New Orleans.

The playwright describes his heroine Blanche as mothlike—pale, fragile, and fluttering in her movements. She takes as a symbol of her character the image of her name—"white woods" in French— the new spring blossoms of a laurel tree. The laurel suggests the virgin Daphne, whom Apollo, the god of the sun, attempts to rape. She appeals to Zeus for protection, and he transforms her into the laurel.

Blanche is fleeing from a town called Laurel, Mississippi, where her sexual liaison with one of her high school students has been discovered, resulting in her dismissal from her post as a teacher. All the DuBoises who lived in the Mississippi plantation mansion Belle Reve (Beautiful Dream) seem to have been cursed with an insatiable sexuality—satyriasis and nymphomania—that has brought about the downfall and loss of Belle Reve, a house cursed like the House of Atreus and its dwellers pursued by Furies.

Williams enhances the play poetically with many symbolic allusions and parallels to Greek classical myth and early Christian cosmography. He was well acquainted with Christian cosmology as detailed in Dante's *Divine Comedy,* and in the last two scenes of *A Streetcar Named Desire* he conjures up Blanche DuBois' progression from punishment in Inferno to the beginnings of redemption in Purgatory, the middle ground, with its stairs leading upward to Heaven.

It is in the second ring of the Inferno that Dante places all carnal sinners, including the shade of Francesca da Rimini, killed by her husband for her adulterous liaison with her brother-in-law. The da Rimini triangle suggests the perverse triangle of the sex-tormented Blanche DuBois and her rape by her brother-in-law, Stanley Kowalski.

Blanche's tragic secret is her role in the death of her adored husband, Allan Gray, whom she was shocked and wounded to discover in bed with a man shortly after their honeymoon. That night, as the couple danced to the elegant polka "Varsouviana," Blanche confronted and shamed her husband, whereupon he left the dance floor and shot himself.

According to the playwright, hers was an evil act of "deliberate cruelty," and the "Varsouviana," which plays in the background, alternating throughout the play with the sad music of the blue piano, becomes a symbolic reminder of that cruelty and of approaching evil. Blanche's guilt over Gray's death becomes the mainspring that drives her into sexual relationships with all kinds of men, including her brother-in-law, which now demands, like Francesca da Rimini, her expiation of guilt in Inferno.

Having come to New Orleans, Williams' symbolic Inferno, driven out of Laurel as unfit, Blanche is pursued by chanting Furies in the guise of women calling from the street, selling bouquets of flowers for the dead.

The approaching thunder of the streetcar Desire mixes with the orchestral "Varsouviana," a constant underlying reminder of the elegance of the dead Gray. In the climactic scene, alternating with that refined music, terrifying, wild jungle cries throb inside Blanche's head, like her primitive id. The sound cues supply the increasingly discordant distress of her psyche: "The barely audible 'blue piano' begins to drum up louder. The sound of it turns into the fierce roar of an approaching locomotive."

In the beginning, Blanche is both terrified and thrilled by her sexual attraction to Kowalski, recognizing his virile brutishness which her fetish-sexual self hungers to experience even as she knows it could destroy her.

Contrarily, if Kowalski represents the object in Blanche's carnal/immoral descent, he acts also as the agent initiating Blanche's move toward a diminution and final elimination of desire. He forces her to face the truth of her wanton degeneracy—her debauchery with the soldiers on the local army base, her seduction of a seventeen-year-old student in her high school English class.

In her dramatic confessional to her disillusioned suitor Mitch, Blanche tells about her many sexual intimacies with strangers, and her hope that Mitch would be like a protective brother or father who could shelter her from her uncontrollable, destructive sexual urges. At the very moment that Blanche completes her confession, the Mexican woman, the symbol of the pursuing Furies, begins to chant in the street below, "Flowers for the dead!" By her confession, Blanche has taken the first step toward atonement.

But atonement must come with more pain. Mitch's rejection of Blanche is as callous as her "You disgust me" to Gray. Mitch speaks the most deliberately cruel words a man can say to a woman, that she is not *clean* enough to bring into his mother's house. Mitch's remark cuts Blanche to the heart as the most painful retributive justice.

Intent on gaining redemption and being readmitted into a state of grace, Blanche unconsciously performs urgent and frequent ablutions. Her constant bathing is the metaphor of her need for cleansing her soul. The Christian ritual of immersion is conjoined with the diagnosed Freudian compulsive disorder, like Lady Macbeth's, a little water to wash away the blood of Gray's suicide or the shame of sex. Lady Macbeth fears that Duncan's blood may incarnadine all the seas, but Blanche dreams that when she dies and is buried at sea, she will at last be clean.

Just before the nurse and doctor arrive to take Blanche away at the end of the drama, a seeming Catholic ritual takes place. Blanche dresses herself in pure Madonna della Robbia blue and discovers the grapes Eunice has brought.

Symbolically, partaking of the grape is holy sacrament, and Blanche says it will transport her soul to heaven. Then at three significant moments the cathedral bells chime, confirming the mystery of Blanche's expiation: that the frenzy of desire within her has been quelled.

Like twin Angels of Death, the medical professionals—also referred to as the Strange Man and the Strange Woman—enter to take Blanche to a mental institution, which may be a modern counterpart of Dante's Purgatory.

When she hesitates, Kowalski tears down the paper lantern with which she has taken such pains to disguise the naked light bulb that illuminates the apartment in all its starkness. In offering to give Blanche the paper lantern to take with her, is Stanley making a gesture of kindness? Or is he cruelly reminding her that she is as phony as the paper moon of the popular song?

There are suddenly mysterious voices behind the wall sounding as though they were reverberating through a canyon of rock, voices of the men who have used Blanche's female vulnerability. She utters the plea of the helpless child, the hungry beggar, and the humiliated prostitute: that she has always depended on the kindness of strangers.

But what kindness does Blanche mean? When have strangers ever been kind to her? Does kindness signify sexual intimacy? In Act III, Scene 3, Blanche confesses that after the death of Allan, "intimacies with strangers was all I seemed able to fill my empty heart with."[1] Is this kindness Williams' declaration about his homosexual relationship with strangers?

The streetcar Desire has arrived at the end of the line, but like desire it does not stop, but turns and starts its course again. *A Streetcar Named Desire* ends with the death of desire, but not the desire of death.

The neurotic Blanche DuBois exits into the "otherworld" of the mental asylum, symbolically Dante's Inferno and Purgatory for cleansing and purification, to be burned clean and restored to the vernal freshness of her name.

A Streetcar Named Desire is Williams' masterpiece, projecting his personal vision of human nature. Blanche is a composite portrait of Williams' own promiscuity and the two most important women of his life: his sister Rose, who was lobotomized in an attempt to cure her madness, and his mother Edwina, a super-refined, genteel woman who acted as if she were fragile aristocracy. Williams identified his androgynous self strongly with Blanche and her sexual incontinence—and perhaps also with her longing for redemption.

The play's major theme underscores the truth that not until the extinction of desire in death can human beings resist the unrelenting, demanding control of eros and the libidinal id. For those still struggling in earthly life, who suffer and beg for God's mercy, Williams evokes a frail and hopeful vision of kindness.

CHAPTER SIXTEEN

God and Humanity

Who or what is God? As we examine the world about us, studying human history from artifacts and relics of prehistory, and exploring our ever-expanding universe using the technology that science provides, we ponder the significance of creation and question the character of the Creator, as well as the meaning of the moral terms good and evil.

The appearance of God as a character in two Pulitzer Prize plays, *The Green Pastures* and *J.B.*, indicates American playwrights' serious inquiry into the nature of Divinity. They present a dubiously divine figure that oversees the human condition, only sometimes acting with compassion for those men and women, who believe themselves to have been made in His image.

The Green Pastures concerns the primal fall of man and woman, and the coming of Christ in the new image of the black man Hezdrel. *J.B.* retells the Book of Job, translating the suffering of that pious man into the dilemmas of a twentieth-century Organization Man.

The Green Pastures is a minstrel-type dramatization of the ongoing acculturation process of Americans of African descent living as second-class citizens in the early twentieth-century Christian South. *J.B.* creates a devout religionist out of a modern corporation executive.

Though these plays are unlike in setting, language, structure, and style, both consider the same moral issues: obedience to God, the problem of evil and injustice in the world, and the promise of an afterlife.

The Green Pastures (1929–1930)
by Marc Connelly

A Play in Two Parts. Produced by Laurence Rivers, Inc. Staged by Marc Connelly. Opened on Broadway at the Mansfield Theater, February 26, 1930.

The Original Cast

Mr. Deshee	Charles H. Moore
Myrtle	Alicia Escamilla
First Boy	Jazzlips Richardson, Jr.
Second Boy	Howard Washington
Third Boy	Reginald Blythwood
Randolph	Joe Byrd
A Cook	Frances Smith
Custard Maker	Homer Tutt
First Mammy Angel	Anna Mae Fritz
A Stout Angel	Josephine Byrd
A Slender Angel	Edna Thrower
Archangel	J. A. Shipp
Gabriel	Wesley Hill
The Lord	Richard B. Harrison
Choir Leader	McKinley Reeves
Adam	Daniel L. Haynes
Eve	Inez Richardson Wilson
Cain	Lou Vernon
Cain's Girl	Dorothy Randolph
Zeba	Edna M. Harris
Cain the Sixth	James Fuller
Boy Gambler	Louis Kelsey
First Gambler	Collington Hayes
Second Gambler	Ivan Sharp
Voice in Shanty	Josephine Byrd
Noah	Tutt Whitney
Noah's Wife	Susie Sutton
Shem	Milton J. Willliams
First Woman	Dinks Thomas
Second Woman	Anna Mae Fritz
Third Woman	Geneva Blythwood
First Man	Emory Richardson
Flatfoot	Freddie Archibald

Ham	J. Homer Tutt
Japheth	Stanleigh Morrell
First Cleaner	Josephine Byrd
Second Cleaner	Florence Fields
Abraham	J. A. Shipp
Isaac	Charles H. Moore
Jacob	Edgar Burks
Moses	Alonzo Fenderson
Zipporah	Mercedes Gilbert
Aaron	McKinley Reeves
A Candidate Magician	Reginald Fenderson
Pharoah	George Randol
The General	Walt McClane
First Wizard	Emory Richardson
Head Magician	Arthur Porter
Joshua	Stanleigh Morrell
First Scout	Ivan Sharp
Master of Ceremonies	Billy Cumby
King of Babylon	Jay Mondaaye
Prophet	Ivan Sharp
High Priest	J. Homer Tutt
The King's Favorites	Leona Winkler, Florence Lee, Constance Van Dyke, Mary Ella Hart, and Inez Persand
Officer	Emory Richardson
Hezdrel	Daniel L. Haynes
Another Officer	Stanleigh Morrell

In his prefatory Author's Note, Marc Connelly writes that *The Green Pastures* is an "attempt to present certain aspects of a living religion in terms of its believers."[1]

He notes the "terrific spiritual hunger and the greatest humility in these untutored black Christians [who] have adapted the contents of the Bible to the consistencies of their everyday lives," and he expresses his indebtedness to Roark Bradford, who inspired him with his "here and now" retelling of Old Testament stories in *Ol' Man Adam an' His Chillun.*

After *The Green Pastures*' opening on Broadway in 1929, one of the most prominent African-American intellectual and social leaders, W. E. B. DuBois, praised it, overlooking the playwright's offensive stereotyping of the African-American character. DuBois and other black leaders were delighted that a Broadway production with an entirely black cast was attracting enthusiastic white audiences and presenting aspects of black folk religion.

In retrospect, in 2008, considering the civil rights movement and the affirmative stand of black nationalism of the 1950s and '60s, the play may be deemed deprecating and offensive, an unflattering account of the black life experience in America. It is a white man's take on the African American's spiritual condition in New Orleans, intended for a white audience's entertainment, not unlike a minstrel show.

"Unburdened by the differences of more educated theologians," Connelly writes in his Author's Note to the play, his characters

> . . . accept the Old Testament as a chronicle of wonders which happened to people like themselves in vague but actual places, and of rules of conduct, true acceptance of which will lead them to a tangible, three-dimensional Heaven . . . where the angels do have magnificent fish frys through an eternity, somewhat resembling a series of earthly holidays. [2]

Connelly's presentation of his characters' cute, childlike ignorance is both demeaning and cruel when one considers that until 1865 blacks were kept ignorant and illiterate by Southern state laws that ensured their continued domination by white slaveholders. Slaves were severely punished if they were found to have begun to learn to read or write. And after Emancipation, blacks were segregated into mockeries of schools with inferior or sham educational standards.

The play begins in a Sunday School classroom setting, representing a dramatized educational experience, indoctrinating black children to understand the power of Divinity in the tradition of the medieval plays that re-enacted scenes from the Old Testament.

Until the Protestant Reformation inspired by Martin Luther, the Catholic Church disallowed the reading of scripture by laypeople, but did allow the staging of popular morality plays. Designed to teach moral values, the characters of these plays were embodied abstractions, with the Seven Deadly Sins, Death, and Vice the most popular *dramatis personae*. Christ does not appear as a character in any of the medieval cycles.

In *The Green Pastures*, the playwright recasts all the characters of the Bible, including God Himself, as contemporary African Americans. The play strives for a quaint humor in its characterizations of black life and values, painting an offensive picture of its characters as uniformly untutored, ignorant, and childish. Even the play's vision of heaven is a sad reflection of the inferior quality of teaching and the low standards of educational expectation for blacks that once was. Each graduating angel is ordained to serve as a holy domestic at the throne of God, a menial service.

This cheerful pageant of the black life experience excludes any complaint against white society and avoids any acknowledgment of the physical, economic, and psychological damage engendered by the years of slavery in America. It is only at the end of the play, with the appearance of the white-hooded posse (the major symbol of white society), that a modicum of seriousness is felt. The posse is eager to hang the black hero Hezdrel, a fictional warrior in the mold of Joshua who is also a significant prophet, teaching new values to God.

Hezdrel makes God aware that those who have suffered slavery will not worship the Jehovah of wrath and vengeance, but instead have chosen a God Who, like them, has suffered at the hands of humankind. As a result, God accepts that He must die as a man, and then overcome death to be reborn as a God of mercy, Jesus Christ.

The ability or willingness of America's black population to accept the white Jehovah and Christ presented to them as images of God is an important historical consideration. Slave owners often forced their slaves' conversion from animism or voodooism to Christianity to civilize and make docile the savage breast—or to save their souls. It must have been a very painful, humbling, and depressing experience for a black slave to find himself praying to the same God that his master worshiped, hearing praises for all His love and benefactions. Where might the black man find courage and hope that a loving Divinity was paying attention to his suffering?

The Coptic or Abyssinian Catholic Church resolved this image problem in Egypt in the first century by painting a black Christ, allowing black worshippers to identify completely with that image of God. Similarly, the powerful final scenes of Connelly's play present a new black Christ, tortured on an American Calvary with the symbol of the KKK's justice, the noose.

Before Hezdrel dies, he declares his faith in a new God different from the old Jehovah. He tells his band of black soldiers that when any of them is slain in this holy war against evil, he will "jump right out of his skin" and find a place in the lap of God. Tragically, even Hezdrel does not seem to believe that black skin is as beautiful as white and just as loved by God.

The major theme is clear: the character of a God that allowed blacks to suffer in slavery must change His essential nature. The Jehovah who engineered the Exodus from slavery for the Hebrews and shut His eyes to the American pharaohs is a God who turns his back on his children. The wrathful God of the Old Testament must undergo a transformation in character to become the merciful God of Hosea. In order for God to have compassion, He must be made to suffer just as black people have suffered in America.

The major theme of this Pulitzer Prize play of 1929 seems to herald—even demand—the birth of a true Hezdrel, a black prophet-leader to speak for the morality and faith of African Americans and to change American society itself, giving its black citizens the opportunity to share fully in the American Dream.

On August 28, 1963, the Reverend Martin Luther King—born January 15, 1929—delivered the impassioned "I have a dream" speech on the steps of the Lincoln Memorial. A brilliant Hezdrel-come-to-life, thirty-five years after the Broadway production of Connelly's play, Martin Luther King fought for the Voting Rights Act of 1965, and managed to secure federal examiners to register qualified black voters, suspending the devious literacy tests aimed at preventing African Americans from voting. His triumph was a momentous step on the march to secure civil rights for African

Americans. Let us hope that Hezdrels to come will resolve the race issue in America, and that no further Christ-like sacrifices will be demanded of them.

J.B. (1958–1959)
by Archibald MacLeish

A Play in Two Acts. Produced by Alfred De Liagre, Jr. Staged by Elia Kazan. Opened on Broadway at the Anta Theater, December 11, 1958.

The Original Cast

First Roustabout	Clifton James
Second Roustabout	James Olson
Nickles	Christopher Plummer
Mr. Zuss	Raymond Massey
Prompter	Ford Rainey
J.B.	Pat Hingle
Sarah	Nan Martin
David	Arnold Merritt
Mary	Ciri Jacobsen
Jonathan	Jeffrey Rowland
Ruth	Candy Moore
Rebecca	Merry Martin
The Girl	Janet Ward
Mrs. Botticelli	Helen Waters
Mrs. Leisure	Fay Sappington
Mrs. Adams	Judith Lowry
Mrs. Murphy	Laura Pierpont
Jolly	Lane Bradbury
Bildad	Bert Conway
Zophar	Ivor Francis
Eliphaz	Andreas Voutsinas

The Book of Job in the Old Testament is one of the greatest philosophical inquiries into the presence of evil in the world and undeserved human suffering.

The matter of the Book of Job is presented mostly in Socratic dialogue, very much like a play, as it attempts to understand whether earthly suffering is God's punishment for individual human sin, and whether or not sin is always punished.

Why, Job asks, does God allow terrible things to happen to good and pious people? And why are the doers of terrible deeds unpunished? MacLeish's poetic interpretation strives valiantly to explore humanity's relationship to God.

The play begins with a long Prologue—longer than the succinct one in the Bible—as it begins to tell the story of Job, which MacLeish sets inside an enormous circus tent that the poet-dramatist proposes to be the world of human affairs. The playwright makes an immediate allusion to Shakespeare's *Hamlet* when Mr. Zuss refers to this tent as the Universe and, immodestly, identifies this work as a poetical creation that will deal with more things than have been dreamed of in human philosophy.

Donning the mask of God, Mr. Zuss—the balloon seller in the unattended circus ring—agrees to test the sincerity of God's supposed favorite J.B., who swears absolute faith in the Lord. Nickles, a vender of popcorn, takes the role of Satan, sneering that J.B. has been bought off, given everything by God. Just as in the Bible, the test is a power play, with J.B.'s soul as the ultimate prize.

Reinterpreting the story of Job, MacLeish's J.B. is not a symbolic American everyman; he is a particular American capitalist who has been blessed by God, chosen as a favorite and much rewarded. He himself has bought "millionaires like cabbages," and never doubts God, the System, or his favored position, until catastrophes destroy everything that he possesses—his family, his wealth, even his health. Sitting on a dumpsite of ashes and garbage, the biblical Job asks God, "Why am I struck down and all that You blessed me with taken away?"

This is Job's question, conjecturally composed between 700 B.C. and 300 B.C., and MacLeish's J.B. attempts to find the answer in the twentieth. Are there truly righteous Americans who fit the character of Job before his catastrophes?

With greater artifice in studied poetic verse and less majesty or feeling than its original, *J.B.* rehearses at great lengths the argument that is effectively and economically presented in the Book of

Job. A rich, generous, and righteous man, devoted to God's commands, is smitten with pain and sits on an ash heap after he has lost everything he had in the world. His three friends try to help him understand the reality of a man's life as they see it. Neither Job nor his friends know that Job is a test case, the object of Satan's envy. Satan has wagered with God that Job would renounce his allegiance to God if everything was taken from him and he was left in abject distress.

Ironically, *J.B.* begins during a Thanksgiving Day celebration. The smug, full-bellied arrogance of J.B. is duplicated in his little daughter Rebecca, whom his wife Sarah describes as made in her father's image, believing the whole world is hers for the taking, with no need for thanks. Sarah trusts in her husband's faith but chides him for not showing more humility, suspecting that God wants more from them than simple enjoyment of His gifts. J.B. feels how he is upheld by God, but an easygoing confidence, rather than any devout prayer, reveals his sense of grace.

As J.B.'s woes begin, violence is reported in graphic close-ups of anguish. Messenger after messenger comes with tidings of his children dead in a war, a car crash, a kidnapping, an earthquake. To believe in God now, says Sarah, is to betray their lost children—and when J.B., his health and fortune gone, will not curse God with her, she leaves.

The long Socratic exchanges of the three friends in the Book of Job are intended to help Job search for the meaning of human suffering and where he may have acted unethically. A parallel dialogue in *J.B.* is voiced by three Spokesmen of modern "isms": Zophar represents the institutionalized Church, Eliphaz the sciences; and Bildad the social sciences.

Stubbornly, J.B. rejects each friend's protestations: Zophar's Christian assertion that the primal fall, the disobedience in the Garden of Eden, marks us all eternally and cannot be forgiven; Eliphaz's Freudian belief that God is the unconscious and that human guilt is an everlasting psychophenomenal situation; and Bildad's Marxist fatalism—that God is historical necessity and the individual does not count in the processes of evolving universal justice.

In abject humility, J.B. submits to the Distant Voice (God's voice?) that humbles him, compelling him to repent, even for the audacity of questioning. Yet the drama's resolution disallows despair, since everything in J.B.'s life rights itself.

Sarah, unable to bring herself to suicide, returns to console J.B., offering love, which the playwright asserts is a relationship peculiar only to the human condition. When J.B. tells Sarah that God does not love, he implies that God incorporates but is beyond all passion, that His Being is all-Being.

This reduction of God to a desireless, existential presence, which finds full expression in simply Being, seems to negate all that came before in the play, that evidences God's power to create and destroy. Being is not the power to command, nor is it consonant with the power-seeking character of Mr. Zuss when he dons the God mask and becomes God in the circus ring.

God's declaration of His own Being as the substance and pattern of the universe reduces Descartes' proof of existence to an impossible, negative illogicality: I doubt Him; ergo, He is.

In "Dover Beach," Matthews Arnold asks for fidelity in love because his pessimism senses the "ebbing sea of faith." In this loveless drama, Sarah's appeal to the heart as the only source of light, her offer of love as the consoling answer, seems a contrived resolution, devoid of substance. MacLeish's God is not a God of Love, but an unseen, Distant-Voiced Wizard of Uz (not Oz), the Biblical city where Job lived.

God's desire for penitent souls reflects the inadequacy of His power, remote and disguised in His Whirlwind. Contrarily, Satan's powerful presence is evident everywhere in the world of J.B. The decades before and after this play was written witnessed an endless series of wars upon wars, with certain ignominiously brutal high points: a genocide of Armenians by the Turks, a Holocaust of millions of Jews in Nazi Germany, and the atomic destruction of cities and hundreds of thousands of Japanese lives in a split second. Now, in the twenty-first century, there is Sudan's Darfur genocide, Kenya's tribal warfare, and bitter conflict in Afghanistan and Iraq.

In the Prologue, Nickles speaks of "millions burned, crushed, broken, mutilated, slaughtered, and for what?" And MacLeish cites the hatred of difference that lurks in the human heart: for thinking to bow to a different deity, for speaking a strange tongue, for wanting to live a different kind of sexual life, for walking around the world in the wrong skin, with the wrong-shaped nose or eyelids, for sleeping on the wrong night, in the wrong city, London, Dresden, Hiroshima.

In our lifetime, the ungodly truth is that there never were and never could have been so many innocents who have suffered more for less.

As for the sufferings of J.B., we in the audience do have compassion because of the interminable sequence of losses, and the inflicting of abject pain and suffering. However, the plight of modern man and woman can not be represented by J.B. in his search for personal salvation, because J.B. does not represent the universal man.

MacLeish's J.B. is a man of the capitalist West: smug, self-centered, self-righteous, self-seeking, a corporate executive, evidenced in his declaration that never since he learned to tell his shadow from his shirt, not once, not for a watch-tick, has he doubted God was on his side and good to him. From the first fine silver dollar in his fist to the last controlling interest in some company, he saw he could get anything he wanted—and he knew it wasn't luck.

How unlike is J.B., with his Protestant ethic, to the pious herdsman Job, "a perfect and upright man," about whose nobility and generosity Eliphaz can say, "Thou hast instructed man, and thou hast strengthened the feeble knees."[3]

Indeed, *J.B.* loses its impact in direct proportion to our inability to identify sympathetically with the play's major theme, turned off by what is essentially J.B.'s lack of compassion for others, egoistic smugness, and endless greed in his capitalist success.

In the end, J.B.'s affirmation becomes, in effect, solely the affirmation of self and gratitude for God's ultimate goodness to him.

The dramatic message of *J.B.*'s dismissal of any earthly help for humankind—whether social, scientific, or political—is blind subservience to God's will in all matters. Rather than work to improve the human condition, we may pass the buck to a dubious God and His even more dubious Grace—as long as we pay for the privilege with our obsequious reverence.

As poet and thinker, MacLeish has received well-deserved world acclaim for dramatic, thoughtful, and poetic philosophical writing. He discusses *J.B.*'s willing acceptance of life-as-it-is in an article in *Theater Arts*: "[J.B.'s] willingness is as pure and naked an affirmation of the fundamental human thing—the fundamental human belief in life in spite of life, the fundamental human love of life as life and in spite of all the miseries of life—as I have ever found."[4]

As *J.B.* says, one must have faith in something beyond oneself. Does this mean faith in a mercenary Church that has established itself politically in this economic-driven world? Where can one place one's faith and not be fooled? How are we to know anything for certain where God is concerned?

Where is the Voice in the Whirlwind today, when belief in God is a choice rather than a given, and the creation of the universe can be explained by astrophysicists without reference to supernatural powers?

As mortal beings, we live our lives in the valley of the shadow of death, forever seeking to understand the mystery of life's meaning (if it has any meaning beyond itself). J.B. confronts these unanswered questions with faith—faith that is unshakeable even to dying in the garbage heap. Steadfast faith *is* J.B.'s answer.

CHAPTER SEVENTEEN

Life and Death

The mystery of human existence, life and death, is the theme of *Our Town* and *The Skin of Our Teeth*. Thornton Wilder's writings reflect his concern with ethics, spirituality, and even saintliness, expressing his belief that the inner core of humanity's essential nature is moral because of our ability to love.

The last line of Wilder's Pulitzer Prize–winning second novel, *The Bridge of San Luis Rey* (1927), reads: "There is a land of the living and a land of the dead and the bridge is love, the only survival, the only meaning." *Our Town* is the dramatic setting that gives the reality to this proposition; the life of Emily Webb represents the particular, personal goodness that infers the human universal. In *The Skin of Our Teeth*, love is expressed in parenting, nurturing, educating, and protecting.

Both deal with love of life and affirm that human beings were created to live in harmony with one another, courageous in the face of all adversity, including Nature's violence. This optimistic philosophy, directly expounded by the philosophers in Act III of *The Skin of Our Teeth*, contrasts with the existential despair presented in the literature of European contemporaries like Jean-Paul Sartre and Samuel Beckett. Yet Wilder agrees with fellow playwrights Sartre and Beckett on the premises of existential philosophy: that each human being is individually responsible for his or her character, with the development of character evolving from an individual's actions, moral or immoral. The living experience of the human being meets the multifarious dynamics of family and culture and, over a lifetime, develops a unique, mature persona.

For Wilder, born in Madison, Wisconsin, on April 17, 1897, this process began from a number three position in the family constellation, behind an older brother and sister, and followed by two younger sisters. His austere Congregationalist father, Amos Parker Wilder, was a Yale graduate who served as editor of various newspapers in New Haven, New York, and Madison, Wisconsin, before he became involved in Wisconsin politics and was appointed U.S. Consul General at Hong Kong and Shanghai by President Theodore Roosevelt.

Being born into the close-knit, matriarchal Wilder household meant excellent educational opportunity as well as economic, emotional, and moral security. All the Wilder siblings, nurtured by the shining example of their mother, Isabella Niven Wilder, were prolific and creative writers. Yet Thornton, deeply saddened by his long separations from his father, and perplexed by his own inner pangs of homosexual longing, experienced what he described in his later journals as a lonely childhood:

> Starved of the environment of love: hence forever after exhibiting so greedy and omnivorous an expectation of love that no affection they *receive* is adequate, and (what is worse) their affection for others is not truly love but a demand and command to be loved. (I am more and more willing to agree with certain authorities that homosexuality is negative—that it is, even when apparently aggressive, a submission to solicitations. These solicitations are not necessarily those coming from the outside; they come from within also, from an exorbitant need for tenderness, i.e., to be valued by another.)[1]

While his personal letters indicate a reserved and reticent social life, Wilder's art communicates passionately, affirming our need and ability to love as an antidote to despair. His characters, reflective of average human beings, are educable because of love, capable of change, possessing a power of goodness intrinsic to their creature-nature that can erase any evil festering within, just as the sun each day erases the night.

The acronym WOW-M corresponds to the four greatest American playwrights to date: Thornton Wilder, Eugene O'Neill, Tennessee Williams, and Arthur Miller. Of the four, Wilder deserves special citation as a well-read classical scholar, a good stage actor in his own plays, an excellent teacher with a gentle sense of caring about his audience's sensibilities, and, of all the Pulitzer Prize playwrights, probably the most patriotic, having served in both the First and Second World Wars.

As one of America's most brilliant creative minds, Wilder informs the world of America's positive and meaningful life experiences that make this nation unique in human history. Playwright and teacher, Wilder is the model of the creative artist that Joseph Pulitzer had in mind when he wrote in his will that the prize in drama should be given to that American playwright whose play about American life best exemplifies the educational value and power of the stage.

Our Town (1937–1938)
by Thornton Wilder

A Play in Three Acts. Produced and Staged by Jed Harris. Opened on Broadway at the Henry Miller Theater, February 4, 1938.

The Original Cast

Stage Manager	Frank Craven
Dr. Gibbs	Jay Fassett
Joe Crowell	Raymond Roe
Howie Newsome	Tom Fadden
Mrs. Gibbs	Evelyn Varden
Mrs. Webb	Helen Crew
George Gibbs	John Craven
Rebecca Gibbs	Marilyn Erskine
Wally Webb	Charles Wiley, Jr.
Emily Webb	Martha Scott
Professor Pepper	Arthur Allen
Mr. Webb	Thomas W. Ross
Woman in the Balcony	Carrie Weller
Man in the Auditorium	Walter O. Hill

Lady in the Box	Aline McDermott
Simon Stimson	Philip Coolidge
Mrs. Soames	Doro Merande
Constable Warren	E. Irving Locke
Si Crowell	Billy Redfield
Baseball Players	Alfred Ryder, William Roehrick, and Tom Coley
Sam Craig	Francis G. Cleveland
Joe Stoddard	William Wadworth

Our Town is an early-twentieth-century portrait of an idealized America, of a New England village and the life and death of a simple American woman, Emily Webb. Thornton Wilder creates an omniscient narrator-guide, the Stage Manager, who, just as Virgil guides Dante in *The Divine Comedy*, helps us explore this Yankee town, Grover's Corners.

In the Preface, Wilder considers the issue of theatrical realism on a proscenium stage, contending that the box-set stage, loaded with props, does not promote the audience's imaginative ability to suspend disbelief. Choosing instead to set his play on an empty stage, he claims to have taken the idea from the post–World War I, German Expressionist theater, particularly the work of Max Reinhardt. But Shakespeare centuries ago used the Globe's bare, open stage to bring forth warring armies and ships tempest-tossed and wrecked in storms.

To establish the setting, Wilder may have been influenced by one of Hollywood's cinematic techniques: wide-angle panning. The camera views a broad cityscape, then zeroes in on one of several tall buildings, then on one of its windows, which takes the viewer into an interior. In this play Wilder paints verbally the panoramic landscapes of all American Our Towns in imitation of the works of Naïve painters like Grandma Moses. The Stage Manager also reports the latitude, longitude, and geological composition of Grover's Corners, linking this minute piece of Earth and the action of the play to the greater cosmos. Whatever the influences, it is with remarkable innovation that Wilder touches the playgoer with his magic wand and stirs the imagination so that each member of the audience, irrespective of his or her unique life experience, can see and believe in Grover's Corners and the events taking place on the bare stage.

Whenever Wilder performed in *Our Town*, he always played the Stage Manager—the factotum, an amalgamation of a twentieth-century sociologist, the voice of a Shakespearean Prologue, a fifth-century Greek chorus, and an Actor's Equity substitute for actors who were indisposed and couldn't get to the theater to play their parts.

The Stage Manager's major responsibility is to make clear that a degree of immortality has come to Grover's Corners, New Hampshire, because of what is being laid in the cornerstone of the new Cartwright Bank Building on Main Street.

Into the bank's cache, to be sealed for a thousand years, for archaeologists of that distant time to uncover and analyze, are items that tell of living and dying in the first part of the twentieth century in the United States of America. As does this play.

Beginning with the turn of the twentieth century, 1901, from the horse-and-buggy days to the advent of the automobile in New Hampshire, about 1911, Wilder's play recreates the innocence of a past era, which will never be again, making *Our Town* its own everlasting memorial.

Much like a medieval morality play, *Our Town* is composed of stations as it focuses on the lives of the inhabitants of Grover's Corners and their daily doings. The downtown Main Street is an unpaved roadway that passes the railroad station and depot, going straight past a livery stable where sturdy, wagon-drawing horses are kept for hire or for stabling. There is one elementary school, one high school, and one bank; four Protestant churches, a Unitarian church, and, across the railroad tracks in Polish Town, one Catholic church. Most people have a reason each day to visit the drugstore and the single grocery store, and most people who are born here are buried in the cemetery on the hill.

Wilder gives no hint of any sinning or immorality or antisocial behavior among the town people, except for the alcoholism of Simon Stimson and one inebriated Pole who nearly dies in a snow pile. There are no incidents of marital infidelity in town and no evidences of sexual deviation, like homosexuality, which seems, however, to be hinted at in Simon Stimson's statement that when young men come too close to him, he feels uncomfortable. Dr. Gibbs says he knows the organist's problem, that Simon shouldn't live in a small town because he has a dilemma that no one here can help. Can it be helped in a large city where anonymity allows sexual freedom?

The vaguely delineated character of Simon Stimson may come more clearly into focus as a self-portrait of the artist, as a gay man living in fear of his being exposed in a small community. In *The Enthusiast: A Life of Thornton Wilder*, Gilbert A. Harrison describes Wilder—an indisputably successful artist, who at the age of thirty won his first Pulitzer Prize for his great novel *The Bridge of San Luis Rey*—as an emotionally reclusive man who could not establish deep and long-lasting relationships. Wilder never married and never came out, but spent the last thirty to forty years of his monkish but highly creative life in Hamden, Connecticut, living with his younger, unmarried sister Isabel.

Almost as if he were trying to convince himself, Wilder's plays and other literary works seem to have a particular psychological and philosophical focus, presenting the artist's message for mankind: *while you are alive and living, live, sensitively appreciative of the gift of life itself.* Did Wilder live by his stated credo?

Like Emily Dickinson's homely philosophy, Wilder's play stresses the value-beyond-any-price of the smallest events in one's daily life. Emily Webb's Lazarus-like return to life on her twelfth birthday is played with an intense ecstasy that is almost unbearable, as Emily asks herself: Does any person alive realize the value of every second of one's life as one lives it on this wonderful, wonderful earth? This moment of theater is one of the most significant educational experiences of any drama.

Having hoped at first to revisit a day from her married life or her short motherhood, Emily is surprised when the other shades of Grover's Corners urge her to choose an *unimportant* day. Longing to see some happiness at least, she settles on a childhood birthday. Yet a girl's twelfth birthday is rich with significance, implying as it does the beginning of womanhood, with the mysterious advent of the body's power to create life. With indescribable love Emily looks to her entire family knowing that she is to be a link in the Webb chain of being.

Our Town, even as it shuns sentimentality, is essentially a play about survival and renewal, remembering Grover's Corners and the significance of Emily Webb's life. Though the playwright would have us believe that Emily's memory of her life experiences will fade away as she passes into eternity, she does not fade from the audience's memory, but lives to reiterate the sober message that one must appreciate life.

The major theme of *Our Town* formulates a socio-philosophical portrait of our relationship to our fellow human beings and to eternity. In the beginning of the play the playwright says he will focus on the "smallest events in our daily life," but before the end he has dramatized the deaths of a large part of that rural community, all seeking a vision of eternity, which is the orderly continuum of all lives in the cosmic hereafter.

Probably the most powerful symbol of the relatedness of all things is dramatically presented in a letter Jane Crofut's minister sent her once when she was sick. The address on the envelope read: Jane Crofut; The Crofut Farm; Grover's Corners; Sutton County; New Hampshire; the United States of America; Continent of North America; Western Hemisphere; the Earth; the Solar System; the Universe; the Mind of God. And Wilder would have us believe that the postman delivered it, though he perhaps believes the letter landed as undeliverable in the U.S. dead letter office.

Like Wilder's other works, *Our Town* is concerned with the interrelatedness of all things in the universe. Traveling outward link by link—the body, the farm, the town, the county, the state—the dead souls in the Grover's Corners cemetery can follow the route of transit for Jane Crofut's letter, at the end of which they will become one with God. The memories of Earth, says the Stage Manager, fade rapidly for those who are luckily elected to dwell in Heaven's eternity. Yet tiny Grover's Corners, barely a nano-speck in the vastness of the cosmos, remains a microcosm that implies the macrocosm: a heavenly, hospitable place where God is a fatherly neighbor in the next house on the hill.

The Skin of Our Teeth (1942–1943)
by Thornton Wilder

A Play in Three Acts. Produced by Michael Myerberg. Staged by Elia Kazan. Opened on Broadway at the Plymouth Theater, November 18, 1942.

The Original Cast

Sabina	Tallulah Bankhead
Mr. Fitzpatrick	E. G. Marshall
Mrs. Antrobus	Florence Eldridge
Dinosaur	Remo Buffano
Mammoth	Andrew Ratousheff
Telegraph Boy	Dickie Nan Patten
Gladys	Frances Heflin
Henry	Montgomery Clift
Mr. Antrobus	Fredric March
Doctor	Arthur Griffin
Professor	Ralph Kellard
Judge	Joseph Smiley
Homer	Ralph Cullinan
Miss E. Muse	Edith Faversham
Miss T. Muse	Emily Lorraine
Miss M. Muse	Eva Mudge Nelson
Ushers	Stanley Prager and Harry Clark
Girls	Elizabeth Scott and Patricia Riordan
Fortune Teller	Florence Reed
Chair Pushers	Earl Sydnor and Carroll Clark,
Conveeners	Stanley Weede, Seumas Flynn, Stephan Cole, Aubrey Fassett, Stanley Prager, and Harry Clark
Broadcast Official	Morton Dacosta
Defeated Candidate	Joseph Smiley
Mr. Tremayne	Ralph Kellard
Hester	Eula Belle Moore
Ivy	Viola Dean
Fred Bailey	Stanley Prager

The Skin of Our Teeth dramatizes the history of human life from the caveman and the Ice Age to World War II, incorporating the Book of Genesis and the evolutionary science of Darwin.

The play's major theme examines the human capacity for survival. Despite awesome pain and suffering, the annihilating forces of nature, and the murderous nature of humanity itself, we hold determinedly, tenaciously, to life. Depicting the continuity of the human experience within the context of family life amid bizarre and challenging outer circumstances, Wilder illuminates a universal hope for peaceful living and the search for essential and enduring values, and possibly God.

As in *Our Town*, the playwright is influenced by German Expressionist drama. He enlists an Announcer—a stage manager figure, not included in the cast list—who comes forward to work a projection screen with lantern slides presenting "news events of the world." Among these, a ring that may have married Adam to Eve has been found in the theater, a moving glacier has pushed the Cathedral of Montreal southward into Vermont, and George Antrobus, a married father of two children in the suburb of Excelsior, New Jersey, has just invented the wheel.

The curtain rises on the interior of the Antrobus home. The maid, Sabina, waits at the window with a feather duster under her arm, hoping to catch sight of Mr. Antrobus, who is late coming home from across the Hudson River but, it is hoped, he may be bringing home something for the family to eat. As Sabina holds forth in a frantic soliloquy about the sometimes rather serious moral failings of her employers, a wall of the house becomes unhinged and tilts, then rights itself. Suddenly a rear wall-flat flips up and out of the scene and disappears into the flies. Sabina is unfazed by any of these bizarre occurrences, saying that the Antrobuses and she have managed to survive despite all the close calls they've had—with dinosaurs nearly trampling them to death or the many times of near-starvation when the locusts ate everything in the garden. Yes, she goes on, it was by the skin of their teeth that the Antrobuses have lived through perilous eons on this earth. But they have survived.

Sabina has reached the end of her soliloquy and looks anxiously toward the kitchen door. She repeats the line, obviously awaiting a response. Then, flustered and angry because Mrs. Antrobus hasn't come in on cue, Sabina walks back to her original position with her feather duster at the curtain's rise and begins the scene again, a ridiculously funny embarrassment for Sabina and a belly-laugh for the audience.

A clearly audible offstage voice instructs Sabina to improvise, make something up—and now that the spell of audience-belief has been obliterated, Sabina comes downstage and speaks directly to the audience. She hates this play, she confesses, and believes that the playwright is absolutely confused about everything, that he can't even make up his mind whether they all are living in New Jersey or in prehistoric caves. But what does it all matter? Where will any person here be a hundred years from now anyhow? If there's one more depression, which everyone came through by the skin of their teeth, where will this all end?

Mrs. Antrobus enters finally, complaining that Sabina has let the fire go out on this coldest day of the year, and asking whether she has milked the mammoth. Yes, she has milked the mammoth, Sabina answers , then steps out of the scene again to inform the audience that she doesn't understand one word of this play!

The Skin of Our Teeth is whimsical, capricious, and cruel, as the inventive playwright interrupts an action, repeats an action, or revises an action with Time telescoped, transforming trivia into historic moment and vice versa, allowing actors to speak directly to the audience and calling on plants in the audience for real audience participation. Like the Pantaloon clowning in the *Commedia dell' Arte*, the comical activity on stage appears as a masquerade disguising the dead-seriousness of the playwright. Wilder is most intensely philosophical and spiritual when he seems most antic.

And the major theme of the play *is* deadly serious: survival is survival is survival (dramatizing Gertrude Stein's rhetorical power of stated truth). Historically kaleidoscopic and anachronistic, with elements of vaudeville, slapstick, carnival, and sideshow, like no other American play, *The Skin of Our Teeth* transforms this harsh and gritty pronouncement into a masterpiece of theater—seriously frenetic, imaginatively provocative, and exciting.

In Act I, prehistoric animals knock on the door, begging to come in out of the Ice Age cold to warm up at the Antrobuses' fireplace. Mr. Antrobus, Wilder's Everyman, asks the audience to pass up their wooden folding chairs so his family can chop them up to keep the fire burning and preserve the species *Homo sapiens*. Like a gaudy three-ring circus with animals and conventioneers, the action in Act II on the Boardwalk at Atlantic City is bawdy, as Esmeralda the Fortune Teller foretells the world's extinction in a universal Flood with Antrobus-Noah as savior. And there is the plague of universal war in Act III, with Evil evolving into the persona of Cain. But in the last hour, the great philosophers attempt to establish good judgment and civility within the individual and in the State. And, at last, at the midnight hour, the playwright cites the belief in the miracle of God's power to create light where there was once only darkness, as a source of hope that there can be peace on the Earth He created.

Wilder sees human existence as a conglomeration of patterns, both horrific and sublime, that promise some sort of mystical enlightenment. Without disillusionment or panic, Wilder views death—the great terror of our existence—with stoic fortitude, reason, and pragmatism as simply a part of the continuum, the next phase in the natural order.

As in his other Pulitzer-winning play, *Our Town*, in *The Skin of Our Teeth* Wilder calls on the dead to intuit the meaning of existence. Given a dispassionate timelessness in the art form of theater, Wilder's characters represent an ethereal reservoir of souls, like Emerson's Oversoul, telling us that civilization without reason becomes chaos, and that to understand truly and fully the experience of being alive, one must realize that the Chain of Being links, without end, generation to generation and to God.

Added to Brecht's manipulative techniques are the basics of Max Reinhardt's expressionistic drama demanding universal significance. The play abounds with grand allusions—scientific, historical, religious, psychological, literary, and sociological.

Wilder takes concepts from the Book of Genesis and combines them with an H.G. Wells–like compendium of world history commenting on human nature and social institutions. His genius adds comic elements that suggest the Marx Brothers, and in the cute mammoth and dinosaur one is reminded of the baby sheep in the Wakefield Master's *Second Shepherd's Play*. Homer, Moses, and the Muses come into the house out of the cold, provided survival by the fire with the American family-for-all-time, the Antrobuses. The wisdom of the philosophers Plato, Aristotle, and Spinoza is presented by backstage personnel who don't even resemble actors. The magic of Creation in Genesis is read by the Stage Manager, introducing for the first time in the play the notion that God may not have had any hand in directing the Ice Age, or any Age in the Earth's evolution before or concurrent with human life.

In three acts, a triptych of very mixed-up geological, Biblical and contemporary time-settings, the major theme of *The Skin of Our Teeth* underscores survival. But is life worth all the suffering? the play asks repeatedly. Why did the whole thing start in the first place and who did it? Where is the Master Designer?

Dramatizing different eras in historical time simultaneously, George and Maggie Antrobus, the eternal Man and Woman, primal Adam and Eve of Creation, search for an answer with a deep spirituality, imbued with the love of "Mind" that links George Antrobus in both a platonic and religious sense to the "Mind of God."

George believes that the human experience has meaning though he can't fathom what it is. He is heaven-bent to discover it. His faith is expressed in inventions, his love for his fellow man and woman, and the beautiful, constructive thoughts he finds in philosophy and literature. He never turns to despair, the sickness unto death of the existentialists. Without self-doubt, George has the intellectual energy and drive to discover alphabetical clues and practical inventions, hinted to him by the "Original Creative Mind."

Intellectual pleasures and lusty hedonism both delight George; his watchword "Have fun" allows him to stray into immoral paths with the seductress Sabina, who aspires to enslave all men to her powerful allure. She and Maggie Antrobus represent the duality of the Eternal Feminine, with Maggie as the breeding, moral, caregiving Mother who promises continuity of the species. Living by her own watchword, "Save the family," Maggie gives voice to a fiercely protective and optimistic maternal love, believing that the kids will "turn out OK"; while George despairs over the sexual impulsiveness of his daughter and the inherently sadistic nature of his son Henry that promises war will always exist.

Henry-Cain, the personification of human wickedness, his forehead marked with the indelible biblical emblem of murder, via Wilder's transformation becomes the Nazi whose hatred and killer instincts are directed against his own father.

The moral values in the play are presented variously—in the most casual way or in the most absurd improvisations. The Expressionistic technique of having characters step out of character to become impersonations of impersonations or abstractions brings the biggest laughs at the most serious moments of the action. Ingeniously, Wilder presents the spiritual message of the play in imitation of a medieval Book of Hours.

The first-hour spokesman-thinker is Spinoza, concerned with self-examination, exhorting his listeners to discover what is both human and good in themselves. Spinoza describes God as the sum total of all natural forces that rule the universe, and theorizes that God governs by way of conscience and free will, which lay the responsibility on each individual for his or her own morality, accounting each human being a unique experiment.

Wilder cites Spinoza, optimistic that the evil in men and women, the mark of Cain, will become fainter as it is confronted constantly with itself. Evil, beholding its own image, will one day fade and disappear. This mystical psychic phenomenon is suggested as Henry steps out of character to confess how his adolescent feelings of emptiness, of being unwanted and unloved, filled him with hatred for everyone. (Is this Wilder's personal confession as well?) Suddenly Henry experiences the self-conscious realization of Spinoza's resolution: "I saw that all the objects of my desire were in themselves nothing good nor bad, save insofar as the mind was affected by them."

Plato's Socrates searches for order in the state, for a just ruler whose decisions are beyond the impress of passion. In Act III Wilder poses the problem of a single man, a megalomaniac like Hitler, whose hate and anger can catch up an entire nation and be multiplied a hundred millionfold to wreak a world-horror of destruction. Socrates offers no solution to prevent this hateful megalomania that nourishes evil even as it infects a whole nation. It is a pity, Wilder suggests, that humanity has no means to appeal to a Divine court for justice. People of good will must collectively struggle as best they can to sustain civilization in the face of the worst horrors.

Aristotle asserts that human intellect must be treasured, for it is the sole energy we share with God. Is that perhaps the meaning of being created in God's image? Wilder's Antrobus is devoted to learning and invention, like Shakespeare's Prospero, in love with books, and his hope is that mind, not might, will triumph, that persuasion by education can change the brutish nature of man.

The last dramatic quotation is spoken at the "dreariest hour of midnight": the first words of Genesis—which represents Wilder's spiritual affirmation of the living presence of the Master Planner. He asserts that the metaphysical problem of existence cannot be answered by the simplistic notion of accident, or by a God that has forsaken His creation, or by a God Who has died. More than theatrical entertainment, Wilder's plays are truly testaments of faith, very personal, but at the same time universally approved by audiences.

The Skin of Our Teeth does not despair of the human condition, despite the ceaselessness of murder, rape, and war. With anguish, guilt, and the negation of human values near the end of Act III, Wilder introduces the philosophers' words and through them attempts to communicate his faith to all the American Antrobuses who are living now, and those to come, that through the anxious hours of Earth's brutal nights, we human beings will survive by the skin of our teeth.

Epilogue

The Pulitzer Prize Plays: An Evaluation

The Pulitzer Prize plays portray an America that is essentially humane, affirming positive human values, essentially against nihilism and depersonalization. Some critics have come forward to speak positively on behalf of the philosophy of theater as life-relevant.

A 1943 editorial by Burton Rascoe in the *New York World-Telegram* commends the Pulitzer Prize as a value to the theater arts:

> Prizes in the arts are a good thing. The more of them, I think, the better. They are a stimulant as well as a bounty; they promote an interest in the theater and the other arts; they are a legitimate means of making the general public conscious of good work, and they usually arouse dissension and controversy, which are, in themselves, signs of health and vigor in the arts.[1]

In 1935, when Akins' *The Old Maid* won over Hellman's *The Children's Hour*, critic Arthur Pollock took exception to the false values and the presumptuous attitudes that he felt governed the selection of the Pulitzer Prize (and focused his ire on Yale professor William Lyon Phelps as representative of those standards):

> Of course, the whole trouble with the selection of this Pulitzer Prize play is the number of William Lyon Phelpses in the world, of old fogies with hermetically sealed minds and egos made sick by the

adulation of nice old ladies and vapid young ones who live to look up wide-eyed to antiquated lecturers spouting banalities from a platform. Prof. Phelps got *The Children's Hour* thrown out by hitching to it the word, found somewhere in an old tin can, "unpleasant."[2]

Ex-Pulitzer Prize juror Walter Prichard Eaton, in *The Theater Annual of 1944*, expressed milder critical reservations about the selection process:

> *De gustibus non est disputandum*, perhaps. That it is difficult to tell until Time has come to one's aid, what is enduring art and what is a flash in the pan. That there is a fear, sometimes, on the part of the administrators of a trust (and even the Pulitzer jurors are, in a sense, such administrators) of departing too violently from conservatism in making their judgments. That, possibly, there is a somewhat greater sense of the underlying moral responsibility of art on the part of such men as constitute the Pulitzer juries than on the part of such men as constitute Broadway critics. And, of course, that, now and then, there is just plain esthetic dumbness, as when we preferred *They Knew What They Wanted* to *What Price Glory?* But, on the whole and in recent years, matched award for award with the Critics' Circle's choices, the Pulitzer Prize has not been unworthily administered. When one considers that the French Academy did not admit Molière till he had been dead a century, one might even say that the Pulitzer Prize has been awarded with some distinction.[3]

There were eight years in the first half-century of Pulitzer Prizes when no award was given, when no play on Broadway was thought worthy of the prize by the jurors. But the most contentious times for the Pulitzer jurors was when there were several prize-worthy contenders. Often the jurors' selection was challenged by a chorus of angry theater critics who felt that poor judgment, politics, or favoritism (sometimes maybe all three) had led the advisory board into error.

What were the criteria that finally determined the winners in controversial years? Why have the notes, critiques, and evaluations of past and present jurors not been published? Theater critics are hardly secretive or shy about their positions on performance, character development, theme-significance, and production values. Why this secrecy among the Pulitzer jurors?

For that matter, several organizations in New York City award annual prizes in the theater, including the Drama Critics' Circle, the Drama Desk, and the American Theater Wing (which awards the Tonys). None of these have published any criteria for what they believe makes a play "the best." The judgment is obviously a matter of personal prejudice evolved from the individual juror's education, personal predilection and maturational life experiences.

The distinctive qualifications for excellence set forth by Alfred Pulitzer in his will served well for most of the fifty years of prize awards examined in this study. It is our contention, with Joseph Pulitzer, that a play's greatness is its intrinsic "educational value and power," that if it is a great play it will provoke powerful emotions and thoughts in its audience. This means that the audience will have been mesmerized by the playwright to identify with one of the characters in the dramatic conflict, experiencing that conflict subconsciously. The playwright and the players on stage have caused the audience, like a hypnotist with a willing subject, to suspend disbelief and accept the belief that what is being performed on the stage is real. We are made to forget that we are sitting in a theater. We are living a strange, unique experience, as though we are watching a dream unfold—a dream we have no power to change, but one that intrigues us by its meaningful message.

When the conflict is resolved on stage, the emotional release is cathartic, similar to what Freud characterizes as the tension-release that comes about in dreaming. But dreams are most often surreal confusions of thoughts and feelings couched in symbolic images controlled by the stage-manager-superego in the unconscious. A play, on the other hand, is the conscious product of a real and rational mind, recreating the problems of reality in such a way that when the dramatic problem is resolved, the conflict no longer oppresses us.

The drama is the most difficult art form to create; it demands a mature, creative integrity. Playwrights must know themselves fully, unashamedly, to be in close touch with their thoughts and feelings. They must be able to divide themselves into other selves as they become each character, leaping like an electric spark from the brain of one character to another, animating the reality between them with passionate words and the body-language of conflict.

Following Hamlet's advice to the players, playwrights must create suitable action with appropriate diction to recreate the reality that would necessarily exist if there were no stage and the players were real people. In words they hear spoken internally, playwrights conceive a reality that springs to life on the stage.

The significant questions are: Is the integrity of the playwright evident in the resolution of the conflict? Does the play matter to your life?

There is no finality—only continuity—to the American historical process, and to the awarding of the annual Pulitzer Prize for excellence in Drama.

It is this author's hope that the gallery of unforgettable portraits and narratives in the library of forty-two American plays reflecting American life from 1917 to 1967 will be deemed a national treasure.

A great nation like ours deserves the establishment of a federally funded National Theater, a theater center in Washington, D.C., with several stages in its complex, much like Lincoln Center in New York City. It could be allied with the current National Council for the Arts. The National Theater would devote itself to on-going repertory productions of the Pulitzer Prize plays. Unlike the renowned Shaw Festival in Niagara-on-the-Lake or the Royal Shakespeare Theater of Stratford-upon-Avon offering a range of classic and contemporary plays, the National Theater of America would be a company of artists—directors, actors, and stage designers—presenting each year a repertory of at least three of the Pulitzer Prize plays, whose major themes reflect comparative portraits of American life.

The ever-increasing library of the Pulitzer Prize plays would serve as the keystone treasury for the National Theater's productions with fine actors, stimulating a new enthusiasm in all Americans to read and reread plays.

A theater center in the nation's capital would draw audiences from across the country and provide continuous work and development for theater personnel. Planned and programmed after-performance study-seminars with playwrights and directors would examine the vision of the American way of life as it is reflected in the prize plays.

Summoning glorious echoes of the theater of Athens in 500 B.C.E., with its competitive playwrights, Aeschylus, Sophocles, and Aristophanes, a federally funded National Theater would inspire today's playwrights to strive for true excellence in their dramatic depictions of America. A National Theater would encourage and demand a playwright's mature creativity to provide an American audience's passionate understanding of the human condition in this nation.

Appendix One

Chronologies 1917–1967: The Plays

1916–1917

The Pulitzer Prize drama jurors, Augustus Thomas, Richard Burton and Hamlin Garland, chosen by the National Institute of Arts and Letters, did not believe that any of the season's plays met the Pulitzer will requirements.

1917–1918

Jesse Lynch Williams' *Why Marry?* was given the first Pulitzer Prize, amid acclaim by all the critics, with the exception of John Corbin of the *New York Times*, who objected to the play's contrived ending as it declaimed against modern marriage and the attitude of men toward women. Corbin maintained that *Why Marry?* was a playwright's sleight-of-hand trick to produce a happy ending. [1]

1918–1919

The Pulitzer advisory committee made no award for drama, passing over Winchell Smith and Frank Bacon's *Lightnin'*. Bacon's starring role as the drunken hero Lightnin' Bill Jones delighted audiences in nearly thirteen hundred performances; but his example did not serve to raise "the standards of good morality, good taste, and good manners."

1919–1920

Beyond the Horizon, by Eugene O'Neill, received the Pulitzer Prize. The play opened in special matinee performances on February 3,

1920, and won the acclaim of all the critics. Alexander Woollcott wrote in the *New York Times*: "Certainly, despite a certain clumsiness . . . the play has greatness in it, and marks O'Neill as one of our foremost playwrights."[2] J. Ranken Towse in *The New York Evening Post* wrote that the play was "a work of uncommon merit and definite ability, distinguished by general superiority . . . But it is not quite a masterpiece."[3]

1920–1921

Zona Gale's *Miss Lulu Bett*, a play adapted from her novel of the same title, won the Pulitzer accolade, despite the fact that the Pulitzer will specified "that the winner should be an *original* American play." The advisory board justified its choice on the grounds that the play's original conception and the adaptation were both Miss Gale's.

1921–1922

In 1922, Eugene O'Neill's *Anna Christie* won the Pulitzer Prize, even though the story of an ex-prostitute did not seem to suit the moral stipulation of the Pulitzer will. Burns Mantle in the *New York Mail* asserted the rightness of art: "Whether the art of *Anna Christie* be rejected because of its ugliness or its ugliness be accepted as art, the thrill of its playing will long be the boast of those who see it." [4]

1922–1923

Icebound, by Owen Davis, won the Pulitzer Prize. It was easy for American audiences and the Pulitzer Prize committee to recognize it as a moral play depicting the real old fashioned values of farm life in New England.

1923–1924

It was not so easy to justify *Hell-Bent fer Heaven*, Hatcher Hughes' play, taking the prize. A major controversy arose when the drama jurors, William Lyon Phelps, Clayton Hamilton, and Owen Johnson, recommended that George Kelly's *The Show-Off* be given the prize instead.

Brander Matthews, Professor of Drama at Columbia, protested the jurors' recommendation. Hatcher Hughes had served as an assistant to Matthews at Columbia, and Matthews wrote a personal letter to the university president, Nicholas Murray Butler, in which he set forth arguments in favor of awarding the Pulitzer Prize to the Hughes play.

President Butler presented the letter to the advisory board, which persuaded them to agree with Professor Matthews' choice. *The New York Times* carried Owen Johnson's reaction on his discovering that the jurors' selection had been overruled:

> Our recommendation is supposed to be secret. How did Dr. Brander Matthews find out . . . ? What right did he have to interfere . . . in behalf of a member of the Columbia faculty who was a junior in his own department? . . . Prof. Phelps and myself feel we were treated with gross discourtesy . . . and we will never serve on a Pulitzer jury again. We do not dispute the power of the advisory board to overrule our verdict, but, where there is interference at Columbia in favor of a Columbia man, we feel that an explanation certainly should have been made to us. [5]

No explanation was forthcoming. It was Hughes' prize.

1924–1925

They Knew What They Wanted, by Sidney Howard, was selected by drama jurors Clayton Hamilton, Jesse Lynch Williams, and Hamlin Garland over the close contender *What Price Glory?* by Maxwell Anderson and Laurence Stallings. According to Walter Prichard Eaton in *The Theater Annual of 1944,* the jurors deliberated long before deciding that the Howard play was a more lasting contribution than *What Price Glory?* which the jurors curiously decided was merely "topical."[6]

1925–1926

George Kelly's *Craig's Wife* was awarded the prize. *The New York Telegram* disagreed with this choice, lauding Marc Connelly's *The Wisdom Tooth* as:

. . . not only better written, with a touch of beauty utterly lacking in *Craig's Wife*, and having a far greater power to stimulate and reflect on American life, but it has a much wider appeal. Possibly Marc Connelly will be attended to next year, when he will be granted the prize for a play not so good as his current one. . . . The Pulitzer Prize committee seems to be just about a year behind in their wash. [7]

1926–1927

The Pulitzer committee honored Paul Green's *In Abraham's Bosom*, produced by the Provincetown Players. The Off-Broadway play garnered the praise of all the critics and moved uptown to the Garrick Theater. Walter Prichard Eaton, commenting about the committee's choice in *The Theater Annual of 1944*, wrote:

> Our choice lay between *The Silver Cord* by Sidney Howard and the new play by young Green, his first play to reach New York . . . Because this play came up out of the soil of the South, and with a passionate sincerity tried to say something important about the Negro problem, and because it seemed to us that the prize, if given to Green, might be a great encouragement to regional American drama, we recommended *In Abraham's Bosom*. [8]

1927–1928

Eugene O'Neill was awarded the Pulitzer Prize for the third time. It was the unique and experimental *Strange Interlude*, the nine-act play—with a dinner recess—that held audiences spellbound in the John Golden Theater from 5:15 to 11:00 P.M. The critics were at great variance. Alexander Woollcott and Brooks Atkinson were negative. Atkinson asked disparagingly in the *New York Times*: "What, in fine, distinguishes *Strange Interlude* from the old three-decker novel?"[9]

However, in the *New York World*, Dudley Nichols' praise for the play was effusive: "the most important event in the present era of the American theater."[10] And Gilbert Gabriel, in the *New York Sun*, named *Strange Interlude* "the most significant contribution any American has made to the stage."[11]

In what appears to be an anti-O'Neill campaign, Alexander Woollcott followed his first harsh criticism of O'Neill's *Strange Interlude* in the *New Yorker* with a second damning column a short time later, entitled "Second Thoughts on First Nights."

When, subsequently, the Pulitzer Prize was awarded to O'Neill, Woollcott printed an ironic letter by writer Ben Hecht describing *Strange Interlude* as "a theatrical pomposity."

1928–1929

Elmer Rice's *Street Scene* won the Pulitzer award. The play, whose setting is the front stoop of a tenement house on the Lower East Side of New York City, portrays lower-class characters, most of them ignorant and mean-spirited. The selection of this play prompted a profound change in the requirements for the Pulitzer Prize. At the request of the jurors, the advisory committee finally eliminated the clause in the original Pulitzer will requiring a prize play to be instructive in raising the standard of good morals, good taste, and good manners.

Drama juror Clayton Hamilton applauded the change: "You can't get up on the stage and cry about manners and morals today and by doing so to expect to raise the standards of the American people. Any good play is a moral play, and the only immoral play is a poor play." [12]

Indeed, immorality, bad taste, and bad manners are intrinsic to the realistic portrait of urban life in Rice's *Street Scene*. Percy Hammond, theater critic of the *New York Herald Tribune*, concurred with the Pulitzer committee's choice of *Street Scene* and was elated that the executors of Pulitzer's will could "disapprove his mouldy standards . . . and that they are justified in upsetting the founder's last will and testament, and probating it according to the better and easier Broadway laws." [13]

1929–1930

The Green Pastures, Marc Connelly's adaptation of Roark Bradford's *Ol' Man Adam an' His Chillun*, was awarded the prize. Brooks

Atkinson in the *New York Times,* called it "a play of surpassing beauty."[14]

That it was an adaptation, like Zona Gale's *Miss Lulu Bett,* seemed to pose a problem. The drama juror Walter Prichard Eaton wrote in *The Theater Annual of 1944*:

> Before recommending *The Green Pastures,* which was based on Roark Bradford's stories, we consulted Mr. Pulitzer's son, who said: "Does it add something original, making the work a new and perhaps larger thing, as Shakespeare added to the stories he took?" We said we thought it did. "Then give it the prize," said he.[15]

1930–1931

Maxwell Anderson's masterfully written *Elizabeth the Queen* lost to Susan Glaspell's *Alison's House.* Brooks Atkinson, in the *New York Times,* took exception to the choice:

> Every few years the drama committee insists on publishing its ignorance. *Alison's House* is a play of flat statements—of assertions, of sentimentally literary flourishes and of perfunctory characterizations. No matter how earnestly the characters talk, in a strangely stereotyped prose, the image of Alison never appears for an instant. Prize committees are always unpopular and under suspicion. But sometimes the drama committee for the Pulitzer Prize goes out of its way to make its glory hollow.[16]

Though the judges might have agreed that *Elizabeth the Queen* was theatrically superior to *Alison's House,* Anderson's play did not convey an American theme.

But even with this contention satisfied, there was cause for complaint. Theater audiences had roared with laughter at George S. Kaufman and Moss Hart's first collaboration, *Once in a Lifetime,* a derisive satire on Hollywood. Theater critics wrote that this comedy surely merited the drama jurors' earnest consideration for the Pulitzer.

1931–1932

The drama jurors, as if correcting the oversight of the previous year, awarded the prize to George S. Kaufman, Morrie Ryskind, and Ira Gershwin's collaborative musical effort, *Of Thee I Sing*. Though many of the critics were content with the Pulitzer choice, Brooks Atkinson in the *New York Times* expressed his disbelief that Eugene O'Neill's *Mourning Becomes Electra*, Elmer Rice's *Counselor-at-Law*, and Paul Green's *The House of Connelly* had been overlooked. Atkinson wrote: "When the committee turns its back on the drama in a season that has yielded several excellent plays and starts equivocating about the book of a musical comedy, the Pulitzer Prize loses a great deal of value. There is more whim than judgment in this year's award."[17]

The critic Gilbert Gabriel disagreed: "*Of Thee I Sing* is gold-flecked with virtuoso cleverness in all its departments, and with such a caustic courage in tune and talk as comes close to Offenbach at his best." [18]

1932–1933

Both Your Houses, by Maxwell Anderson received the Pulitzer Prize. The theatrical season had been a lean one in both the number and the quality of plays on Broadway, and Richard Lockridge, drama critic of the *Evening Sun*, described the problem very well when he quipped:

> The award of the Pulitzer Prize to Maxwell Anderson's *Both Your Houses* can best be applauded on the assumption that it is really an award to Mr. Anderson, who so clearly stands well forward among the country's playwrights. The cantankerous may urge that the committee has seen fit to honor Mr. Anderson's worst play.[19]

1933–1934

Maxwell Anderson's *Mary of Scotland* was the unanimous choice of the three Pulitzer jurors, Clayton Hamilton, Walter Prichard Eaton, and Austin Strong. It was a shock to the jurors when their selection was set aside by the advisory board in favor of Sidney Kingsley's *Men in White*. Eaton was indignant:

> The Pulitzer advisory board consists of a group of newspaper editors, mostly from out of town, who come up to Columbia once a year. I have no doubt they are excellent men, but they don't know a thing about the theater. They don't want dramatic experts any more—they want office boys. No self-respecting, intelligent critic would serve on such a jury.[20]

The jurors resigned in a body.

It was a theatrical *cause célèbre* in all the newspapers. The spokesman who answered for the Pulitzer Advisory Board was Columbia's President Frank D. Fackenthal. He stated that the Pulitzer drama jurors were retained only in an advisory capacity, and, though their vote for *Mary of Scotland* was unanimous, the board reserved the right to exercise its own judgment. *Mary of Scotland* did not deal with an American theme. *Men in White* did. A new set of jurors was appointed: John Erskine, William Lyon Phelps, and Stark Young. And, to avoid any further controversy between the jurors and the advisory board, the jurors were redirected:

> The advisory board has, therefore, directed that hereafter the Juries of Selection and Recommendation shall be invited not to propose a definite recipient for a prize but to submit what the members of the jury regard as an eligible list of possible recipients, with a summary of their reasons for the recommendation in each case. . . . By refraining from making a distinct recommendation, the embarrassment which the Advisory Board has sometimes felt would be avoided.[21]

1934–1935

The furor of the critics was intense in 1934 when the Pulitzer Prize was given to Sidney Kingsley's *Men in White* rather than to Maxwell Anderson's *Mary of Scotland*. But now the critics' wrath rose to a new and shriller pitch when the Pulitzer Prize went to Zoe Akins'

The Old Maid rather than to Lillian Hellman's *The Children's Hour*, a serious drama dealing daringly with lesbianism and enthusiastically extolled by all the critics.

The New York Times printed the gist of the story:

> In 1934, the Pulitzer Advisory reversed the jurors' unanimous decision for Anderson's *Mary of Scotland* and gave it to *Men in White*. Last Spring's uproar was the loudest of all. The jury simply offered four names to the committee. They were *The Old Maid, Personal Appearance, Merrily We Roll Along*, and *Valley Forge*, and the committee picked the first named.[22]

The consensus of the critics was that *The Old Maid* was the least worthy of the plays. Burns Mantle had earlier assessed its odds as a Pulitzer selection as forty to one, against Lillian Hellman's *The Children's Hour*, nine to five. [23] Clayton Hamilton, an ex-juror, reflected caustically on the Pulitzer choice in a broadcast over radio station WJZ:

> The Prize jury has labored and brought forth a mouse. Miss Zoe Akins herself very likely would be the last to claim that this is an original American play. The characters were created by Miss Edith Wharton; the atmosphere was created by Miss Edith Wharton, and the emotions and sentiments were worked out by Miss Edith Wharton.[24]

Actually, the Pulitzer jurors had not even considered the Hellman play as a possible candidate because of its "controversial" lesbian theme. Angry editorials by the New York critics grew increasingly intense and spurred the foundation of a competing awards committee, the Drama Critics' Circle.

In October 1935, the New York Drama Critics' Circle, a group of seventeen theater critics, met at the Algonquin Hotel and resolved to attend to what they termed their own official business. In their capacity as theater critics who reviewed every play on Broadway and off, they claimed the right and responsibility to be the arbiters of excellence in theater. And so they conceived a new prize, the

Drama Critics' Circle Award "for the best new play by an American playwright produced in New York during the theatrical season."

Amidst all of this confusion, the Pulitzer Advisory Committee issued a new, controversial—even meaningless ruling. Unexpectedly, in October 1935, they announced that hereafter, the Pulitzer Prize could be received only once by any one playwright. No reason was given for this exclusion. However, the confusion and contention that this rule might have caused was forestalled when, seven months later, in May l936, the board wisely nullified the unwarranted restriction. The board also changed the wording of the prize criteria from "which shall best represent the educational value and power of the stage" to "which shall represent in marked fashion the educational value and power of the stage." The reformulation seemed to suggest a more liberal tendency and a less presumptuous tone by the board.

It was fortunate that the board rescinded the briefly held stipulation that a playwright could not win more than one Pulitzer award. Robert Sherwood said that he would have rejected the prize for *Idiot's Delight* if that had been a condition. In a trans-Atlantic interview, he explained that the elimination of competition with major playwrights who were former Pulitzer winners would have made the winning of the prize a doubtful honor.[25]

In "Topic of the Times" in October 1935, the matter of two competing prizes in the drama—the Pulitzer and the Drama Critics Circle—was discussed in statesmanlike terms, attempting a reconciliation of the objectives of the Drama Critics' Circle Award and the Pulitzer Prize Advisory Committee for all time. The article reported that the criteria for the selection of the Pulitzer Prize were self-contradictory in citing the ethical and social service motive of the work of art. The Drama Critics, considering themselves specialists in the field, took exception to these limiting criteria, which they agreed did not serve the communal interest and inspire "a stronger faith in American ideals."

The *Times* article attempted to define the *raison-d'être* for the new committee of prize-awarding experts:

The new line-up [between the Pulitzer Award and the Drama Critics' Circle Award] clears the air for everybody. The professional reviewers can go ahead and pick a play which is the best theater in
absolute terms. The Pulitzer committee can pick a play which is the
best theater for our American democracy. Most of the time the two
agencies will likely be in agreement, but if they differ too often, it will
only stimulate healthy discussion of what does constitute a good play
these days in the United States.[26]

The prize choices of the Drama Critics' Circle and the Pulitzer
have differed to some extent over the years, though not completely;
during the years 1935 to 1965, the two awarding groups concurred
in their choices of award-winning plays on eleven occasions. And
for two disappointing theatrical seasons, 1942 and 1944, both
groups abstained from naming a Pulitzer Prize play. It is difficult, if
not impossible, to say whose selections have been the superior. But
it seemed that honoring more plays encouraged more theatergoing
and spurred American playwrights to greater productivity.

1935–1936
There were excellent choices for the prizes: *Winterset*, by Maxwell
Anderson, for the Drama Critics' Circle, and *Idiot's Delight*, by Robert Sherwood, for the Pulitzer. Both are romantic, artificially styl-
ized tragedies.

Winterset takes a stand against the American courts for their
failure to enact justice. The play is based on the famous 1920 Sac-
co-Vanzetti case in which two immigrant Italians, suspected of
radical anarchist views, were tried and condemned to death for
murder and the theft of $15,000.00 at a Massachusetts shoe fac-
tory. Despite their pleas of innocence and the many stays of execu-
tion that stirred a public concern for justice, the men were put to
death.

Idiot's Delight condemns the rise of Fascism and the Fascist preparation for war in Europe, even as it glorifies the American democratic tradition.

1936–1937

The prize plays were the Drama Critics' Circle choice, *High Tor,* by Maxwell Anderson, and the Pulitzer's, *You Can't Take It with You*, by George S. Kaufman and Moss Hart. Both plays are critical of American life, dramatizing the joylessness of the American capitalist.

The contention of some of the critics was that Kaufman and Hart's *You Can't Take It with You* was purely box-office comedy and that a serious antiwar play like Paul Green's *Johnny Johnson*, which was overlooked, truly merited the award. Burns Mantle in the *New York Daily News* wrote of the critical problems in judging for prizes:

> The trouble with prize play awards is, ever has been and always will be, that it is quite impossible to define actually just what specific virtues in a play are to be considered. The theater fulfills its truest function only so long as the actions it inspires are 90 percent emotional reactions, and emotional reactions are as varied as the humans who experience them. Hence every award is a compromise of sorts. [27]

1937–1938

The Drama Critics' Circle choice was John Steinbeck's dramatization of his novel *Of Mice and Men*, a California ranch tragedy in which the childlike, half-witted Lenny Small, unaware of his tremendous strength, accidentally kills his seductress. In the same year, *Our Town*, by Thornton Wilder, was the Pulitzer choice; it presents a cosmic vision of America, past and present and future, set in the microcosm of New Hampshire's Grover's Corners, a land blessed by the "Mind of God."

1938–1939

Robert E. Sherwood's *Abe Lincoln in Illinois* was honored by the Pulitzer committee. The Drama Critics' Circle members were unable to reach the necessary number of nominating votes as they considered Lillian Hellman's celebrated *The Little Foxes*, Clifford Odets' powerful *Rocket to the Moon*, S. N. Behrman's delightful *No*

Time for Comedy, and Philip Barry's sophisticated *The Philadelphia Story*. Stymied, they made no award. But critic Heywood Broun was enthusiastic for the Pulitzer Committee's choice that year. He said: "The Pulitzer Prize has double-crossed me; I'm sore this year because l have nothing about which I can holler. Not only is *Abe Lincoln in Illinois* a magnificent play, but it represents the peak of a fine artist who has constantly grown in stature through several seasons."[28]

1939–1940

The Drama Critics' Circle and the Pulitzer Prize committee both selected as prize winner William Saroyan's *The Time of Your Life*. However, the Pulitzer committee was faced for the first time in its history with a prize recipient's rebuff.

The power of Saroyan's *The Time of Your Life* shines through in its theme of total rejection of the materialist values of capitalism and middle- and upper-class society. The play glorifies the poor, the immigrant, the ignorant, the immoral, the shiftless, the destitute, and the renegade—those who, even in abject poverty, still dream that life can be beautiful.

Saroyan returned the $1,000.00 check, declaring he had not written the play to have it approved by the social groups he wished to condemn. He said, "I would be no more guilty of bad taste, if I made an annual William Saroyan award to one or another of the great magnificently organized industries for most effectively profiting more than any other similar industry during the year."[29]

1940–1941

Lillian Hellman's *Watch on the Rhine* was the winner of the Drama Critics' Circle Award, and Robert E. Sherwood's *There Shall Be No Night* won the Pulitzer award. Both plays are powerfully concerned with the cruelty of Nazism and the obligation of Americans to recognize its evil and destroy it. The competition was keen; both plays were equally worthy candidates for the Pulitzer award, but the choice of *There Shall Be No Night* probably depended upon the late opening of *Watch on the Rhine*. The Hellman play opened on

Broadway on April 1, one day after the Pulitzer's eligibility period closed.

1941–1942
Judging that none of the Broadway offerings merited an award, neither the jurors for the Pulitzer committee nor the Drama Critics' Circle named a prize play.

1942–1943
The Drama Critics' Circle Award was given to Sidney Kingsley's *The Patriots* and the Pulitzer Prize to Thornton Wilder's *The Skin of Our Teeth.* A formal protest was immediately lodged with the Pulitzer Prize committee by Henry Morton Robinson, senior editor of *Reader's Digest,* and Professor Joseph Campbell of Sarah Lawrence College against this choice. Robinson said that Wilder had committed "literary grave robbing" and that the play was a "bold and unacknowledged appropriation" of *Finnegans Wake* (1939) by James Joyce.[30] However, the exception was put aside, and the "Joycean borrowings"—such as they are—do not in any way diminish the excellence of Wilder's play. The petty professional envy reflected by Robinson and Campbell must be recognized. They have forgotten Shakespeare's borrowings and overlooked the fact that their own works are borrowings, even rehashes of borrowings.

1943–1944
The theatrical season was so disappointing that there was neither a Pulitzer Prize for drama nor a Drama Critics' Circle award. No Broadway plays were deemed worthy.

1944–1945
Mary Chase's *Harvey* won the Pulitzer Prize; the Drama Critics' Circle's choice was Tennessee Williams' *The Glass Menagerie.* It is difficult to understand how Williams' first masterpiece, *The Glass Menagerie,* blessed with the magnificent performance of Laurette Taylor, failed to impress the Pulitzer jurors or the advisory board. Not awarding the prize to Williams represents possibly the biggest

error the Pulitzer committee has made in its assessment in any theater season. The whimsy of a drunkard who hallucinates a six-foot tall rabbit simply cannot compare in dramatic value to the passionate, fully realized portrait of American life that Williams presented in his great memory play, *The Glass Menagerie*.

1945–1946
The Pulitzer committee awarded the prize to Howard Lindsay and Russel Crouse's *State of the Union*; the Drama Critics made no award.

1946–1947
There was no Pulitzer Prize awarded for drama. The Drama Critics' Circle selected Arthur Miller's *All My Sons*. Completely overlooked, unaccountably, was Eugene O'Neill's masterwork *The Iceman Cometh*. The three Pulitzer jurors, Mrs. Mary M. Colum, Joseph W. Krutch, and Oscar J. Campbell, were astute drama critics and fully recognized the power of Miller's well-made play and the poignancy of the actor Jason Robards in O'Neill's brilliant *The Iceman Cometh*. Unaccountably, the Pulitzer advisory board rejected the jurors' recommendation of either of these plays and decided to give no award.

1947–1948
The Pulitzer Prize and the Drama Critics' Circle Award were both given to Tennessee Williams for his superb *A Streetcar Named Desire*.

1948–1949
Arthur Miller's masterpiece *Death of a Salesman* won both the Pulitzer Prize and the Drama Critics' Circle Award.

1949–1950
The Pulitzer advisory committee gave the prize to *South Pacific* by Richard Rodgers, Oscar Hammerstein II, and Joshua Logan. The musical had been chosen the previous year by the Drama Critics'

Circle in its category of Best Musical. *South Pacific* was selected over William Inge's poignant *Come Back, Little Sheba*, Maxwell Anderson and Kurt Weill' s powerful collaboration, *Lost in the Stars*, and Carson McCullers' superb *Member of the Wedding*, which was honored by the Drama Critics' Circle as Best Play.

1950–1951

The Broadway theatrical season was brilliant with many exciting plays that deeply explored the psyche of American life. Among them were Abe Burrows and Frank Loesser's *Guys and Dolls*, Louis Coxe and Robert Chapman's *Billy Budd*, Clifford Odets' *The Country Girl*, and Tennessee Williams' *The Rose Tattoo*. Yet, unaccountably again, no Pulitzer Prize for drama was awarded. Sidney Kingsley and Arthur Koestler's *Darkness at Noon*, won the Drama Critics' Circle Award.

1951–1952

The two Broadway plays honored for excellence were both dramatic studies of emotionally disturbed women with weak and introverted men. They were Joseph Kramm's *The Shrike*, the Pulitzer Prize winner, and John Van Druten's *I Am a Camera*, the choice for the Drama Critics' Circle Award.

1952–1958

For six consecutive years the Pulitzer Prize and the Drama Critics' Circle Award were given to the same plays:
  1952–1953: *Picnic*, by William Inge
  1953–1954: *Teahouse of the August Moon*, by John Patrick
  1954–1955: *Cat on a Hot Tin Roof*, by Tennessee Williams
  1955–1956: *The Diary of Anne Frank*, by Frances Goodrich and Albert Hackett
  1956–1957: *Long Day's Journey into Night*, by Eugene O'Neill
  1957–1958: *Look Homeward, Angel*, by Ketti Frings
  The 1956 Pulitzer choice, *The Diary of Anne Frank*, raised some serious contention among the jurors because it was not, in its subject matter, an American play. Eight years later it was to be revealed that the jurors, in following the Pulitzer will "to the letter," had put

aside *The Diary of Anne Frank,* and had voted unanimously for Clifford Odets' *The Flowering Peach,* but their choice had been overruled by the advisory board.[31]

1958–1959
Archibald MacLeish's *J.B.,* a poetical, dramatic retelling of the biblical story of Job (recast as an American CEO) was the Pulitzer choice. Lorraine Hansberry's significant *A Raisin in the Sun,* dealing with the problems of the African American in the urban ghetto, was cited for excellence by the Drama Critics' Circle.

1959–1960
The Drama Critics' Circle Award went to Lillian Hellman's Freudian-based play, *Toys in the Attic.* The Pulitzer award went to Jerome Weidman and George Abbot's musical *Fiorello!*

1960–1961
All the Way Home, by Tad Mosel, won both prizes. The play, adapted from James Agee's Pulitzer Prize novel *A Death in the Family,* was the singular shining star in a dim theatrical season.

1961–1962
Jack Weinstock, Abe Burrows, Willie Gilbert, and Frank Loesser's barbed satire *How to Succeed in Business Without Really Trying* won the Pulitzer Prize and the Drama Critics' Circle Award for Best Musical. This same year, Tennessee Williams' *Night of the Iguana* won the Drama Critics' Circle Award for Best Play.

1962–1963
The Drama Critics' Circle named Edward Albee's *Who's Afraid of Virginia Woolf?* the best play. The Pulitzer advisory committee made no award, refusing their jurors' unanimous recommendation of the Albee play, which portrayed two couples on a college campus in a grotesque evening of alcoholism and debauchery.

An editorial in the *New York Times* suggested that the "immoral" aspect of the play may have offended the advisory committee.[32]

Who's Afraid of Virginia Woolf? portrays a ruthless, nihilistic struggle between the sexes, very similar in theme to the earlier prize-winning plays *Craig's Wife* and *The Shrike.*

Critic Stanley Kauffmann of the *New York Times,* in writing about the Albee play, observed that many of the plays on Broadway at the time seemed to be homosexual charades and that the female characters had not originally been conceived by the playwrights as female. Changing the sex of the characters, he suggested, was requisite to satisfy theatrical producers who did not believe audiences would come to the theater to see a homosexual play. Kauffman held the belief that *Who's Afraid of Virginia Woolf?* was actually a disguised homosexual play.[33]

When *Who's Afraid of Virginia Woolf?* was rejected, by the Pulitzer advisory board, John Mason Brown and John Gassner, who had served as Pulitzer drama jurors for nearly seven years, both resigned, denouncing the Pulitzer advisory board as having devaluated the prize "with zeal and muddleheadedness on the one hand, and with timidity and disingenuousness on the other." The first remedy for this problem, Mr. Gassner suggested, would be to abolish the advisory board.[34]

The Pulitzer committee's rejection of Albee's play caused bitter discord in theatrical and literary circles. Behind the scenes at the Columbia University School of Journalism the "Albee problem" prompted much discussion about the need for further revision of the Pulitzer Prize criteria.

1963–1964

The Pulitzer Prize committee again made no award in the drama. *Luther,* by the British John Osborne, was awarded the Drama Critics' Circle Prize.

1964–1965

The Subject Was Roses, by Frank Gilroy, was chosen by both the Drama Critics' Circle and the Pulitzer committee. At this time the Pulitzer committee announced that the terms for the Pulitzer Prize had once again been amended, to omit the clause "which shall represent in marked fashion the educational value and power of the stage." It was necessary to eliminate this clause, the advisory board announced, because it represented a stumbling block for the critics who wanted greater flexibility in determining which plays were prize-worthy.

The implication was clear: the revision was made to allow awarding a prize to a play whose theme might seem morally controversial to the general public. "Greater flexibility" seemed to mean that the Pulitzer jurors did not want to be restricted by a rule that they believed encouraged an old-fashioned and Sunday-school-moralizing variety of drama. With this poorly considered emendation, the committee turned its back on what they saw as the "controversial" and "moralistic" criteria that Joseph Pulitzer's will had established nearly fifty years before.

The change nullified Pulitzer's essential reason for having established the prize in drama in the first place. Pulitzer believed that the drama, though essentially a form of entertainment, was an educational experience reflecting life. In his newspapers Pulitzer had sought objectively to report the human condition without moralizing, but he took great pride in the belief that he was *educating* his readers.

With the elimination of these initial criteria, the Pulitzer Prize committee had discarded its anchor and seemed willing to drift in the same rudderless boat as the Drama Critics' Circle, navigating on their jurors' collective critical consensus without any particular directive or purpose.

Pulitzer's original will had attempted to establish educational value as a serious reason for a playwright to write a play. (This same raison d'être for the drama was the basis for the prize awarded to the great Greek playwrights at the Panathenian Festival Athens in 500 B.C.E.) This value tested the dramatic and compelling powers of a theatrical work to move an audience emotionally. The prime consideration was that a play should be a meaningful reflection of reality with the power to move the hearts and minds of the American audience to examine itself.

Now the Pulitzer Prize award was to be based solely on the individual judgment of the jurors, subject to approval of the advisory board, which body, in turn, was to be governed by its members' unique social and educational backgrounds, and personal prejudices.

1965–1966

There was no Pulitzer Prize award. *The New York Times* reported that the Pulitzer jurors had considered William Alfred's *Hogan's Goat*, a play of violence, sex, and politics in a wild nineteenth-century Brooklyn, and Dale Wasserman's *Man of La Mancha*, a musical dramatization of Cervantes' *Don Quixote*.[41] The Drama Critics' Circle saw fit to honor *Marat/Sade* by Peter Weiss.

1966–1967

Possibly in an attempt to make up for its rejection of Edward Albee's *Who's Afraid of Virginia Woolf?* four years before, the Pulitzer committee awarded the prize to *A Delicate Balance*. The Drama Critics' Circle chose Harold Pinter's *The Homecoming*.

Again, the wrathful voices of the press were heard, this time labeling the Albee play second-rate and the Pulitzer Prize now a prize for mediocrity.[36] Albee accepted the prize, claiming that taking the prize allowed him to criticize it as a waning honor. [37]

Though *A Delicate Balance* is indeed less focused than *Who's Afraid of Virginia Woolf?*, the winning Albee drama explores—in a mix of realism and surrealism—the dysfunctional aspects of one American family's life. The award satisfied onetime juror and drama critic John Mason Brown. In an article in the *New York Times*, he comments on Albee's award: "I found *A Delicate Balance* the most fascinating new American play of the season. I am sure Mr. Gassner would have shared my delight at the current award for Mr. Albee. I talked with him about the play before his death and he took the trouble . . . to send me a written review of it. A favorable one, as I recall."[38]

After fifty years of prizes, the changed criteria for awarding the Pulitzer Prize will have had significant effects. For playwrights, for the moment, there are now no restrictive guidelines, except that the play be written by an American and possibly deal with some aspect of American life.

In a 1931 article, drama critic Harold Clurman delineated what he conceived to be good theater and its purpose:

> A good play . . . is the image or symbol of the living problems of our time. These problems . . . chiefly moral and social . . . must be faced with an essentially affirmative attitude, in the belief that . . . there may be some answer. . . that should be considered operative for. . . the humanity of our time and place. Such plays may be tragedy or comedy, fantasy or farce; . . . identified with any aesthetic category; but they must be directly relevant to the audience for which they are presented.[39]

The Pulitzer Prize plays seem to epitomize Harold Clurman's vision of what makes "a good play."

The original Pulitzer criteria for prize-worthiness is different from that of the Drama Critics' Circle. In establishing the Pulitzer Prizes, Joseph Pulitzer sought to encourage American playwrights to create great art, to award them a prize of honor, as they explored American life in dramatic terms. He may have hoped that these plays would give shape to a uniquely American National Theater, with the Pulitzer plays as repertory reflecting American cultural traditions. Certainly, the Pulitzer Prize plays are collectively representative of America's best dramas—a national treasure, both as a library of American plays and a mirror-study of the American character.

Appendix Two

Chronologies 1917–1967: The Jurors

Listed here in chronological order are the Pulitzer Prize plays' jurors (varying in number from two to four) appointed for each year with an indication of significant qualification. In years that no award was made, either the jurors deemed no Broadway offering worthy of the Pulitzer Prize, or, if they did name one, the advisory committee rejected their suggestion.

1917 No award
1918 *Why Marry?* by Jesse Lynch Williams
Jurors: (3) Augustus Thomas, Chair, Playwright: *The Witching Hour*; Richard Burton, Critic: *The New American Drama*; Hamlin Garland, Novelist: *Daughter of the Middle Border* Pulitzer Prize, 1923
1919 No award
1920 *Beyond the Horizon*, by Eugene O'Neill
Jurors (3): Hamlin Garland, Chair; Richard Burton; Walter Prichard Eaton, Critic: *The American Stage of Today*
1921 *Miss Lulu Bett*, by Zona Gale
Jurors (3): Hamlin Garland, Chair; Richard Burton; William L. Phelps, Critic: *The Twentieth Century Theater*
1922 *Anna Christie*, by Eugene O'Neill
Jurors (3): William L. Phelps, Chair; Hamlin Garland; Jesse Lynch Williams, Playwright: *Why Marry?* Pulitzer Prize, 1918

1923 *Icebound*, by Owen Davis
Jurors (3): William L. Phelps, Chair; Clayton Hamilton,
Drama Critic; Owen Johnson, Novelist

1924 *Hell-Bent for Heaven*, by Hatcher Hughes
Jurors (3): William L. Phelps, Chair; Clayton Hamilton;
Owen Johnson

1925 *They Knew What They Wanted*, by Sidney Howard
Jurors (3): Jesse Lynch Williams, Chair; Clayton Hamilton;
Hamlin Garland (asked to be released)

1926 *Craig's Wife*, by George Kelly
Jurors (3): A. E. Thomas, Chair; Walter. P. Eaton; Owen
Davis, Playwright: *Icebound*, Pulitzer Prize, 1923

1927 *In Abraham's Bosom*, by Paul Green
Jurors (3): A. E. Thomas, Chair; Walter P. Eaton; Clayton
Hamilton

1928 *Strange Interlude*, by Eugene O'Neill
Jurors (3): A. E. Thomas, Chair; Walter P. Eaton; Clayton
Hamilton

1929 *Street Scene*, by Elmer L. Rice
Jurors (3): A. E. Thomas, Chair; Walter P. Eaton; Clayton
Hamilton

1930 *The Green Pastures*, by Marc Connelly
Jurors (3): Clayton Hamilton, Chair; Walter P. Eaton; Austin
Strong, Playwright

1931 *Alison's House*, by Susan Glaspell
Jurors (3): Clayton Hamilton, Chair; Walter P. Eaton; Austin
Strong

1932 *Of Thee I Sing*, by George S. Kaufman and Morrie Ryskind;
Music by George Gershwin and Lyrics by Ira Gershwin
Jurors (3): Clayton Hamilton, Chair; Walter P. Eaton; Austin
Strong

1933 *Both Your Houses*, by Maxwell Anderson
Jurors (3): Clayton Hamilton, Chair; Walter P. Eaton; Austin
Strong

1934 *Men in White*, by Sidney Kingsley
Jurors (3) Clayton Hamilton, Chair; Walter P. Eaton;

Austin Strong. All resigned to protest advisory committee's overruling Maxwell Anderson's *Mary of Scotland*

1935 *The Old Maid*, by Zoe Akins
Jurors (3): William L. Phelps, Chair; Stark Young, Critic: *The New Republic*; John Erskine, Novelist, Educator

1936 *Idiot's Delight*, by Robert E. Sherwood
Jurors (2): William L Phelps, Chair; Mary M. Colum, Poet, Critic

1937 *You Can't Take It with You*, by Moss Hart and George Kaufman
Jurors (3): William L. Phelps, Chair; Mary M. Colum; Arthur Hobson Quinn, Biographer

1938 *Our Town*, by Thornton Wilder
Jurors (3): William L. Phelps, Chair; Mary M. Colum; Schuyler Watts, Critic

1939 *Abe Lincoln in Illinois*, by Robert E. Sherwood
Jurors (3): William L. Phelps, Chair; Mary M. Colum; Schuyler Watts

1940 *The Time of Your Life*, by William Saroyan
Jurors (3): William L. Phelps, Chair; Mary M. Colum; Schuyler Watts

1941 *There Shall Be No Night*, by Robert E. Sherwood
Jurors (3): William L. Phelps Chair; Mary M. Colum; Schuyler Watts

1942 No award
Jurors (3): William L.Phelps, Chair; Mary M. Colum; W. Somerset Maugham, Novelist, Playwright: *The Constant Wife*

1943 *The Skin of Our Teeth*, by Thornton Wilder
Jurors (3): W. Somerset Maugham, Chair; Mary M. Colum; Glenway Wescott, Novelist

1944 No award
Jurors (3): W. Somerset Maugham, Chair; Mary M. Colum; Glenway Wescott

1945 *Harvey*, by Mary Chase
Jurors (3): Mary M. Colum, Chair; Joseph W. Krutch,

Columbia University Faculty, Critic: *The Nation*; Oscar J.
Campbell, Columbia University Faculty

1946 *State of the Union*, by Russel Crouse and Howard Lindsay
Jurors (3): Mrs. Mary M. Colum, Chair; Joseph. W. Krutch;
Oscar J. Campbell

1947 No award.
Jurors (3): Mrs. Mary M. Colum, Chair; Joseph W. Krutch;
Oscar J. Campbell

1948 *A Streetcar Named Desire*, by Tennessee Williams
Jurors (3): Joseph W. Krutch, Chair; Oscar J. Campbell;
Maurice J. Valency, Columbia University Faculty,
Playwright: *Madwoman of Chaillot*

1949 *Death of a Salesman*, by Arthur Miller
Jurors (3) Oscar J. Campbell, Chair; Joseph W. Krutch;
Maurice J. Valency

1950 *South Pacific*, by Richard Rodgers, Oscar Hammerstein II,
and Joshua Logan
Jurors (3): Oscar J. Campbell, Chair; Joseph W. Krutch;
Maurice J. Valency

1951 No award
Jurors (2): Oscar J. Campbell, Chair; Maurice J. Valency

1952 *The Shrike*, by Joseph Kramm
Jurors (2): Oscar. J. Campbell, Chair; Maurice J. Valency

1953 *Picnic*, by William Inge
Jurors (2): Oscar J. Campbell, Chair; Maurice J. Valency

1954 *The Teahouse of the August Moon*, by John Patrick
Jurors (2): Oscar J. Campbell, Chair; Maurice J. Valency

1955 *Cat on a Hot Tin Roof*, by Tennessee Williams
Jurors (2): Oscar.J. Campbell, Chair; Maurice J. Valency

1956 *The Diary of Anne Frank*, by Frances Goodrich and Albert
Hackett
Jurors (2): Oscar J. Campbell, Chair; John Mason Brown,
Critic: Saturday Review

1957 *Long Day's Journey into Night*, by Eugene O'Neill
Jurors (2): Oscar J. Campbell, Chair; John Mason Brown

1958 *Look Homeward, Angel*, by Ketti Frings

Jurors (2): John Mason Brown, Chair; John W. Gassner, Critic and Editor

1959 *J.B.*, by Archibald MacLeish

Jurors (2): John Mason Brown, Chair; John W. Gassner

1960 *Fiorello!* by George Abbott, Jerome Weidman, Jerry Block, and Sheldon Harnick

Jurors (2): John Mason Brown, Chair; John W. Gassner

1961 *All the Way Home*, by Tad Mosel

Jurors (2): John Mason Brown, Chair; John W. Gassner

1962 *How to Succeed in Business Without Really Trying*, by Frank Loesser and Abe Burrows

Jurors (2): John Mason Brown, Chair; John W. Gassner

1963 No award

Jurors (2): John Mason Brown, Chair; John W. Gassner. Both resigned in the controversy with the advisory committee over *Who's Afraid of Virgina Woolf?*

1964 No award

Jurors (3): Walter Kerr, Chair, Critic: *The New York Herald Tribune*; Elliot Norton, Critic: *Boston Record*; Maurice J. Valency

1965 *The Subject Was Roses*, by Frank D. Gilroy

Jurors (3): Walter Kerr, Chair; Elliot Norton; Maurice J. Valency

1966 No award

Jurors (3): Maurice J.Valency, Chair; Walter Kerr; Elliot Norton

1967 *A Delicate Balance*, by Edward Albee

Jurors (3): Maurice J. Valency, Chair; Walter Kerr; Elliot Norton

Notes

Introduction

1. Henri Fluchere, *Shakespeare and the Elizabethans* (New York: Hill and Wang, Inc., 1956), p. 182.

Family Life

Youth in Parental Conflict

1. Virginia Floyd, ed., *Eugene O'Neill at Work* (New York: Frederick Ungar Publishing Co., 1981), p. 296.
2. Ibid., p. 74.

The Unmarried Woman

1. Frederick Lewis Allen, *Only Yesterday* (New York: Harper, 1931), p. 79ff.

The Conflict of the Sexes

1. M. F. Ashley Montagu, "Marriage—A Cultural Perspective," in *Neurotic Interaction in Marriage*, ed. Victor W. Eisenstein (New York: Basic Books, Inc., 1956).
2. See Lawrence S. Kubie, "Psychiatrists on a Shrike—Other Views," *The New York Times*, March 16, 1952, Sec. X2, p. 6.

The Drive for Generation

1. Warren Freedman cites a Talmudic document that discusses this subject in *Society on Trial* (Springfield: Chas. Thomas Co., 1965), p. 78.
2. Friedrich Nietzsche, "Natural History of Morals," in *The World's Great Thinkers, Man and Spirit: The Speculative Philosophers*, ed. Saxe Commins and Robert N. Prescott (New York: Random House, 1947), p. 519.
3. Gilbert Murray, *Five Stages of Greek Religion* (New York: Doubleday, Inc., 1951), p. 34.
4. Arthur and Barbara Gelb assert in their study *O'Neill* (New York: Harper Bros., 1962, p. 635) that O'Neill, like the world at large, was impressed with the youthful courage of Charles Lindbergh, who may have served as inspiring model for the Superman.
5. Tad Mosel, *All the Way Home* (New York: Samuel French, 1961), p. 32.
6. Louis Kantor, "O'Neill Defends His Play of Negro," *The New York Times*, May 18, 1934, Sec. IX, p. 1.

7. Tennessee Williams, *Cat on a Hot Tin Roof* (New York: Signet Books, 1955), p. 136.

Social Protest

The Nonconformists

1. *The William Saroyan Reader*, 1958. (Fort Lee: Barricade Books, 1994), p.497.

Against Prejudice

1. Oscar Handlin, *Race and Nationality in American Life* (New York: Doubleday, 1957), p. 76.
2. Israel Zangwill, "The Melting Pot," quoted in *Planning for a Nation of Cities*, ed. Sam Bass Warner, Jr. (Cambridge: M.I.T. Press Paperback Edition, 1966), p. 148.

Against War

1. Franklin Delano Roosevelt, "Quarantine Speech," reprinted in *Builders of American Institutions*, ed. F. Freidel and N. Pollack (Chicago: Rand McNally Co., 1963), p. 491.
2. Benito Mussolini, "Fascism," in *Encyclopedia Italiana*, 1932, quoted in *Europe in Review*, ed. G. L. Mosse et al. (Chicago: Rand McNally, 1964), p. 458.
3. Robert Emmet Sherwood, *There Shall Be No Night* (New York: Charles Scribner's Sons, 1941), pp. xxviii-xxi.

Political Heroes

The Charismatic Historical Hero

1. Abraham Lincoln, "First Inaugural Address," in Builders of American Institutions by F. Freidel and N. Pollack (Chicago: Rand McNally Co., 1963), p. 257.
2. Max Weber, *The Theory of Social and Economic Organization*, trans. A. M. Henderson and Talcott Parsons (New York: Free Press of Glencoe, l957), pp. 360–363.
3. Robert E. Sherwood, *Abe Lincoln in Illinois*, in *Best Plays of the Modern American Theater*, ed. John Gassner (New York: Crown Publishers, 1947), pp.756–757.
4. Abraham Lincoln, "First Inaugural Address," in *Builders of American Institutions* by F. Freidel and N. Pollack (Chicago: Rand McNally Co., 1963), pp. 256–57.

The Fictional Political Hero

1. Herbert Hoover, *The Challenge to Liberty* (New York: Charles Scribner's Sons, 1934), p. 13.
2. David A. Shannon, *Twentieth Century America* (Chicago: Rand McNally Co., 1963), p. 303.
3. *Online Journal*, February 5, 2004.

Morality and Survival in a Materialistic Society

The Capitalist Hero

1. Gustave de Beaumont, *Marie* or *Slavery in the United States*, translated by Barbara Chapman (Baltimore: Johns Hopkins University Press, 1994), appendix 2.
2. Arthur Miller, *Death of a Salesman* (New York: Penguin Books, 1976), p. 132.
3. Rostow, *Stages of Economic Growth* (Cambridge: Cambridge University Press, 1962), p. 139.

The Spiritual Condition of Humankind

Inferno and Purgatory

1. Tennessee Williams, *A Streetcar Named Desire* (New York: New Directions, 2004), p. 146.

God and Humanity

1. Marc Connelly, *The Green Pastures* in *Pulitzer Prize Plays, 1918–1934*, ed. Kathryn Coe and William H. Cordell (New York: Random House, 1934), pp. 602ff.
2. Ibid.
3. Book of Job, 4:4.
4. Archibald MacLeish, "The Men Behind *J.B.*," *Theater Arts*, April 1959.

Life and Death

1. Thornton Wilder, *The Journals of Thornton Wilder, 1939–1961* (New Haven: Yale University Press, 1985), p. 183.

Epilogue

1. Burton Rascoe, "Prize Awards Help Theater," *New York World-Telegram*, May 3, 1943.
2. Arthur Pollock, "Plays and Things," *Brooklyn Daily Eagle*, May 12, 1935.
3. Walter Prichard Eaton, *The Theater Annual* (New York: Published under the auspices of The Theater Library Assn. 1944), p. 29.

Appendix One

1. Either John Corbin, "The Katydid Comedy," *The New York Times*, February 3, 1918, Sec. 5, p. 8.
2. Alexander Woolcott, "Second Thoughts on First Nights: The Coming of Eugene O'Neill," *The New York Times*, February 8, 1920, Sec. 8, p. 2.
3. J. Ranken Towse, "The Drama," *The Evening Post*, February 4, 1920, p. 11.
4. Burns Mantle, "The New Plays," *The Mail*, November 3, 1921, p. 13.
5. Owen Johnson, "Pulitzer Jurors Overruled on Play," *The New York Times*, May 17, 1924, p. 7.
6. Walter Prichard Eaton, *The Theater Annual* (New York: Published under auspices of the Theater Library Association, 1944), p. 25.

7. John L. Toohey, *A History of the Pulitzer Prize Plays* (New York: The Citadel Press, 1967), p. 51.

8. Walter Prichard Eaton, *The Theater Annual* (New York: Published under auspices of the Theater Library Association, 1944), p. 2.

9. Brooks Atkinson, "Strange Interlude Plays Five Hours," *The New York Times*, January 31, 1928, p. 28.

10. Dudley Nichols, "The New Play," *The New York World*, January 31, 1928, p. 11.

11. Gilbert Gabriel, "Last Night's First Night," *The New York Sun*, January 31, 1928, p. 16.

12. John L. Toohey, *A History of the Pulitzer Prize Plays* (New York: The Citadel Press, 1967), p. 74.

13. Percy Hammond, "*Street Scene* Wins the Pulitzer Prize for Morals.and Manners," *The New York Herald Tribune*, May 19, 1929, Sec. 7.

14. Brooks Atkinson, "*The Green Pastures*," *The New York Times*, March 9, 1930, Sec. 9, p. 1.

15. Walter Prichard Eaton, *The Theater Annual* (New York: Published under auspices of The Theater Library Association, 1944), p. 27.

16. Brooks Atkinson, "Pulitzer Laurels," *The New York Times*, May 10, 1931, Sec. 8. p. 1.

17. Ibid.

18. Gilbert Gabriel, "New Offerings on Broadway," *The New York American*, December 28, 1931, p. 9.

19. John L. Toohey, *A History of the Pulitzer Prize Plays* (New York: The Citadel Press, 1967), p. 111.

20. Ibid., p. 115.

21. "Pulitzer Juries Shorn of Power," *The New York Times*, May 12, 1934, p. 17.

22. "Reviewers to Give Best Play Award," *The New York Times*, October 24, 1935, p. 23.

23. Burns Mantle, "Which is the Season's Prize Play?" *The New York Daily News*, April 21, 1935, p. 74.

24. "Clayton Hamilton Assails Pulitzer Prize Selection," *The New York Herald Tribune*, May 7, 1935, p. 3.

25. Burns Mantle, "Another Playwright Wins a Prize," *Sunday News*, May 10, 1936, p.78.

26. "Topics of the Times," *The New York Times*, May 25, 1935, p. 20.

27. John L. Toohey, *A History of the Pulitzer Prize Plays* (New York: The Citadel Press, 1967) p. 146.

28. Heywood Broun, "It Seems to Me," *The New York World Telegram*, May 3, 1939.

29. "Saroyan Spurns Pulitzer Prize," *The Sun*, May 7, 1940, p. 12.

30. "Protest Award to Wilder," *The Sun*, May 4, 1943, p. 5.

31. "Pulitzer Jury Chose Odets Play," *The New York Times*, August 18, 1963, p. 80.

32. Editorial, "Pulitzer Prizes, Minus One," *The New York Times*, May 7, 1963, p. 42.

33. Stanley Kauffmann, "Homosexual Drama and Its Disguises," *The New York Times*, January 23, 1966, Sec. 2, p. 1.

34. John Gassner, "Too Many Judges," *The New York Times*, July 21, 1963, Sec. 2, p. 7.

35. "Pulitzer Board Omits '66 Drama Award," *The New York Times*, May 3, 1966.

36. John Simon, "Should Albee Have Said, No Thanks?" *The New York Times*, August 20, 1967, Sec. 2, p. 1.

37. Dan Sullivan, "Albee Criticizes Pulitzer Board," *The New York Times*, May 3, 1967, p.49.

38. "Albee Play Wins a Pulitzer Prize," *The New York Times*, May 2, 1967, p. 40.

39. Harold Clurman, "What the Group Theater Wants," Program Notes, Mansfield Theater, December 1931.

Bibliography

Adams, James Truslow. *The Epic of America*. New York: Little, Brown & Co., 1931.

Akins, Zoe. *The Old Maid*. Unpublished play. First performed January 7, 1935.

Alighieri, Dante. *The Divine Comedy*. Translated by H. F. Cary. New York: Oxford University Press, 1957.

Allen, Frederick Lewis. *Only Yesterday: An Informal History of the Nineteen-Twenties*. New York: Harper, 1931.

———. *Since Yesterday; the Nineteen-Thirties in America*. New York: Harper & Bros., 1940.

———. *The Big Change: America Transforms Itself, 1900–1950*. New York: Harper, 1952.

———. *The Lords of Creation*. New York: Harper & Bros., 1935.

"America in the '60's," *Fortune*, December 1960.

Anderson, Maxwell. Both Your Houses. In *Pulitzer Prize Plays 1918–1934*, edited by Kathryn Coe and William H. Cordell. New York: Random House, 1934.

Argyris, Chris. *Personality and Organization*. New York: Harper, 1957.

Banfield, Edward C., and James Q Wilson. *City Politics*. New York: Vintage Books, 1963.

Barck, Oscar Theodore, Jr., and Nelson Manfred Blake. *Since 1900*. New York: Macmillan, 1947.

Barnay, Ralph. "Alcoholism Can Begin at Home," *Collier's Magazine*, December 11, 1948.

Barnes, Harry E., and Oreen M. Ruedi. *The American Way of Life*. New York: Prentice Hall, Inc., 1942.

Barzun, Jacques. *The Energies of Art*. New York: Harper, 1956.

Beard, Charles A. and Mary R. *America in Midpassage*. New York: Macmillan, 1939.

———. *The Idea of National Interest*. New York. Macmillan, 1934.

——— and George H. E. Smith. *The Old Deal and the New*. New York: Macmillan, 1940.

———. *The Rise of American Civilization*. 2 Vols. New York: Macmillan, 1928.

Bendix, Reinhard, and Seymour M. Lipset. *Class, Status, and Power*. Glencoe, IL: Free Press, 1953.

Bennett, Lerone, Jr. *What Manner of Man*. New York: Pocket Books, Inc., 1955.

Bentley, Eric. *Dramatic Event*. Boston: Beacon, 1956.

——. *Life of the Drama*. New York: Athenaeum, 1954.

——. *Playwright as Thinker*. Cleveland: Meridian, 1955.

Berg, Jan Hendrick Van den. *The Changing Nature of Man*. New York: W. W. Norton & Co., 1961.

Berle, Adolf A., Jr. *The 20th Century Capitalist Revolution*. New York: Harcourt, 1954.

Billington, Ray A. *The Protestant Crusade*. New York: Macmillan, 1939.

Boorstein, Daniel J. *The Genius of American Politics*. Chicago: University of Chicago Press, 1953.

Brogan, D. W. *Politics in America*. New York: Harper, 1954.

Brustein, Robert. *Theater of Revolt*. Boston: Little, Brown, & Co., 1964.

Burke, Kenneth. *Attitudes Toward History*. 2 vols. New York: New Republic, 1937.

——. *Permanence and Change*. New York: New Republic, 1935.

Burrows, Abe, Jack Weinstock, and Willy Gilbert. *How to Succeed in Business Without Really Trying*. Unpublished play. First performed October 14, 1961.

Cargill, Oscar, et al., eds. *O'Neill and His Plays: Four Decades of Criticism*. New York: New York University Press, 1961.

Cary, Joyce. *Art and Reality*. New York: Harper & Bros., 1958.

Cash, Wilbur. *The Mind of the South*. New York: Knopf, 1941.

Chase, Mary. *Harvey*. New York: Dramatists Play Service, 1944.

Chase, Stuart. *The Proper Study of Mankind*. New York: Harper, 1956.

Clark, John Maurice. *Alternative to Serfdom*. New York: Alfred Knopf. 1948.

——. *Economic Institutions and Human Welfare*. New York: Alfred Knopf, 1957.

——. *Guideposts in Time of Change: Some Essentials for a Sound American Economy*. New York: Harper, 1949.

Coe, Kathryn, and William H. Cordell, eds. *Pulitzer Prize Plays 1918–1934*. New York: Random House, 1934.

Commager, Henry S. *The American Mind*. New Haven: Yale University Press, 1950.

Connelly, Marc. *The Green Pastures*. In *Pulitzer Prize Plays 1918–34*, edited by Kathryn Coe and William H. Cordell. New York: Random House, 1934.

Cooper, Charles W. *Preface to Drama*. New York: Donald, 1955.

Corrigan, Robert W., ed. *Theater in the Twentieth Century*. New York: Grove, 1961.

Curti, Merle. *The Growth of American Thought*. New York: Columbia University Press, 1946.

——. *The Making of an American Community*. Palo Alto: Stanford University Press, 1959.

Daiches, David. *Critical Approaches to Literature*. Englewood Cliffs, NJ: Prentice Hall, 1956.

Davis, Owen. *Icebound*. In *Pulitzer Prize Plays 1918–1934*, edited by Kathryn Coe and William H. Cordell. New York: Random House, 1934.

Degler, Carl N. *Out of Our Past*. New York: Harper & Row, 1962.

De Tocqueville, Alexis. *Democracy in America*. New York: Vintage Books, 1959.

Dewey, John. *Democracy and Education*. New York: Macmillan, 1916.

Dollard, J., et al. *Frustration and Aggression*. New Haven: Yale University Press, 1939.

DuBois, W. E. B. *The Souls of Black Folk*. New York: Blue Heron Press, 1953.

Eisenstein, Victor, ed. *Neurotic Interaction in Marriage*. New York: Basic Books, 1956.

Eliot, T. S. "Baudelaire in Our Time." *Essays Ancient and Modern*. London: Faber & Faber, 1949.

Erikson, Erik H. *The Challenge of Youth*. Garden City, NY: Doubleday, 1965.

———. "The Concept of Identity" in *Daedalus*, Winter 1966.

Faulkner, Harold U., and Mark Starr. *Labor in America*. New York: Oxford University Press, 1953.

Felkner, Bruce L. *Dirty Politics*. New York: W. W. Norton & Co., 1966.

Fergusson, Francis. *The Human Image in Dramatic Literature*. Garden City, NY: Doubleday, 1957.

———. *The Idea of a Theater*. Princeton: Princeton University Press, 1949.

Fishwick, Marshall W. *American Heroes—Myth and Reality*. Washington, D.C.: Public Affairs Press, 1954.

Florovsky, George. "Faith and Culture." *The Christian Idea of Education*, edited by Edmund Fuller. New Haven: Yale University Press, 1957.

Floyd, Virginia, ed. *Eugene O'Neill at Work*. New York: Frederick Ungar Publishing Co., 1981.

Fluchere, Henri. *Shakespeare and the Elizabethans*. New York: Hill and Wang, 1964.

Frankel, Charles. *The Case for Modern Man*. New York: Harper, 1956.

———. *The Love of Anxiety*. New York: Harper & Row, 1965.

Freedman, Warren. *Society on Trial*. Springfield: Charles C. Thomas, 1965.

Freidel, F., and N. Pollack, eds. *Builders of American Institutions*. Chicago: Rand McNally, 1963.

Freidenberg, Edgar Z. *The Vanishing Adolescent*. New York: Dell, 1962.

Frings, Ketti. *Look Homeward, Angel*. New York: Samuel French, 1958.

Fromm, Erich. *Man for Himself*. New York: Holt, Rinehart and Winston, 1964.

Fuller, Edmund. *Man in Modern Fiction*. New York: Random House, 1958.

Galbraith, John Kenneth. *The Affluent Society*. Boston: Houghton Mifflin, 1968.

———. *American Capitalism*. Boston: Houghton Mifflin, 1956.

———. *The Great Crash, 1929*. Boston: Houghton Mifflin, 1955.

Gale, Zona. *Miss Lulu Bett*. In *Pulitzer Prize Plays 1918–1934*, edited by Kathryn Coe and William H. Cordell. New York: Random House, 1934.

Galloway, David D. *The Absurd Hero in American Fiction*. Austin:University of Texas, 1966.

Gassner, John, ed. *Best American Plays*, 4th series. New York: Crown, 1958.

———. *Twenty Best Plays*. New York: Crown, 1939.

———. *Directions in Modern Theater and Drama*. New York: Holt, 1965.

———. *Theater in Our Times*. New York: Crown, 1954.

Geismer, Maxwell. *American Moderns*. New York: Hill and Wang, 1958.

Gelb, Arthur and Barbara. *O'Neill*. New York: Harper & Row, 1962.

Gilroy, Frank D. *The Subject Was Roses*. New York: Random House, 1952.

Ginger, Ray. *American Social Thought*. New York: Hill and Wang, 1961.

Glaspell, Susan. *Alison's House*. In *Pulitzer Prize Plays 1918–1934*, edited by Kathryn Coe and William H. Cordell. New York: Random House, 1934.

Goldberg, Gerald G. and Nancy M. *The Modern Critical Spectrum*. Englewood Cliffs, NJ: Prentice Hall, 1962.

Goldman, Eric F. *The Crucial Decade*. New York: Random House, 1960.

———. *Rendezvous with Destiny*. New York: Knopf, 1952.

Goodrich, Frances, and Albert Hackett. *The Diary of Anne Frank*. New York: Dramatists' Play Service, 1956.

Green, Paul. *In Abraham's Bosom*. In *Pulitzer Prize Plays 1918–1934*, edited by Kathryn Coe and William H. Cordell. New York: Random House, 1934.

Griffith, Thomas. *The Waist High Culture*. New York: Grosset & Dunlap, 1959.

Grinder, R. E., ed. *Studies in Adolescence*. New York: Macmillan, 1963.

Hacker, Louis M. *The Triumph of American Capitalism*. New York: Columbia University Press, 1940.

Haggard, Howard W., M.D. *Devils, Drugs, and Doctors*. New York: Pocket Books, 1940.

Hamilton, Edith. *The Greek Way*. New York: W. W. Norton & Co., 1930.

Handlin, Oscar. *Race and Nationality in American Life*. New York: Doubleday, 1957.

Hansen, Alvin H. *The American Economy*. New York: McGraw-Hill, 1961.

———. *Economic Issues of the 1960s*. New York: McGraw-Hill, 1961.

Hansen, Marcus. *The Immigrant in American History*. Cambridge: Harvard University Press, 1940.

Harris, Herbert. *American Labor*. New Haven: Yale University Press, 1939.

Harrison, Gilbert A. *The Enthusiast: A Life of Thornton Wilder*. New York: Ticknor and Fields, 1983.

Hart, Moss, and George S. Kaufman, *You Can't Take It with You*. In *Twenty Best Plays*, edited by John Gassner. New York: Crown, 1939.

Hatterer, Lawrence J., M. D. *The Artist in Society*. New York: Grove Press, 1965.

Heilbroner, Robert L. *Great Ascent*. New York: Harper & Row, 1963.

———. *Making of Economic Society*. New York: Prentice Hall, 1962.

Hession, Charles H., and S. M. Miller. *The Dynamics of the American Economy*. New York: Alfred Knopf, 1960.

Hofstadter, Richard. *Social Darwinism in American Thought*. Boston: The Beacon Press, 1964.

———. *The American Political Tradition*. New York: Knopf, 1948.

Hohenberg, John, ed. *The Pulitzer Prize Story*. New York: Columbia University Press, 1959.

Hoover, Herbert. *The Challenge to Liberty*. New York: Charles Scribner's Sons, 1934.

Horney, Karen. *Neurotic Personality of Our Time*. New York: W. W. Norton & Co., 1937.

———. *Our Inner Conflicts*. New York: W. W. Norton & Co., 1945.

Howard, Sidney. *They Knew What They Wanted*. In *Pulitzer Prize Plays 1918–1934*, edited by Kathryn Coe and William H. Cordell. New York: Random House, 1934.

Hoyt, Edwin P. *The Tempering Years*. New York: Scribner, 1953.

Hughes, Hatcher. *Hell-Bent fer Heaven*. In *Pulitzer Prize Plays 1918–1934*, edited by Kathryn Coe and William H. Cordell. New York: Random House, 1934.

Hunt, Morton M. *The Natural History of Love*. New York: Alfred Knopf, 1959.

Hutchins, Robert M. *The Conflict in Education*. New York: Harper, 1953.

Huxley, Aldous. *Ape and Essence*. New York: Harper & Bros., 1948.

Hyman, Stanley Edgar. *The Armed Vision*. New York: Alfred Knopf, 1948.

Inge, William. *Picnic*. In Best American Plays, 4th series, edited by John Gassner. New York: Crown, 1958.

Janowsky, Oscar I., ed. *The American Jew*. New York: Harper & Bros., 1942.

Jaspers, Karl. *Man in the Modern Age*. Garden City, NY: Doubleday, 1957.

Jersild, Arthur T. *The Psychology of Adolescence*. New York: Macmillan, 1963.

Johnstone, Paul H. "Old Ideals Versus New Ideas in Farm-Life." *Yearbook of Agriculture*. Washington, D.C.: Government Bureau of Publications, 1940.

Kaufman, George S., and Morrie Ryskind. *Of Thee I Sing*. In *Pulitzer Prize Plays 1918–1934*, edited by Kathryn Coe and William H. Cordell. New York: Random House, 1934.

Kelly, George. Craig's Wife. In *Pulitzer Prize Plays 1918–34*, edited by Kathryn Coe and William H. Cordell. New York: Random House, 1934.

Kendall, Willmore, and Austin Ranney. *Democracy and the American Party System*. New York: Harcourt, 1956.

Keniston, Kenneth. *The Uncommitted*. New York: Harcourt, Brace and World, 1960.

Kennan, George F. *American Diplomacy 1900–1950*. Chicago: University of Chicago Press, 1951.

Kerr, Walter. "Gossamer in Your Eyes." *The New York Times*, Section 2, July 16, 1967.

———. *Theater in Spite of Itself*. New York: Simon and Schuster, 1963.

Kierkegaard, S. *Fear and Trembling*. Translated by W. Lowrie. NewYork: Doubleday, 1954.

Kingsley, Sidney. *Men in White*. In *Pulitzer Prize Plays 1918–34*, edited by Kathryn Coe and William H. Cordell. New York: Random House, 1934.

Konvitz, Milton R. *Expanding Liberties*. New York: Viking, 1966.

Kramm, Joseph. *The Shrike*. New York: Dramatists Play Service, 1952.

Langer, Susanne K. *Philosophy in a New Key*, 3rd ed. Cambridge: Harvard University Press, 1957.

Laski, Harold. *The American Democracy*. New York: Viking, 1948.

Lawson, John Howard. *Theory and Technique of Playwriting*. New York: Hill and Wang, 1960.

Leighton, Isabel, ed. *The Aspirin Age 1919–1941*. New York: Simon and Schuster, 1949.

Lerner, Max. *America as a Civilization*. New York: Simon and Schuster, 1957.

Levi-Strauss, Claude. "Essay." *Time Magazine*. June 30, 1967.

Lindsay, Howard, and Russel Crouse. *State of the Union*. In *Best American Plays*, 3rd series, edited by John Gassner. New York: Crown, 1950.

Lindsey, Judge Ben B., and Wainwright Evans. *The Companionate Marriage*. Garden City, NY: Garden City Publishing, 1929.

Link, Arthur S. *American Epoch*. New York: Alfred Knopf, 1955.

Lippmann, Walter. *A Preface to Morals*. New York: Macmillan, 1929.

Lovejoy, Arthur O. *Essays in the History of Ideas*. Baltimore: Johns Hopkins University Press, 1938.

———. *Great Chain of Being*. Cambridge: Harvard University Press, 1936.

Lowenthal, Leo. *Literature, Popular Culture and Society*. Englewood Cliffs, NJ: Prentice Hall, 1961.

Lubell, Samuel. *The Future of American Politics*. New York: Doubleday, 1952.

Lynd, Robert S. "The Myth of Diffused Power." Introduction to *Business as a System of Power* by Robert A. Brady. New York: Columbia University Press, 1943.

MacLeish, Archibald. *A Time to Speak*. Boston: Houghton Mifflin, 1941.

———. *J.B.* Boston: Houghton Mifflin, 1958.

———. *Poetry and Experience*. Cambridge: Riverside Press, 1960.

———. "Thoughts on an Age that Gave Us Hiroshima." *The New York Times*, Section 2, July 9, 1967.

Marcus, Herbert. "The Ideology of Death" in *The Meaning of Death*, edited by Herman Feiffel. New York: McGraw-Hill, 1965.

Mencken, H. L. *Prejudices*. New York: Vintage Books, 1959.

———. "On Politics." In *A Carnival of Buncombe*, edited by Malcolm Moos. New York: Vintage Books, 1956.

Menninger, Karl A. *Man Against Himself*. New York: Harcourt Brace and Co., 1938.

Miller, Arthur. *Death of a Salesman*. In *New Voices in the American Theater*. New York: Random House, 1955.

Miller, Perry, ed. *American Transcendentalism*. New York: Doubleday, 1957.

Morison, S. E., and H. S. Commager. *Growth of the American Republic*, vol. 2. New York: Oxford University Press, 1942.

Mosel, Tad. *All the Way Home*. New York: Samuel French, 1961.

Mosse, G. L., et al., eds. *Europe in Review*. Chicago: Rand McNally, 1964.

Murray, Gilbert. *Five Stages of Greek Religion*. New York: Doubleday, 1951.

Nelson, Lowry. *American Farm Life*. Cambridge: Harvard University Press, 1954.

Nevins, Allan. *The United States in a Chaotic World*. Washington, D.C.: U.S. Publications, 1950.

Niebuhr, Reinhold. *Moral Man and Immoral Society.* New York: Scribner, 1932.

Nietzsche, Friedrich W. *Thus Spake Zarathustra.* New York: Dutton, 1951.

O'Neill, Eugene. *Plays.* 3 vols. New York: Random House, 1941.

Osgood, Robert E. *Ideals and Self-Interest in America's Foreign Relations.* Chicago: University of Chicago Press, 1953.

Packard, Vance. *The Hidden Persuaders.* New York: McKay, 1957.

———. *The Pyramid Climbers.* New York: McGraw-Hill, 1962.

———. *The Status Seekers.* New York: Pocket Books, 1961.

Parrington, Vernon. *Main Currents in American Thought.* Vol. 3. New York: Harcourt, 1956.

Patrick, John. *Teahouse of the August Moon.* New York: G. P. Putnam, 1952.

Paxson, F. L. *American Democracy and the World War.* 2 vols. Boston: Houghton Mifflin, 1936.

Perkins, Frances. *The Roosevelt I Knew.* New York: Harper, 1946.

Perkins, O. *The New Age of Franklin Roosevelt: 1932–1945.* New York: Rand McNally, 1957.

Peterson, Shorey. *Economics.* New York: Henry Holt, 1954.

Petersen, William, ed. *American Social Patterns.* Garden City, NY: Doubleday, 1955.

Polanyi, Karl. *The Great Transformation.* New York: Farrar, Straus and. Cudahy, Inc., 1944.

Price, Roy A., ed. *New Viewpoints in the Social Sciences.* Washington, D.C.: Twenty-Eighth Yearbook of the National Council for the Social Studies, 1958.

Rabkin, Gerald. *Drama and Commitment.* Bloomington: Indiana University Press, 1964.

Raglan, Lord. *The Hero.* New York: Vintage, 1956.

Rice, Elmer. "American Theater and the Human Spirit." In *American Playwrights on Drama*, edited by Horst Frenz. New York: Hill and Wang, 1965.

———. *Street Scene.* In *Pulitzer Prize Plays 1918–1934*, edited by Kathryn Coe and William H. Cordell. New York: Random House, 1934.

Riessman, David. *The Lonely Crowd.* New York: Pocket Books, 1953.

Robinson, James H. *The Human Comedy.* New York: Harper & Bros., 1937.

Roche, John P. *The Quest for the Dream.* New York: Macmillan, 1963.

Rodgers, Richard, Oscar Hammerstein II, and Joshua Logan. *South Pacific—Six Plays.* New York: Modern Library, 1959.

Rodnick, David. *Postwar Germans.* New Haven: Yale University Press, 1948.

Rolo, Charles, ed. *Psychiatry in American Life.* New York: Dell, 1963.

Rosenberg, Bernard, and David M. White, eds. *Mass Culture: The Popular Arts in America.* Glencoe, IL: Free Press, 1957.

Rostow, W. V. *The Stages of Economic Growth.* Cambridge: Cambridge University Press, 1962.

Ruttenberg, Harold. *Self-Developing America.* New York: Harper, 1960.

Santayana, George. *The Philosophical Poets.* Garden City, NY: Doubleday, 1938.

Saroyan, William. *The Time of Your Life*. New York: Samuel French, 1941.

Saveth, E. N., ed. *American History and the Social Sciences*. Glencoe, IL: Free Press, 1964.

Schneider, Herbert. *Religion in 20th Century America*. Cambridge: Harvard University Press, 1952.

Scholem, Gershom. "Jews and Germans." *Commentary*, November 1966.

Schur, Edwin M. "Psychiatrists Under Attack: The Rebellious Dr. Szasz," *Atlantic*, June 1966.

Seldes, Gilbert. *The Public Arts*. New York: Simon and Schuster, 1957.

Shannon, David A. *Twentieth Century America*. Chicago: Rand McNally, 1963.

Sherwood, Robert E. *Abe Lincoln in Illinois*. In *Best Plays of the Modern American Theater*, edited by John Gassner. New York: Crown, 1947.

———. *Idiot's Delight*. In *20 Best Plays of the Modern American Theater*, edited by John Gassner. New York: Crown Pub., 1939.

———. *There Shall Be No Night*. New York: Charles Scribner's Sons, 1941.

Shirer, William L. *Rise and Fall of the Third Reich*. New York: Simon and Schuster, 1961.

Sievers, V. David. *Freud on Broadway*. New York: Hermitage House, 1955.

Smith, Adam. *Wealth of Nations*. Canaan ed. New York: Modern Library, 1937.

Snell, Bruno. *Poetry and Society*. Bloomington: Indiana University Press, 1961.

Soule, George. *Prosperity Decade: From War to Depression, 1917–1929*. New York: Holt, Rinehart and Winston, 1947.

Spencer, Thomas. *Shakespeare and the Nature of Man*. New York: Macmillan Co., 1942

Steward, Samuel. *Dear Sammy: Letters from Gertrude Stein and Alice B. Toklas*. Boston: Houghton Mifflin, 1977.

Stewart, George R. *American Warp of Life*. New York: Doubleday, 1934.

Stokes, Anson P., and Leon Pfeffer. *Church and State in the United States*. New York: Harper, 1954.

Strauss, Anselm L. *Mirrors and Masks*. Glencoe, IL: Free Press, 1959.

Stringfellow, William. *My People Is the Enemy*. New York: Holt, Rinehart and Winston, 1954.

Stynan, J. L. *Dramatic Experience*. Cambridge: Cambridge University Press, 1955.

Sussman, Marvin. *Sourcebook in Marriage and the Family*. 2nd ed. Boston: Houghton Mifflin, 1955.

Sweet, William W. *The Story of Religion in America*, rev. ed. New York: Harper, 1950.

Sypher, Wylie. *Loss of the Self*. New York: Random House, 1952.

Tawney, R. H. *Religion and the Rise of Capitalism*. London: Smith, Peter Co., 1925.

Theater Annual. New York: Published under the auspices of the Theater Library Association, 1944.

Tillich, Paul. *The Courage to Be* New Haven: Yale University Press, 1959.

———. *Theology of Culture*. New York: Oxford University Press, 1959.

Tillyard, E. M. W. *The Elizabethan World Picture*. New York: Macmillan, 1961.

"The Transformation of American Capitalism" *Fortune*, February, 1951.

Toohey, John L. *A History of the Pulitzer Prize Plays*. New York: The Citadel Press. 1967.

Trilling, Lionel. "Eugene O'Neill" in *The New Republic*, September 1936.

Truxal, Andrew G., and Francis E. Merrill. *The Family in American Society*. New York: Prentice Hall, 1953.

Veblen, Thorstein. *Theory of the Leisure Class*. New York: Modern Library, 1934.

Warner, Sam Bass, Jr., ed. *Planning for a Nation of Cities*. Cambridge: MIT Press, 1966.

Warner, W. Lloyd. *Social Class in America*. New York: Harper & Row, 1960.

Weales, Gerald. *American Drama Since World War II*. New York: Harcourt Brace and Co., 1962.

Weber, Max. *The Protestant Ethic and the Spirit of Capitalism*. London: Smith, Peter Co., 1930.

———. *The Theory of Social and Economic Organization*. New York: Free Press of Glencoe, 1957.

Wecter, Dixon. *The Age of the Great Depression, 1929–1941*. New York: Macmillan, 1948.

Weidman, Jerome, and George Abbott. *Fiorello!* New York: Popular Library, Inc. 1960.

Wellek, Rene, and Austin Warren. *Theory of Literature*. New York: Harcourt Brace and Co., 1956.

West, Roy B., Jr., ed. *Essays in Modern Literary Criticism*. New York: Rinehart and Co., 1952.

Whyte, William H., Jr. *The Organization Man*. New York: Doubleday Anchor Books, 1957.

Wilder, Thornton. *The Angel That Troubled the Waters, and Other Plays*. New York: Coward-McCann, 1928.

———. *The Journals of Thornton Wilder, 1939–1961*. New Haven: Yale University Press, 1985.

———. *Our Town*. New York: Coward McCann, 1939.

———. *The Skin of Our Teeth*. New York: Samuel French, 1944.

Williams, Jesse Lynch. *Why Marry?* In *Pulitzer Prize Plays 1918–34*, edited by Kathryn Coe and William H. Cordell. New York: Random House, 1934.

Williams, Tennessee. *Cat on a Hot Tin Roof*. New York: Signet Books, 1955.

———. *A Streetcar Named Desire*. Mount Vernon, NY: New Directions, 1947.

Wolfe, Thomas. *Look Homeward, Angel*. New York: Modern Library, 1929.

Wright, Quincy. *A Study of War*. Chicago: University of Chicago Press, 1964.

Wylie, Philip. *Generation of Vipers*. New York: Holt, Rinehart and Winston, 1942.

Wyllie, Irvin O. *The Self-Made Man in America*. Trenton: Rutgers Press, 1954.

Young, Whitney M., Jr. "A Vanishing Era." in *Harper's Magazine*, April 1965.